"A must-read for anyone in equality for women. Millicent   e in her fight for a better deal for women on many fronts. Clever, determined and energetic, she was a feminist whose battles are still relevant today."

HARRIET HARMAN, CHAIR OF THE FAWCETT SOCIETY
AND FORMER LEADER OF THE HOUSE OF COMMONS

"A lively and readable account of the rich and varied life of a leader whose gender shut her out of mainstream politics. Today, it seems extraordinary that until 1918, not only were women barred from being MPs – they could not even vote. Undaunted by the power and status of Prime Ministers, Millicent Fawcett led a fifty-year campaign to persuade them to change their minds, and Tessa Blackstone explores this fascinating story with verve."

DAVID BLUNKETT, FORMER HOME SECRETARY

"A must-read for anyone curious about a great feminist activist. Tessa Blackstone's admiration and respect for Millicent Garrett Fawcett have resulted in an intimate, engaged biography, showing how one woman can change the world."

PROFESSOR JOANNA BOURKE, BIRKBECK,
UNIVERSITY OF LONDON

"Never forget how hard-fought women's rights have been. This excellent biography is a reminder that all progress begins with a minority campaign regarded as eccentric at the time but which is only later seen as heroic."

POLLY TOYNBEE, JOURNALIST AND AUTHOR

"A wonderfully readable account of a seminal period in British protest history, when it was proved that it does not take violence to win an argument."

SIMON JENKINS, JOURNALIST AND AUTHOR

"No one is in a better position than Baroness Blackstone to revisit the life and work of Millicent Fawcett, Britain's most famous fighter for women's suffrage. This carefully and compassionately written biography reveals a woman who campaigned fiercely and tirelessly for a wide range of emancipatory causes for over half a century. Above all, the book brings Fawcett to life as a person enmeshed in a network of close and supportive family relationships, and as a key member of those social and political circles that helped to bring (and sometimes drag) Victorian society into the modern age."

ANN OAKLEY, AUTHOR OF *FORGOTTEN WIVES: HOW WOMEN GET WRITTEN OUT OF HISTORY*

"Tessa Blackstone's fascinating biography of Millicent Fawcett is both scholarly and highly engaging. It provides an insight into not only the multifaceted life of this extraordinary campaigner for women's rights but also the hugely talented and influential family of which she was part and the social and political times in which she played a leading role."

HELENE HAYMAN, FORMER LORD SPEAKER

THE FIGHT FOR VOTES FOR WOMEN

MILLICENT GARRETT FAWCETT

TESSA BLACKSTONE

Biteback Publishing

First published in Great Britain in 2024 by
Biteback Publishing Ltd, London
Copyright © Tessa Blackstone 2024

ISBN 978-1-78590-855-2

10 9 8 7 6 5 4 3 2 1

A CIP catalogue record for this book is available from the British Library.

Set in Adobe Caslon Pro and Copperplate Gothic Condensed

Printed and bound in Great Britain by
CPI Group (UK) Ltd, Croydon CR0 4YY

CONTENTS

PREFACE

When I was appointed to be the Master of Birkbeck College in the late 1980s, I did not realise at first that with the job came a 'tied cottage'. The college leased from the University of London 2 Gower Street as a residence for the master. As soon as I could, I arranged to go and see it. I discovered a tall, white, stuccoed house at the south end of Gower Street, close to Bedford Square, with an English Heritage blue plaque on it reading:

Dame Millicent Garrett Fawcett (1847–1929),
pioneer of women's suffrage, lived and died here.

Nobody had told me that for forty-four years, the great campaigner for women to be able to vote had lived in the house which was about to become my home. I was delighted. For the next ten years, while I was the Master of Birkbeck, I told anyone who would listen what an honour it was to live in the place from which the campaign for women's suffrage had been fought for four decades.

The house was on five floors, with a large basement that led into a garden at the back, and a ground floor, which I used for college dinners and seminars. I lived in the top two floors. However, my study was at the back on the first floor in a room with a beautiful painted ceiling, which I later discovered had been designed and painted by Millicent's sister Agnes and her cousin Rhoda. I imagined that Millicent might well have worked there too. I looked for a recent biography to read more about her. None had been published since the 1930s and I was tempted to write one myself.

It was around this time that I also became aware that Elizabeth Garrett Anderson, Britain's first female doctor, was Millicent's sister. I was curious about what had led these unusual sisters to be pioneers and campaigners for change, but many other commitments at that time prevented me from investigating their backgrounds. It was not until the unveiling of the statue of Millicent in Parliament Square in 2018, which marked the 100th anniversary of the first Act allowing some women to vote in general elections, that I thought again about writing her story. As I read about her life and her wider interests beyond women and suffrage, some of which I shared with her, such as higher education and the employment of women, I realised how much of what she had fought for beyond votes for women is still relevant today. But what triggered my interest in the first place was that for nearly ten years, I lived in what had been her home.

Bloomsbury was her London home as well as mine, but her family home was in Aldeburgh, a small town on the Suffolk coast, and Millicent stayed connected to it throughout her life. I too became linked to Suffolk. In the early 1980s, I bought a small cottage in the village of Bures, near Sudbury, as a place to escape from London and to allow me to walk in the Stour Valley. Unlike Millicent, I was not born in Suffolk, but it has become more important to me than my childhood home in Hertfordshire.

My own childhood, growing up in a middle-class family in the Home Counties, had some similarities to Millicent's. Independence was encouraged and the expectations of my parents for their daughters were only a little different to the expectations they had for their sons. I was pushed to do well at school and to take my education seriously, as well as being sent off for summer holidays away from my parents. In my teens in the 1950s, I became aware of my mother's restlessness and frustration with the restrictions of marriage and motherhood on women's opportunities, but I did not embrace the concept of feminism nor read any of the literature about it, yet I almost subconsciously became a feminist. I started to believe that there should be no barriers to women joining the professions, participating in politics and travelling the world. I knew nothing about the young Millicent Garrett, but had I done so, I would have identified strongly with her ambitions and applauded her for her determination to break down barriers and to promote the rights of women. The strength of her convictions and her persistence in pursuing her goals would have drawn me to her then, as it does now.

In writing this book, I have aimed to reach readers who know little about Millicent but might be inspired by her as I have been, as well as those interested in what it was in her family background, in her education and in her early marriage which propelled Milly, as she was known by her relations, into being a lifelong feminist campaigner. It is also the story of a long, slow, arduous campaign mounted against indifference and prejudice, which was ultimately successful in enfranchising women. Millicent's life also demonstrates that it is possible to have a hinterland beyond politics and policy-making and to know how to enjoy life too. Although honourable, intelligent and astute, she sometimes made mistakes and pursued causes which might have better been left alone, but she was all the more interesting because she was not always a paragon of virtue.

In 2028, the centenary of all women being able to vote will be held. The story I tell here will provide the context for a celebration, which should take place to remind us of what it took to secure this victory. Those who fought so hard for it should not be forgotten, so I hope this book will help to put Millicent Garrett Fawcett on the centre stage where she belongs.

Tessa Blackstone
September 2024

1

FAMILY LIFE IN ALDEBURGH

In the early nineteenth century, the youngest sons of moderately successful, small manufacturers or tradesmen usually had to seek a living outside the family firm. Commonly, the eldest brother inherited a business which was not large enough to accommodate several others. Newson Garrett, born in 1812, was the third son of Richard Garrett, who owned a small works at Leiston in East Suffolk. It manufactured agricultural machinery and implements needed by farmers in East Anglia. Newson's oldest brother, also called Richard, inherited the firm; his middle brother, Balls, had been apprenticed as an ironmonger; Newson had to seek his fortune elsewhere. He went to London. Unlike many others who had taken this route, he had a contact who might be able to help and guide him. In 1828, his brother Richard had married Elizabeth, the elder daughter of John Dunnell, who came from a family of Suffolk smallholders but had moved to London, where Dunnell prospered as an innkeeper, owning more than one inn as well as pawnbroking shops. Newson was welcomed by Dunnell at the Beehive Inn in Crawford Street in Marylebone, as his son-in-law's brother and a Suffolk man.

Although Newson had been to school and could read and write, he had not been a studious pupil, nor had he acquired any training after he left school. However, he did not lack ambition and was confident and enthusiastic about his various schemes and how he might earn his living. His ebullience and energy impressed Dunnell and endeared him to his younger daughter, Louisa. Newson was twenty-two years old, blue-eyed, fair-haired and unusually handsome. Louisa was twenty years old and, in spite of her gender, better educated than Newson, although where she acquired her neat hand- and letter-writing skills is not clear. She was very small and slight, probably less than five feet tall. Although shy, she was intelligent and resourceful and was drawn to a man brimming with ideas and determination. The pair fell in love and Newson was given Dunnell's consent to marry Louisa.

So it was that two brothers married two sisters, six years apart, but at the same church, St Mary's in Bryanston Place. Whereas the older of the two couples returned to Suffolk after their wedding, Newson and Louisa stayed in London. They settled in Whitechapel at 1 Commercial Road, where Dunnell owned a pawnbroker's shop. Newson ran it for the next four years. To be a pawnbroker was not an especially auspicious beginning, but it provided a secure base for the young couple. There was plenty of business in a neighbourhood where poverty was rife. The poor brought their worldly goods in exchange for cash to keep them going for a few days until they could be redeemed. The shop's site was close to the Thames and thieves often came up from the river to pawnshops to dispose of their swag, which they had stolen or smuggled.

Just under a year after their marriage, Louisa gave birth to her first child, a girl who they called Louisa too, although perhaps to distinguish her from her mother, she became known as Louie.

Sixteen months later, in June 1836, she had a second daughter, who was christened Elizabeth at the great Hawksmoor church St George-in-the-East. Only seventeen months passed before a third child was born in November 1837. This time it was a boy, who they named Dunnell Newson. He lived for only six months, dying the following May. Louisa was consumed with grief and prayed that she could die too. She never forgot the enormity of her loss, despite the many children who were to follow. Perhaps she felt the loss so keenly because he was her firstborn son. However, it was not long before she had another son in 1839, simply reversing the names of the baby who had died to Newson Dunnell. By the time he was born and christened in another great church, St Martin-in-the-Fields, the family had moved.

While Louisa's hard work and skills as a homemaker had created a comfortable, warm and cosy home for her family, the junction of Commercial Road and Whitechapel High Street was far from salubrious. The noise of the iron-bound wheels of the drays carrying sugar from the West India Docks along the granite-paved roads was incessant. The raw sugar was boiled in the sooty buildings which surrounded the Garretts' home; and the atmosphere was polluted by sulphurous smoke. There was nowhere outside to take the little children, no park where they could toddle and no trees where they could watch the wind rustle their branches. The move to a much larger pawnshop and silversmiths in Long Acre must have been a welcome opportunity to improve their circumstances. It was a big step up from Whitechapel. St James's Park was within reach and St Martin's Lane was far from the industrial slum of the Commercial Road. Instead of watching drays of raw sugar passing, they could observe carts from the country on the way to Covent Garden Market.

Although Newson had moved to managing a larger enterprise by adding silversmith as well as pawnbroker after his name, he had plans for a business with more potential. Moreover, he was not a Londoner and did not want to settle there permanently. His wish was to return to his native Suffolk. After the birth in 1840 of another son, Edmund, Newson had a family of four children to support. The death of his father in 1837 had resulted in a small inheritance, though the bulk of his father's estate had gone to his older brother and was needed for the works at Leiston to flourish. In addition, Newson had some savings and some money his wife had been given by her father. With these funds, he bought corn and coal warehouses at Snape, a few miles inland from Aldeburgh, a small town on the coast that he would have been familiar with when he grew up in nearby Leiston.

For a family of six, with all their possessions, the easiest way to travel to Aldeburgh from London in 1841 was to go by sea. The journey took them into the North Sea up the Suffolk coast, then a further six miles up the River Alde, anchoring at Slaughden Quay, where they were ferried ashore in open boats. They had still not reached their destination. The final part of their journey involved loading all their baggage and furniture into carts, climbing in themselves and trundling down a track from the harbour into Aldeburgh itself. According to the 1841 census, the population was 1,557. As such, Aldeburgh was little more than a large village. However, it was big enough to have two inns to accommodate tourists, especially those in ailing health who came to benefit from its pure sea air and its quiet environment. Those who could not get into one of the inns could rent rooms in as many as fifty houses offering lodgings. Many of Aldeburgh's inhabitants made their living from fishing and were the Garretts not too tired from their long and arduous journey on a Suffolk hoy, they would have noticed fishermen's boats and nets along the beach. They would have seen three windmills higher up above the town, a Martello tower and a small moot hall, which dated back to the Tudors. Much of the town's housing was in two parallel streets which ran along the coast.

The family soon moved into a Georgian house, the Uplands, where, nearly a century earlier, the poet George Crabbe had served his apprenticeship as an apothecary. Their new home compared well with the houses of most of their neighbours and looked out onto the embattled square tower of the flint parish church of St Peter and St Paul. Initially, it was large enough to accommodate a growing family, with many eighteenth-century panelled rooms. The walled garden had mulberry, quince and medlar trees to supply the family with fruit for jam-making. After their arrival at the Uplands, Louisa's pregnancies followed in rapid succession. Alice was born in 1842. Next came two more daughters, Agnes in 1845 and Millicent in 1847, and then a son, Samuel, in 1850. The size of the family, not untypical in mid-nineteenth-century Britain, no doubt put some pressure on Newson and Louisa to seek a bigger house with more space for eight children. Newson's solution was to build a much larger, grander house on land that he purchased overlooking the town. To do so required business success to pay for the construction and then the maintenance of this bigger property.

The warehouses at Snape became the basis for a successful business transporting raw materials, mostly coal and corn, up and down the east coast between Newcastle and London. The boats did not return empty to Snape: they came back from London laden with coal and lime picked up on the journey along the Thames Estuary. Newson soon began to diversify. He established a boat-building yard at Snape to augment his fleet of sailing boats, later adding a fleet of barges. His lack of education and training was no impediment to his exploitation of new opportunities to broaden his business. He soon recognised that he could make more money from higher-value cargo. To do so, he built a maltings at Snape, turning barley into malt, for which there was a growing demand in the burgeoning brewing industry. By the middle of the nineteenth century, the consumption of beer had grown. More people could afford it and scientific improvements in brewing had improved both the supply and the quality of beer. Newson's father-in-law was a publican and other members of his wider family made their living from beer. His older brother Richard had also diversified into brewing, owning a brewery in Camden Town. Since competing successfully with his brother was an important motivation in Newson's entrepreneurial projects, never wanting to be outdone by him, Newson followed him into brewing in partnership with another established London brewer.

The production of malt and beer were linked, but Newson branched out into another enterprise, having bought a brickyard. He built terraces in Aldeburgh, having designed them himself, so that he owned a number of houses as well as a dozen ships, which constituted half the ships in the port. His largest construction project was to double the size of the maltings at Snape in a little over ten years from the mid-1840s until 1856. He used the red bricks from his own brickyard. The Snape buildings became the largest construction for many miles and could be seen from a considerable distance across the flat Suffolk landscape. By 1850, he had also been appointed agent for Lloyds, carrying out the work associated with this role in his counting house. He was forceful, argumentative and driven. Anyone who stood in his way learnt quickly that he would not give up. After a quarrel with his brother, he did not speak to him again for many years despite the fact that Richard was married to his wife's sister, and the sisters remained in touch with each other, as did the cousins.

The new property Newson built for himself and his family was named Alde House. It was no more than half a mile from their first home opposite the church and it looked over the town from the west. It had a large conservatory, many rooms and extensive grounds. Two more children were born there: Josephine in 1853 and George in 1854. Louisa had borne eleven children between 1835 and 1854, from the age of twenty-one until she was forty-one. Her tiny build did not seem to be a hindrance. Although there is no evidence that she was worn out by a family of this size, nor that she suffered ill health, she must have been tired at the end of each day by the sheer physical demands a family of this size made on her. She was deeply religious and sustained by her evangelical Christianity. She regularly read the Bible and Charles Spurgeon's sermons, which were published every week. Though central to her life, she did not seem to have imposed her faith on her children in a forceful or relentless way. The family went to church together on Sundays and said grace at mealtimes like most middle-class Victorians. She and her husband, along with some of the children, are buried in the family plot in the churchyard. Inside the church, there is a large plaque commemorating Newson, placed there by his children after his death in 1893. The dedication says:

His Life from early Manhood was spent at Aldeburgh
Where for upwards of Half a Century
He took a Leading Part
In All that Concerned the Welfare of the Town.
GOD GAVE HIM LARGENESS OF HEART.

Louisa, who outlived him by a decade, dying in 1903 at the age
of eighty-nine, is not commemorated by a plaque in the church
where she worshipped. 'Largeness of heart' would have been an apt
description of her too. Moreover, much of the work Newson did
both as a successful businessman and as a leading figure in the Aldeburgh community would have been impossible without her dedicated support and without her skills as the manager and organiser
of a large household. She, like so many of her peers, received no
formal recognition for what she did to assist her husband's achievements, and we know far less about her than about him. However,
when her daughter Millicent was a young married woman, she said
of her mother that she would have made 'a very capable organiser
of a big business'. Gentle as Louisa was, it was also Millicent's view
that she was a stronger personality than the argumentative and as-
sertive Newson. If she was publicly in his shadow, privately she was
immensely influential and helped to defuse some of his conflicts
with those who crossed him in the many projects he pursued as an
important figure in Aldeburgh. At Christmas, she sent turkeys as
presents to neighbours and friends. When Newson remonstrated
that he had had a row with one of the people on her list, she told
him it did not matter, she was sending the turkey anyway. This suggests that she could do what she thought was right without him
necessarily preventing her. In her home, she was in charge of buying
the provisions they needed and keeping careful accounts of what
she spent. She wrote letters regularly to her children when they
grew up and left home, as well as composing and writing letters
for her husband. When her children were young, she taught them
to read and write. When they were older, tutors were employed to
teach her sons and a governess joined the household to teach her
daughters.

How she found the time to do everything she took on is not clear. There were both inside and outside servants, but it was Louisa's responsibility to supervise them. There is also little evidence that the children were handed over completely to nannies and nursemaids, as happened so frequently in richer and more aristocratic families. Washing, dressing and feeding ten children with small gaps in age between them was no small task, even with the help of a nursemaid. Organising their time and teaching them, settling their quarrels and tending to them when they were ill would have been taxing too. She may have had some help from her elder daughters with the care of the younger children. There is some evidence of this in their late teens, when supporting her was perceived to be a role for them.

The census of 1851 shows that seven of their eight children were living with them, ranging from Louie aged sixteen years to four-month-old Samuel. Their oldest son was presumably away at school. A governess and just three servants are listed, none of whom were nursemaids. By the 1861 census, when the older children had left home or were away at school, the same governess is still a member of the household, along with a cook and three other servants, two of whom are described as housemaids. The outside servants such as the coachman, grooms and gardeners were not listed in the census as they did not live in, so we do not know how many there were. Also unlisted were those who worked under Louisa's supervision in the family dairy, as they lived outside the household too.

Louisa was the centre of all that happened in the house. As well as ensuring that provisions were purchased, she oversaw the many activities which kept such a large family going. Everyday cooking and baking and bringing food to the table required planning. There was a dairy to run and a laundry to supervise, where masses of clothes and bed linen had to be washed and ironed. Garden produce had to be picked and transport arranged for the family on outings and visits in the neighbourhood and beyond. When money was short, as sometimes happened when one of Newson's business ventures failed, Louisa had to cut back spending and run a more austere family regime until financial security was restored. Her children would have observed how important she was as a lynchpin in all that took place in the family. It may well have contributed to their feminism as they grew older. They must have perceived too the constraints on her life and, when they became adults, wanted something different for themselves.

A further complication for Louisa followed from the decision that the family should spend the winter months five miles away in Snape from the mid-1850s. A house was built at Snape Bridge to accommodate the family from late October to early May. During the winter, the process of turning the stored barley into malt took place. The malt was then shipped to London from Snape. While this happened, it was more convenient for Newson to be based in Snape, however inconvenienced his wife was by moving backwards and forwards. It is not clear for how long this division of the year between Aldeburgh and Snape lasted.

Louisa's organisational skills allowed Newson time and space to pursue a public role as a leading figure in Aldeburgh on top of his commercial activities. He was public-spirited and wanted the community to flourish. It was easy to obtain a formal position in the borough, which had not been affected by the local government reform in the 1830s and therefore the Aldeburgh Corporation remained a self-elected group of men. Newson paid a fee of £5 to purchase his election as a burgess. His feuds were many and public. He was impatient and forceful in his determination to get his own way. One of his main antagonists was the rector of Aldeburgh, who was also the bailiff and capital burgess. During especially heated battles with him, Newson blocked his own family from attending the church on a Sunday and sent them down the hill to the Dissenters' Union Chapel instead. This amused the children, as they were treated with deference in this humbler place of worship.

A number of Newson Garrett's commercial initiatives had both direct and indirect benefits for the town and its citizens. He was an innovator and a progressive. Millicent, many years later, said of her father, 'Everything new appealed to him. He welcomed railways with both hands, though they destroyed his carrying trade at Aldeburgh.' In 1859, he insisted that the East Suffolk railway opened a branch line from Saxmundham, a few miles to the north-west, to Snape. His brother and greatest rival, Richard, promoted another branch line to Aldeburgh from Woodbridge. A railway station in the town opened it up to visitors and helped the development of the tourist trade. The terraces Newson built provided lodgings for visitors, who wanted to benefit from the sea air. In the mid-1850s, with two or three other local landowners, Newson formed the Aldeburgh Gas Light Company; and in 1870, the Aldeburgh Waterworks Company Ltd. His vision was to modernise living conditions, greatly improving the quality of life of both residents and visitors. In the 1880s, he formed the Aldeburgh Land Company Ltd, an umbrella body which promoted both the acquisitions of leases and the purchase of land and buildings. His immediate family and other relatives became shareholders in all these companies. Embracing change and believing in the benefits it could bring was a feature in the Garrett sisters' lives as they grew up. It was later manifested in various ways when they campaigned for reforms.

In spite of the town's expansion and its more diverse economy, which accompanied the growth, fishing remained central to

Aldeburgh's economic activity. Fishing was a dangerous occupation on an exposed North Sea coast, subject to sudden storms when boats could be overturned or driven onto the rocks. A lookout in the form of a slender tower stood on the edge of the beach to spot vessels in danger, and the lives of the fishermen received some protection from the lifeboat which went out into rough seas to rescue those in danger of drowning. The coastguard's gun would bring the crew running from their various occupations to launch the lifeboat. Newson was the local chairman of the Royal National Lifeboat Institution (RNLI) and there are records of him personally taking part in rescues when he went into the water waist-deep to be part of the human chain along a rope that was formed to rescue the shipwrecked fishermen one by one. According to Millicent, he received 'official thanks from the RNLI engrossed on vellum' for what he had done. He was prepared to risk his life for the seamen with whom he formed a close bond.

He loved the sea and wanted to pass this on to his children by taking them out in his boats. An anecdote is told about one of the family's dogs retching on one of these outings, as the boat lurched from one side to the other in the swell. Newson had always said that seasickness was an affectation. Millicent quotes him as saying, 'God rest my soul, look at that poor thing; then it is not an affectation after all.' Millicent also tells a story about being taken out on the lifeboat itself. After the gun had been fired for a practice run, she went down to the beach holding her father's hand. When invited to join the crew on the boat, her father said he could not as he had his small daughter with him. The sailor replied, 'Little miss would like to come too, Sir.' So they set off together, putting on cork jackets to help them stay afloat if they capsized. Though they did not fall into the water, the sea broke over them soaking Milly.

This is an early example of how Newson exposed his children to adventure rather than pampering them and protecting them from possibly risky experiences.

The little seaside town in which the Garrett children grew up might justly be described as a backwater. Despite this, their lives were enriched by the freedom they were given to explore their environment and to engage with life in the town and its surroundings. Newson loved horses and either rode them or drove them to go from place to place. As soon as they were old enough, the children were put onto the backs of Shetland ponies and taught to ride. Newson then proudly took them out as a family on horseback, giving them the opportunity to become confident in the saddle and to explore more distant areas that could not be reached easily on foot. In the winter, they learnt to skate and raced along the salt marshes. In the summer, they went sailing on the sea, although there is no record of them learning to swim in the sea or even in the River Alde. Along with physical activities, which must have contributed to their good health and their energy, the children also got to know the local people with whom they were free to talk and to acquire an understanding of how they lived.

East Suffolk was a relatively poor part of East Anglia and there were few members of the gentry in the town with whom the children could mix. The Garretts were well known for several generations for the success of the iron works at Leiston, which Newson's brother Richard expanded with the manufacture of more advanced machinery which improved agricultural productivity. However, Newson was a self-made man who acquired his wealth through his own drive and inventiveness. As such, in the class-conscious era of mid-Victorian Britain, he was not likely to socialise with the two or three families Millicent identified as belonging to the 'aristocracy'.

She described them as being 'aloof from people of the town' and not making 'the smallest impression on our lives', probably in part because they were often absent as they also had properties elsewhere. In her memoirs, she identifies one or two individuals who became family friends, such as Percy Metcalf and his wife. He was a shipbuilder from Tyneside who was contracted by her father to build some ships at Snape. She singles him out because of his passion for music, 'It was he who introduced us to the great world of music – Bach, Mozart and Handel.' This friendship led to the Garrett sisters' lifelong love of classical music.

There was no barrier put up by their parents to the Garrett children making friendly contacts with fishermen and their families, with men who worked for Newson and their wives and with local characters such as Bob Wilson, the old seaman who sat in the tower as a 'look-out man'. These men and women entertained and amused them. The children's lives were not restricted by snobbery. They acquired an understanding of how people struggled to survive on low incomes, of their punishing long hours and of the strength of body and mind they needed in the unrelenting demands of their arduous jobs.

Millicent is the best source on these contacts as she describes them in the first two chapters of her memoir. There is no reference to the housemaids who worked for her mother, but she describes with warmth and admiration a couple who spent many years in her parents' service. Barham was the carriage driver, groom and gardener who also looked after the pigs and turned them into bacon. On Sundays, Barham's only day of rest, he walked three miles there and back to a Dissenters' chapel where he worshipped. In spite of her devout mother, religion never featured much in Millicent's later life, so her best explanation for this was that he was an out-and-out outdoor man who loved the walk through gorse and heather with the sea shining in the distance. The Garrett children also walked and rode through this landscape and, like music, walking was one of the pleasures they enjoyed throughout their lives.

Millicent's book includes a long anecdote about Barham which reveals another aspect of the sisters' lives. One of Barham's tasks was to drive the children in the family carriage when they were visiting somewhere too far away to walk. On one occasion, he took Agnes and Millicent to a ball in Saxmundham, eight miles from Aldeburgh. On the way back, the carriage overturned when the horses wandered off the road and went up a bank. Barham guarded the carriage and its contents, but the girls had no other option than to walk two miles home at night in their satin slippers. Their father was appalled. He accused Barham of being drunk or having fallen asleep, which he indignantly denied. Newson was unconvinced and unforgiving, so Barham was sacked. Within a few days, however, he was back in his job after an intervention from Mrs Barham, who persuaded him to admit he was asleep. The sisters were delighted and none the worse for their long walk at night.

Mrs Barham ran their mother's dairy. Millicent described her as remarkable. She and her sisters visited her often so that they could enjoy conversations with her and the amusing anecdotes she recounted. She claimed they never left the company of Mrs Barham without coming back with something worth remembering. Millicent recognised that although uneducated, Mrs Barham was clever, with many skills as well as a command over those she was close to, including her husband. Amongst her other achievements was designing and making elaborate quilts in silk. She gave one to all six of the Garrett sisters. Relationships with women like Mrs Barham influenced them and developed their high regard for working-class women. They were later able to empathise with them in ways most middle-class Victorian women found difficult. In Jo Manton's biography of Elizabeth Garrett Anderson, she suggests that from these relationships Elizabeth learnt an 'unaffected simplicity which she kept all through her life'.

Invitations to balls appeared to be part of the girls' social life, where they were able to meet the other young people from families who could afford to entertain in this way. Thus, in spite of their large family and its closeness, they were not confined to interacting with their siblings alone. They mixed more widely and in the absence of their parents.

The girls were also exposed to the rough and tumble of local small-town politics by their father, who talked openly about both friends and foes. When he went out to visit a new house that was being built, he sometimes took one of his daughters with him. He clearly enjoyed their company and was as likely to invite one of them to join him as his sons. Elizabeth accompanied him in an open dog cart when he travelled to markets in the region to buy corn and barley. After women were given the vote in local elections, Newson sent his daughters, who were still living at home, to canvass female voters. By then, he had changed his allegiance from Conservative to Liberal, embracing more progressive values. Although there is little evidence that he was involved in national politics, he read the newspapers and followed events such as the Crimean War. Milly remembers holding his hand while he tried to persuade the leaders of the beachmen in Aldeburgh to volunteer for the navy. Although only six years old, she listened to and absorbed the argument about it. A couple of years later, Newson came into breakfast waving a newspaper, calling to his children, 'Heads up and shoulders down, Sebastopol is taken.'

His daughters were no more confined to the nursery than his sons. They were encouraged to be active and they were free to roam. What kind of diet they had is not clear, but under Louisa's careful management of the kitchen and the dairy and produce from the gardens and orchards, it is likely that they were well-fed. The physical exercise they took in the bracing weather along the Suffolk coast contributed to their good health. In old age, Elizabeth was to say that in seventy years, she had never suffered from a headache.

Newson and Louisa were temperamentally different and they each got on with their daily lives independently, but they were devoted to each other. What they shared was great energy and the determination to succeed in their separate spheres. Their children's environment, and perhaps their genes too, would have disposed them to be persistent and determined and to have the ability to work hard for long hours without being totally drained of energy. The children were also shaped by the model of a deeply happy marriage, which they were able to replicate in their own lives. They observed their mother's orderliness, sense of duty, calmness and morality; and their father's inventiveness and refusal to take no for an answer. It was an inheritance to be envied and one which three of the daughters used to great advantage. Their childhood environment, with so many siblings, meant that they learnt to defend themselves and to speak out to be heard. Most of the education they received in their early years was informal, but their intelligence and their native wit compensated for the limitations of their schooling. When they eventually went to boarding school in their teens, their willingness to learn and their ambition was apparent.

2

EDUCATION AT HOME
AND AT SCHOOL

The Garretts, like many middle-class parents in mid-Victorian Britain, found it a challenge to find ways to provide educational opportunities for their daughters. Tutors were hired to teach the sons before they were sent off to board at boys' public schools, which were being founded from the middle of the nineteenth century. For girls, the solution in most cases was to find a governess. They were women drawn from the unfortunate circumstances of genteel poverty combined with few or no prospects of marriage. They needed a home and they moved in with the strangers who hired them. They were tolerated but rarely appreciated. Their skills as teachers were usually limited, as they had inadequate preparation for the all-purpose educators they were expected to be. They had little or no privacy and rare opportunities for broadening their own experience or for making friends outside the families with whom they lived. They had little leisure and no one to share it with other than the children they tried to befriend as well as to teach.

Amelia Edgeworth was a typical example. Poor and pious, she was hired by the Garretts in 1846 initially to teach Louie and

Elizabeth, aged eleven and a half and ten. By then, Louisa also had four younger children and a fifth was born the following year, so she had little time to give further lessons to the older children. Where Miss Edgeworth came from and how she was recruited is not recorded, but it would have been easy for the family to find and to hire her. The supply of potential governesses easily exceeded the demand. In 1851, there were approximately 25,000 of them. When posts were advertised, there were sometimes several hundred applicants. Most young women stayed at home until they married if their families could afford to support them. If they could not, there were few alternatives to becoming a governess. Higher education for women did not exist and the professions were closed to them. Even school teaching was an unlikely option, as there were so few schools before the 1870 Education Act, which established elementary education, and attendance at school was not compulsory until 1880.

Few young women became governesses because they positively wanted this role. It was forced on them because they had no alternative; more often than not it was a joyless existence but one from which it was rarely possible to escape. Amelia Edgeworth's experience was typical. She slept in a curtained bed in the same room as Louie and Elizabeth, undressing at night and dressing in the morning behind the curtains. Presumably, she found some way of washing, although access to a bath was unlikely. She had her meals with the family and was never able to escape for a holiday. Her routine consisted of spending all morning in the school room, then taking the same walk along the road towards Leiston for a mile, then going back for a mile each afternoon. She was self-effacing and servile and it appears from Elizabeth's comments that her lessons were as dull as her life. At the dining table, she strove to agree with everything Louisa said, on one occasion provoking an irritable response from Newson, 'Miss Edgeworth, you just said the opposite a minute ago.' She replied that the last time she spoke was before she had had 'the pleasure of hearing dear Mrs Garrett's opinion'.

The main content of Miss Edgeworth's lessons was drawn from a book entitled *Historical and Miscellaneous Questions for the Use of Young People*, from which she took a new section each day. It is easy to criticise these governesses, although it is also unfair. They had virtually no teaching materials and few other sources from which to draw on and usually no training whatsoever on how to teach. Unsurprisingly, her instruction was not going to engage a girl as high-spirited and intelligent as Elizabeth, who made the lessons more entertaining by finding ways to trip up Miss Edgeworth. She encouraged her gentler, older sister to do the same. They asked Miss Edgeworth questions she could not answer and poked fun at her when she failed. Like other children of this age whose teachers lacked the skills and the personality to motivate them and were unable to provide material to interest them, they took pleasure in humiliating her.

Attempts were made by the girls' parents to reason with them; and when that failed, to punish them. They were of no avail. The school room was a battleground and the war needed to be ended. Some Victorian parents might have decided that as the girls were by then thirteen and nearly fifteen, their formal education could come to an end. The Garretts took a different view. Just as their younger brothers were sent away to school, so should the girls continue their education. Newson had acquired enough money to afford to give his daughters a secondary education away from home and, unlike many wealthy fathers, he was determined to use his wealth to do so. How he selected the school they eventually went to is not clear, nor can we be sure that Louisa played an equal part in choosing the school. We do know that he began with a choice that was quickly regretted. Louie, not with Elizabeth but with her cousin Betsy Marion Garrett, who was a similar age, was sent to a school in Hampstead. It was an appalling experience. There was not enough to eat and a hamper of good food sent from Suffolk was confiscated; the accommodation was wholly inadequate and the teaching was of poor quality. Fortunately, their grandfather (Louisa's father) visited them and was shocked by what he saw. They were removed indefinitely after only four months there.

The next school was chosen with more care. The Boarding School for Ladies was one of a number of small private schools in Blackheath. It had thirty-seven pupils, according to the 1851 census. It was owned and run by the Misses Browning, who were the step-aunts of the poet Robert Browning. Another of their relatives was Samuel Browning, who was a minister at a chapel in Framlingham in Suffolk, and the owner of a small day school for boys. He may have recommended the Blackheath school to Newson Garrett. By whatever means Newson alighted on it, it was to change the course of his daughters' lives, probably more through the other pupils they met there than through what they were taught. In 1851, about half the pupils came from London, the rest from far and wide across the country. The girls with whom the Garrett sisters became friends were from middle-class families with money from the successful businesses they owned. Louie and Elizabeth were invited to stay with them in the holidays and after they had left the school. These invitations gave them the chance to broaden their experience beyond their home in Suffolk.

Miss Louisa Browning, their headmistress, was eccentric but

amiable. More important, she was convinced that the education of girls should not be confined to accomplishments but should embrace a curriculum, in which they would learn to read widely and to write well. Modern languages were deemed to be important and pupils were required to speak French all the time, although it is doubtful whether that could be effectively imposed outside the classroom. They were introduced to German and Italian literature as well as to French writing. What the Garrett parents made of this is not known. We do know that when visiting the school to decide on whether to select it, Newson made only one request after the extras on the curriculum had been described. He said they would take them all but insisted that his daughters should be able to have another extra: a hot bath once a week. However surprised she was by this unusual request since few houses had baths at the time, Miss Browning organised a washtub in front of the kitchen range on Saturday nights where the girls could wash in hot water, screened by a towel horse. They became known as the 'bathing Garretts'.

It is unlikely that Louie and Elizabeth had read many of the classics before attending school. Their father would have had little inclination to read them; their mother little time; and their governess too little imagination to include them in the school room. In Blackheath, by contrast, they read widely and learnt to enjoy books. In her biography of Elizabeth, Jo Manton said she read poetry as well as prose, including 'not only the fashionable Tennyson but Wordsworth, Milton and Coleridge as well. She read Gibbon and Motley for pleasure, and for relaxation Trollope, Thackeray or her favourite, George Eliot.' This focus not only established the habit of reading, which was to remain an important part of the sisters' lives, it also taught them how to write with confidence and clarity. It was an invaluable skill in the campaigns they pursued later.

Their parents must have been satisfied with the school for they sent Alice, Agnes and Millicent there when they reached their teens. Only Josephine, the youngest daughter, was not exposed to the little Blackheath school. Had she been sent there too, perhaps she might have made her mark in some sphere or other, but unlike her older sisters, she failed to do so. Millicent formed a close bond with Agnes, just as Elizabeth did with Louie. Each pair of sisters had the advantage of their sibling's company at school. This must have lessened homesickness and the misery so many children suffered when sent to boarding school away from the familiar companionship and comfort of their own homes. How Alice fared is not known, but she went alone as her two older siblings nearest in age to her were boys.

The sisters' later views about their schooling were not identical. Millicent said Louisa Browning ruled her school with a rod of iron but said she was a born teacher who was appreciated by her pupils for her 'thoroughness and her method'. The iron rod cannot have been as harsh as it might sound, for she describes Miss Browning's eccentricities with amusement and affection. For example, Miss Browning thought it beneath the school's intellectual aspirations to teach needlework. She thought it should be taught at home. If she saw a girl with a needle in her hand, she would exclaim dismissively, 'A guinea a stitch, my dear, a guinea a stitch!' Millicent also describes her rather bizarre taste in clothes, mixing 'scarlet, purple, green and yellow on her ample person'. Elizabeth was more critical. According to her daughter, Elizabeth said that she remembered the stupidity of the teachers there with shudders. With hindsight, she was disappointed that she was taught no science and little, if any, mathematics. In saying so, she failed to reflect on the unlikelihood of being able to find female teachers who had any knowledge of these subjects. Given the contempt she had for her governess, it is a little surprising that she was not more generous about at least some of the teaching she had at school. While the rules about speaking French all the time were probably irritating and would have compromised the quality of conversations the girls might have had on intellectual issues, at least it gave Elizabeth enough knowledge of the language to live in Paris and study medicine there in her twenties.

One of the school's greatest gifts to her, and indeed to Louie too, were the friendships they were able to make with other girls. There would have been time to get to know other pupils outside the classroom. The only obligatory form of exercise in girls' schools at the time was to go out for walks. Dartmouth Row, where the school was located, was a pleasant road with large houses that accommodated other small boarding schools. While walking in a crocodile could not have matched the freedom of exploring the coast and the fields inland around Aldeburgh, the girls found that Blackheath was an attractive suburban village with its own open space and was close to the Royal Park of Greenwich. If they walked as far as the park, they would have been able to look down onto Sir Christopher Wren's superb master plan for the Royal Naval Hospital and Inigo Jones's Queen's House. Beyond there was the Thames, crowded with vessels taking people and goods in and out of London. It was a pleasing environment to share with their fellow pupils, amongst whom two sets of sisters became lasting friends. The Smith girls were the daughters of a well-off businessman who ran a large drapers' shop and lived in central London but had a country house in Acton, where Louie went to stay. Jane, Sophie and Annie Crow came from Gateshead, where their father owned a chemical factory manufacturing alkali. Both sisters travelled north to stay at

Unsworth Hall, the Crow's house outside Gateshead. These visits had a momentous effect on the sisters, as will emerge later.

After two years, Louie and Elizabeth left the school together. The independence they had acquired through their upbringing in Aldeburgh was enhanced by being away from home and learning to fend for themselves without their parents. They were intelligent and open to new ideas acquired through their wide reading and enthusiasm about new experiences. Louie was gentle and loving; Elizabeth was high-spirited, confident and curious about the world. On their departure from Blackheath, they were rewarded with a short trip to the Continent, starting in Paris and going on to see the scenery as they travelled through the Rhine Gorge. Back in London, they visited the Great Exhibition in the Crystal Palace. Agnes and Millicent, at home in Suffolk, were greatly disappointed at not being included. They were mollified by presents of blue velvet and lace bonnets with pink ribbons, which their older sisters brought home for them. After the excitement of the Great Exhibition, which Elizabeth never forgot and talked about in her old age, returning to the life of daughters at home at Alde House was an anticlimax. However, they took pleasure in encouraging their younger siblings to broaden their interests beyond the limitations of Miss Edgeworth's instruction. They had a social life of sorts with other young people who lived near enough to meet at dances or picnics. Louie, beautiful and sensitive, was pursued by young men looking for a wife. She turned down her uncle Richard's eldest son, causing further friction between Richard and her father.

Elizabeth spent her time pursuing learning that had not been possible at her school. Her parents agreed that a tutor hired to prepare her brother Newson for entry into the army could coach her in Latin and arithmetic. She had the self-discipline and drive to acquire new knowledge without the structure supplied in a school classroom. She also continued to read widely by finding books of interest in the Aldeburgh Public Reading Room, which charged £1 for an annual subscription. She supplemented this with a subscription to a London lending library, which sent her new novels. She also kept up with current affairs by reading her father's newspapers. At some point, although it is not quite clear when, she started Sunday evening sessions in the Alde House drawing room, which she described as 'Talks on Things in General'. This may have been after Louie married in 1857, leaving Elizabeth as the eldest sister at home. Millicent was to describe Elizabeth becoming 'more than ever, therefore, the leader and friend of the younger half of the family'. She remembers Elizabeth sitting on the sofa with George, the youngest in the family, on her lap, with the others sitting around her. The subjects she covered were drawn it seems from her own reading as well as political events at the time. Millicent lists 'Garibaldi and the freeing of Italy from the Austrians, Carlyle's *Cromwell*, Macaulay's *History of England* and modern political events and persons such as Lord Palmerston, and the chances of a Reform Bill, Louis Napoleon and the Haynau incident etc., etc.' This sounds like intellectually demanding fare for the younger children, and it might have gone over some of their heads. Not so Millicent, whose great intelligence was apparent from early on. She claims to have been especially interested in Italian unification and the campaign in Italy against the Austrians in 1857. Apparently, Giuseppe Garibaldi, the Count of Cavour and Victor Emmanuel became her heroes and Millicent tried to find out everything she could about them. She was certainly precocious, as she was only ten years old at the time.

Louie's new husband was James Smith, the brother of her school friend. On her marriage, she left Suffolk to live in London with her husband, first in Bayswater and later in Manchester Square. Within a year, she had given birth to a son. Three more children were born later. Although she had left Aldeburgh, she remained closely attached to her family, especially to Elizabeth, but to her younger sisters too, who were invited to London to stay with her. She was stalwart in supporting them and provided them with opportunities to benefit from London life through going to events such as lectures and through meeting a wider range of people than would have been possible at home in Aldeburgh.

Millicent describes her first visit to London in January 1858, when she would have been ten years old. The railway line to Aldeburgh had not yet been built, so to visit Louie meant travelling in her father's carriage to Ipswich, which was twenty-six miles away. The railway journey was a new wonder for her, as were the streets of London when they arrived. Shop windows were not shuttered at the time and were, as she put it, 'brilliantly illuminated' so it seemed to her 'a sort of fairyland'. On this first visit to London, Millicent remembers being made a fuss of and given a wonderful time. She also recounts being taken out to an event where 'comical stories' seem to have been told. The entertainment was interrupted by the announcement that, on the way to the opera, the Emperor and Empress of France had nearly been blown up by Orsini. She describes it as the first occasion she became aware of what she called 'the tragedy of revolutionary politics', to which she was to remain opposed throughout her life.

Once she had started school in Blackheath, Millicent was sometimes invited by Louie to spend the weekend at her home. Presumably, Alice and Agnes received similar invitations. Once Agnes had left school and returned to Suffolk, Millicent was without her, so the weekends with Louie provided her with welcome contact with her eldest and most motherly of sisters. Louie and her husband took Millicent with them to entertainments on Saturdays and to hear F. D. Maurice, the intellectual churchman and founder of the Working Men's College, preach at St Peter's in Vere Street on Sundays. Louie and Millicent also went on walks together in Kensington Gardens and Louie introduced her to William Wordsworth's poetry. Millicent described her 'as much a mother to me as a sister'. When it came to returning to school early on a Monday morning, Millicent was put on a bus at Marble Arch, getting off at London Bridge Station, where she took a train to Greenwich and walked from the station on to Blackheath. The bus route passed Newgate Prison and Millicent was shocked by the rabble gathering to watch the public executions, which she thought a repulsive form of entertainment. However, she did not question whether this journey across Victorian London on her own in her mid-teens was something she should not have been expected to do. Had she been asked, she would probably have said that it contributed to her independence, her confidence and her experience of life.

At school, she was benefiting from a new teacher. She described her as 'a really competent teacher who was extremely good to me and to whom I was devoted'. Perhaps this unnamed woman was perceptive about Millicent's qualities as a student, for she was certainly curious, highly intelligent and better informed than most fifteen-year-old girls as a result of what she had learnt both from Elizabeth's 'Talks' in Aldeburgh and from her weekends with Louie and her husband, James, in London. It would not be surprising if her teacher had picked her out as a star pupil and was therefore good to her. Millicent also briefly had the company of her eighteen-year-old distant cousin Rhoda Garrett, for whom Louie and Elizabeth secured a role as a pupil teacher at the Blackheath school.

Rhoda was from a branch of the family which became known as the Derbyshire Garretts. Her mother died young, leaving two sons as well as Rhoda. Her father, a poor clergyman, married and had four more children, displacing Rhoda, who appears to have been more or less pushed out of her home. One of her brothers went to New Zealand; the other found work in an office in London. What else was there for Rhoda to do other than become a governess? To provide her with some preparation for the role, Louie organised a spell in Alsace, where Rhoda was able to learn French and German. Rhoda's placement in Blackheath was designed to prepare her to teach English subjects. According to Millicent, 'she immediately became my guide, philosopher and friend, and more particularly, my protector'. Rhoda was later to become Agnes's working partner and close companion and part of the Garrett sisterhood. However, Rhoda's progress to becoming a competent governess was limited and she soon left the Blackheath school. Elizabeth despaired and thought Rhoda was indolent. A better explanation was probably that she dreaded the thought of being sentenced to be a governess and that Elizabeth failed to detect her potential or to see any of her extraordinary qualities, which became more obvious later. Rarely short of ideas, Elizabeth also suggested Rhoda might like to become a photographer, following in the footsteps of Julia Margaret Cameron, who had broken new boundaries in becoming famous for her portraits which were being widely exhibited. This suggestion went nowhere and Rhoda instead became a reluctant governess for a few years before a successful escape eventually materialised, as will be described later.

Elizabeth's eight years in Aldeburgh after leaving school at sixteen were a period not just of applying herself to new areas of knowledge; they were also a time to reflect on her future and the kind of life she wanted to have. In considering her options, she was greatly influenced by Emily Davies. On a trip with Louie to the north-east to stay with their schoolfriends the Crowe sisters, Elizabeth was introduced to their friend Emily, the daughter of the Reverend Dr John Davies, Rector of Gateshead. The small, prim and mousey-looking young woman of twenty-four was to be a huge influence on the eighteen-year-old Elizabeth over the coming years. Millicent described their meeting as a turning point in history. The friendship between the Garrett and Crow sisters and Emily Davies lasted throughout their lives. The part played by Emily was pivotal in Elizabeth's decision to pursue a career. Emily's relentless pursuit of the rights of women to education, to professional work and to roles outside those of wife and mother was to influence not just Elizabeth but a generation of women from the 1850s onwards. Later, it certainly greatly influenced Millicent, who became passionate about extending educational opportunities for women.

The visit to Gateshead in 1854 was for some weeks and long enough for Elizabeth and Emily to talk at length and to get to know each other well enough to be sure that they wanted to stay in contact through letters. Growing up in a rectory had left much to be desired for an ambitious and intellectually able young woman. Emily greatly resented the precedence given to the education of her brothers, on whom money was spent in sending them to public schools and university. She had a minimal education at home, which included writing weekly English essays for her father to criticise or praise and learning Latin with her brothers. She grew up in an environment which was religious, conservative and intellectual. With her three brothers and sister, Emily and her siblings played at being missionaries but more surprisingly at being parliamentary candidates too. Presumably, this helped to hone their skills in the arts of persuasion, whether religious or secular. As a young adult, she was frustrated by the amount of time she had to give to household duties which bored her. She found in Elizabeth a willing listener to her passionate views about the need to release women from the constrictions of their lives in Victorian middle-class families.

Elizabeth had devised for herself a way of life which on a surface level was happy and productive. As well as her wide reading and her disciplined self-education, she gave lessons to the younger children, whom she loved deeply. She accompanied her father on business visits in the vicinity, she rode regularly and she socialised with her cousins and other young people. Yet she was increasingly dissatisfied and bored by provincial life and being her mother's companion, especially after her beloved elder sister had married and left for life in London. Her restlessness grew and turned into a search for occupations which would be more rewarding. Looking back much later at her life in her early twenties, she admitted to her comfortable circumstances but complained that she had nothing to do. She said, 'I was full of energy and vigour and of the discontent which goes with unemployed activities.' It was not true she had nothing to do. What she had to do fell short of her ambition, did not stretch her enough and had no clear long-term purpose.

All this was shared with Emily, who fed her discontent but, in the end, helped to channel it into a truly challenging goal, which would have seemed insurmountable to weaker characters than Elizabeth. Elizabeth returned to visit her in Gateshead and Emily travelled south and visited Elizabeth in Aldeburgh, where she was able to meet the younger Garretts. They did not appreciate her. The Gateshead rectory was probably a less easy-going regime than Alde House and produced in Emily not just resentment but also contributed to her somewhat humourless persona, inclined to priggishness.

Millicent claimed that 'her manner towards us was not winning ... She always seemed to be letting us know of how little consequence we were.' Undoubtedly, Emily's qualities of intelligence, a dry wit and a genuine wish to encourage and support other women were not apparent to Millicent and the others in their childhood. Yet Emily took a genuine interest in the sisters. For example, she suggested that Alice, who had returned sometime earlier from the Blackheath school, where like all the sisters, she had spent two years, might try to become the first female civil servant. This was a very ambitious proposal and highly unlikely to succeed. Moreover, Alice was less daring than her sisters and rejected the idea, but she was by no means idle and she continued to educate herself. She had a particular talent for numbers and was able to calculate with speed and accuracy.

Happily, a relevant alternative to trying to force a way into the all-male preserve of the civil service emerged for Alice. To Elizabeth's delight, she was able to write to Emily telling her that her father Newson was offering Alice a position as a junior clerk in his counting house, where for five or six hours each day, she would work on the accounts and write some of Newson's letters, for which she was paid a small salary. This was hardly a great leap into the cause of professional roles for women. As Elizabeth admitted, some of the work at first would be drudgery, but it did provide an alternative to housekeeping with which the nineteen-year-old Alice was pre-occupied, and the limited hours meant she was still able to provide her mother with support and companionship. However, Alice's work on her father's accounts did not last long, as at the age of twenty-one, she married and left for India to join her husband there.

Alice's choice of Herbert Cowell to be her husband is an enigma.

It is not known whether, like Louie, she had had other offers of marriage, nor how she met him. He came from a Suffolk family but was working in Calcutta at the Indian Bar. Newson was opposed to the marriage and had to be dissuaded from sending back the wedding present of a tea set sent by his brother Richard and his wife, who was Louisa's sister. Although Alice must surely have met Herbert in England, Newson insisted on giving Alice a return fare to India, telling her that when she saw him, she would want to return. As so often, Newson was outspoken. He was not able to tactfully accept her choice. Moreover, he was initially reluctant to welcome some of his other daughters' choices of men to marry. It suggests he found the prospect of them leaving home difficult to embrace. He was both close to them and proud of them, and their company mattered to him. In Alice's case, he even accompanied her as far as Malta, demonstrating his affection and making sure she would have good and reliable company for the rest of the lengthy boat journey to Calcutta.

Once Alice had settled into Calcutta, true to the Garrett sisters' drive to go on acquiring new knowledge, she took German lessons with another Raj wife. What led her to choose to learn German in India is perplexing and unknown. She also helped her husband Herbert who, as well as working as a practising lawyer, wrote a 900-page book on thousands of cases which had been through the Indian courts. Alice edited, proofread and indexed this tome, which became a standard book for Indian law students. Her absence in India during her early adulthood married to a somewhat conservative and rather dull lawyer, although reliable and scholarly, may well have thwarted her development as a feminist activist like her sisters. But at least she was engaged in work beyond household duties, even if on her husband's book rather than one of her own.

Alice kept in close touch with her sisters and with her mother through frequent letters in which she commented favourably on their progress in the roles they had chosen. Early in her marriage, she had a daughter, followed by a stillborn son. She seems to have made friends, although she was not uncritical of Raj life. However, she did not come back to Aldeburgh until her daughter was five years old. True to the prevailing views at the time that it was better for children once they reached this age to go back to relatives in Britain, she left her daughter behind instead of taking her back to Calcutta. It was a terrible wrench and Alice missed her hugely. The birth of a son a little later was of some mitigation. But her pain continued until she finally returned to England after ten years in India.

By the time Alice left for India, first Agnes and then Millicent had returned from their allocated two years at boarding school. In fact, much to her disappointment, Millicent was withdrawn early as a result of a temporary financial crisis Newson was facing because of one or more risky investments in his business activities. Savings had to be made, not just on school fees but on household expenses too. This even included the food the family ate, so that for a short period the meat that usually accompanied their Suffolk dumplings was cut out. However, Millicent's parents were determined to find some way of compensating her for her misery at leaving school sooner than she anticipated. They provided her with her own little bedroom and use of the school room in the mornings, so that she could have a quiet space where she could continue learning. Her friends at school gave her a leaving present of a complete set of Shakespeare's plays, which she kept in her bedroom along with other favourite books. She read the plays on Sunday afternoons, sometimes reading them aloud with Agnes.

Sunday mornings meant church, where she was bored by the

Reverend Dowler's sermons. She described him as 'a pure formalist and a dull one at that' and 'platitudinous to the last degree'. She describes how on the first Sunday of the month, he always said he had to be brief on 'our sacrament morning'. In her memoir, Millicent remarked that 'we hailed the brevity and escaped out of the church glad to have got it over in a shorter time than usual'. While her mother failed to persuade any of her daughters to embrace her evangelical faith, Millicent was much more generous about the Reverend Dowler's successor, saying he was 'the very best kind of clergyman, devout, thoughtful and original'. However, Canon Thompson fell far short of Millicent's high standards when he was dismissive about women, claiming a church in Asia was insignificant because it was almost entirely made up of female worshippers. A few days later, when he was visiting her mother, she told him, 'I nearly called out "Shame" in the middle of your sermon last Sunday.'

Visits to London to stay with Louie were another way in which Millicent's education was continued informally. For example, the family went to the opera for the first time, which delighted Millicent and allowed her to develop her love of music. When her uncle Balls Garrett asked what she and her siblings would like as a treat, they told him they would like to go to a concert. They were thrilled by listening to Joseph Haydn but realised it was probably purgatory for her uncle, whom she called a 'kind old man', because 'he cared no more for music than a mastodon would have done'. Their activities were not focused only on uplifting culture. They went to dances too, which she loved. They were also exposed to political events. For example, in 1865, Louie and her husband took Millicent to an election meeting where the Liberal candidate John Stuart Mill was speaking.

This experience had a huge impact on her. She describes how he spoke with passion and conviction on the importance of the political enfranchisement of women. She noted that this alienated some of the audience but attracted others, including her brother-in-law James Smith, who was an elector. She mentioned that Mill was a strong supporter of extending the franchise to working-class men, who were denied the vote, as well as to women. She admired the way Mill handled questions, especially his candour when faced with a hostile heckler. In a memorable quote from her book, she stated, 'I was a woman suffragist, I may say, from my cradle, but this meeting kindled tenfold my enthusiasm for it.' Staying with her much older sister Louie would have further reinforced her conviction about the suffrage being extended to women. Not long after Mill's election address, Louie had become the secretary of the Kensington Society, whose small committee included Elizabeth. Although this is speculation, it is highly likely that Louie talked to Millicent, who was thirteen years younger, about the injustice of denying women a say on who represented them in Parliament. The sisters would have been as one on this, just as they were on the beauty of Wordsworth's poetry. Talking together, they reinforced each other's feminist ideals.

Meanwhile, Millicent's self-education continued. In her own study of current political developments, she read about the American Civil War, becoming, she said, like her sister Elizabeth, a staunch Northerner. She claimed to have studied all the arguments made that slavery was the real cause of the war. President Abraham Lincoln was one of her heroes for the stand he eventually took on slavery and then the role he played in its abolition in America. On the day on which he was assassinated in 1865, Millicent was seventeen. On that same day, she was taken by Louie to a party in Kensington at the house of a Liberal MP and his feminist wife, both ardent Northerners. The conversation was dominated by the news that Lincoln had been assassinated while watching a play. In spite of her youth, Millicent confidently claimed that his death was the worst loss of a single man that could have hit the world. When challenged she added, 'Yes, greater than the loss of any of the crowned heads of Europe.' Amongst those who were present was Henry Fawcett, a blind academic and Liberal politician. He was immediately taken by this girl, who stood out in a group of older and more experienced commentators in expressing her passionate convictions about the horror of the loss of Lincoln. He asked his host who she was, saying that he wanted to meet her and get to know her. This was a hugely important turning point in Millicent's life.

Henry Fawcett was not alone in being impressed by the Garrett sisters' spirited and surprisingly well-informed views. Their wide reading and their capacity to absorb and interpret what they read was considerable. They demonstrated that, in spite of only two years at school in their teens, they could go on learning under their own auspices. While they were studying at home in Aldeburgh, the younger sisters were also watching with interest what their older sister Elizabeth was doing after she left home.

3

GETTING MARRIED AND
LEAVING HOME

In order to understand what shaped Millicent and why her feminism did not lead to conflict with her family, a short diversion about her much older sister is needed, for it was Elizabeth who paved the way and who won round their father.

Marriage was the route normally taken when young women moved away from their parents' home, as happened in the case of the eldest daughter Louie and the third daughter Alice. Elizabeth had another ambition. She wanted a career of her own. It would give more meaning to her life than her daily routine as the eldest sibling still in Aldeburgh, studying and reading alone, as well as learning how to manage the large household, including the move backwards and forwards to Snape every year. Most young women in the 1860s would have found it extremely difficult, if not impossible, to fulfil this ambition. Elizabeth had three things in her favour: her friendship with Emily Davies, the support of her elder sister and, eventually, the encouragement of her father. Her energy, drive and determination were paramount and would have been obvious to Millicent, who was an observant, perceptive and much younger sister.

Emily Davies had been able to escape from the tyranny of her father's rectory in the north-east and spend time in London, where she had become involved in the early feminist movement, to which she introduced Elizabeth. Louie and her husband lived in central London and were able to offer Elizabeth somewhere to stay, telling her that she was free to come and go from Aldeburgh when she wished. This must have given Louisa Garrett, who opposed her daughter's wish to have a career, some reassurance that Elizabeth would at least be safe in her eldest daughter's home. Newson Garrett was also initially opposed, but he provided financial as well as 'moral' support once he had been won around. He was up for this fight as he had been in many of his own challenging business projects.

The *English Woman's Journal*, which was devoted to feminist issues, first appeared in 1858. A little later, probably encouraged by Emily Davies, Elizabeth started to read it. The key movers and shakers behind it were Barbara Bodichon, who financed it; Bessie Parkes, who edited it; and Jessie Boucherett, who helped to found it, along with the Society for Promoting the Employment of Women, and who wrote articles for it. Two of them came from radical Unitarian backgrounds, marked by progressive values and a commitment to change. Barbara Bodichon, née Leigh Smith, had the advantage of wealth and freedom. She had travelled on unchaperoned holidays, founded a non-denominational school and written two pamphlets on the legal position of women and women and work. Then, in 1857, she married an eccentric French doctor and lived with him for some time in Algiers, although she returned to London every summer to maintain her contacts and to escape the heat. Most of the women involved in the *English Woman's Journal* became part of what was known as the Langham Place Circle; they were young and able and determined to make a success in a variety of occupations. The journal, based in Langham Place, printed contributions women had made to the newly established Social Science Association meetings, in order to disseminate their feminist views more widely. These women formed a core of pioneers, who went on to campaign for the cause of the liberation of women for several decades.

The *English Woman's Journal* did not confine itself to the promotion of women in the professions. It also published articles on the dreadful conditions in which many working-class women lived and worked. It backed the idea of apprenticeships for women, so that they could be trained for work in a variety of trades such as printing, many of which were largely male preserves. However, the article in the magazine which caught Elizabeth's eye was about Doctor Elizabeth Blackwell, who was a relative of the editor Bessie Parkes and had emigrated to America as a child and had trained and become a doctor at a small university in the State of New York.

Elizabeth's decision to pursue a career was motivated by dissatisfaction with her role as her mother's companion and enforced by the domestic preoccupations which did not stimulate her nor engage her interest, rather than by a strong commitment to a particular vocation. She had to escape from the dreary daily chores and the lack of purpose in her life and find something more fulfilling. Elizabeth Blackwell provided her with a model of a woman who had challenged conventional views about suitable work for women by graduating in medicine and then setting up a people's dispensary, which served immigrant women and children in the slums of New York. She was not a campaigner for women's rights, nor was she interested in promoting herself publicly in search of a high profile.

She quietly got on with the job of treating her patients. Nevertheless, she attracted press comment, some of which was dismissive and hostile. One columnist claimed that 'it is impossible that a woman whose hands reek with gore can be possessed of the same nature or feelings as the generality of women'.

Newson Garrett had picked up from the newspapers some of the hostility expressed by commentators about Dr Blackwell. When he repeated it to his family, Elizabeth, confident as she was in taking on her father, sprang to the defence of the female doctor. Elizabeth's daughter, Louisa, recounts this incident in her biography of her mother. Since Newson had not met Dr Blackwell, and knew little about her, how could he rush to judge her, Elizabeth asked? She pushed him further with a suggestion that he should write to a business contact in London, related to Barbara Bodichon, who in turn was a friend of Elizabeth Blackwell. Newson respected his daughter for her spirited intervention and did what she asked. The outcome was a letter of introduction to Dr Blackwell. Elizabeth set off for London to stay with Louie. She then met Emily Davies, who was in London, staying nearby with her brother Llewelyn, who had become the rector of a Marylebone church. Emily and Elizabeth went to tea with Barbara, who told Elizabeth that she should definitely present the letter of introduction, which could be arranged to take place at her house.

Meanwhile, the Society for Promoting the Employment of Women had been set up and was provided with accommodation in the office of the *English Woman's Journal*. The journal had also established a small Ladies' Institute where women could meet to have lunch and read the newspapers and magazines. It was, on a tiny scale, an imitation of the gentlemen's clubs from which women remained excluded until the latter part of the twentieth century.

Emily and Elizabeth were able to enjoy the company of like-minded young women there. Having joined the Society for Promoting the Employment of Women, Elizabeth discovered an organisation which provided her with a context for pursuing her own goal of a career and for campaigning to make this possible for women generally. In her biography of her mother, her daughter Louisa quotes her as saying, 'No one has time for everything ... The passion of my life is to help women.'

In the spring of 1859, Elizabeth went to a lecture organised by the society given by Elizabeth Blackwell. The impression on Elizabeth Garrett was profound. At a party after the lecture, she presented Dr Blackwell with her letter of introduction. Dr Blackwell assumed that Elizabeth would follow her and become a doctor. However, at first, Elizabeth hesitated. In spite of her strength of mind and her willingness to defy convention, she betrayed a typical female modesty about her ability and a lack of confidence about the enormity of meeting the challenge that it would entail. Spending some time in Gateshead with the Crow sisters and Emily Davies allowed her to talk it over with friends who embraced the women's cause. These conversations helped her to put aside her doubts. None of them could have predicted just how huge the barriers would be to the achievement of her goal.

On her return from the north, Elizabeth went home to Aldeburgh and told her seventeen-year-old sister Alice, who met her at the station, 'I am going to be a doctor.' The rest of the family were not told about her ambition. Newson's new business ventures were not thriving and cuts had to be made in the family's outgoings. Elizabeth sensed this was not the time to present her parents with a bombshell, which would shock them and the wider community in Aldeburgh. She realised how expensive it would be to spend many years in training and needed to choose a time when Newson's fortunes were up not down. It was not until the following year, in 1860, that she told them.

At first, her father strongly opposed her wish to study medicine. In letters to Emily Davies, who constantly encouraged her, Elizabeth recounted her parents' reactions. At first, her father said he could not entertain it and her mother shut herself in her room and sobbed. Her conservative brother Edmund joined the opposition too. Millicent was thirteen at the time and was possibly away at school, so her views were not recorded. Probably by the time Millicent heard the news, Newson had relented. Elizabeth had stood her ground and used all the persuasive arguments she could muster to win him round. He loved this most spirited and clever daughter and once he had decided to support her, he joined the fight to get the training and the recognition she needed and financed it generously. Her mother said it would be the death of her and took many years to accept her wilful daughter's resolve. She would have liked Elizabeth to become the governess for the younger children if the conventional route of marriage and children of her own was not to happen. Elizabeth forcibly rejected her mother's suggestion. As to marriage, she thought it incompatible with achieving her ambition to train as a doctor. She could not be distracted from her goal.

Elizabeth was almost certainly right about the hard work it would take to achieve her objective. Wherever she turned, she faced seemingly insurmountable opposition. Her eventual victory after many years of seeking and then finding ways to circumvent the prejudice and rejection of most of the medical profession and the universities is testimony to her determination, her inventiveness and her persistence. In all these respects, she was a role model for Millicent, whose own struggles would come later.

Elizabeth was not without male admirers. Not conventionally beautiful, she had thick auburn hair and regular features, was small and slight and attracted men who admired vigour and energy, wit and intelligence. One of these was Henry Fawcett. In 1864, towards the end of her time as a student, Elizabeth and Harry became friends. He was a Cambridge academic and not yet an MP, although he had stood for Parliament three times and been defeated. He had published in 1863 a long book entitled *Manual of Political Economy*, which was influenced by John Stuart Mill, of whom he was a leading disciple. Harry's blindness was no impediment to his life as a scholar and politician. He lost his sight at the age of twenty-five while out shooting with his father, who accidentally let off his gun, leading to pellets entering both Harry's eyes. After this terrible accident, Harry resolved to continue his active life, presenting papers to the Social Science Association within a year of being blinded. He was also determined to enjoy a sporting life by following the pursuits he enjoyed, including walking, riding, rowing and skating, all physically taxing, as well as fishing. Having met Elizabeth through Jane Crow, Harry ensured that whenever he came from Cambridge to London, he spent time with her.

They had much in common. From an early age, Elizabeth had been interested in politics, had read the same newspapers at home as her father and debated the issues of the day with him, probably welcoming his shift from supporting the Conservatives to becoming a Liberal. Harry was a reformer and, like Elizabeth, a feminist. He was a good speaker, able to communicate with his audience and to convey his passion for change and reform. Elizabeth admired him and greatly enjoyed his company, writing to her mother about his success in keeping up with political issues and the news of the day by being read to for many hours each week. His enthusiasm for life was catching and conversations between them would certainly have ranged beyond her serious interests in reform including a wider role in public life for women. Elizabeth too brimmed with physical energy and loved the countryside of East Anglia. She would have empathised with Harry's Fenland skating and his riding. He would have understood her dedication to her studies and admired her ambition. However, her ambition did not deter him from asking her to marry him.

He had proposed to other women, all of whom had been unusual in their independence and commitment to an unconventional rejection of mere domesticity. One of them was an author and editor of several books, another a campaigner on women's education, but both these engagements were broken off. He also proposed to one of the founders of the *English Woman's Journal*. She rejected him. Harry Fawcett was clearly attracted to intellectually able female achievers. Elizabeth had much earlier decided that marriage was incompatible with her aim of training to be a doctor and establishing herself as a practitioner once qualified. Yet for the first time, she hesitated. Harry was an unusual suitor and would not have expected a conventional marriage. Rather than turning him down immediately, she consulted the woman to whom she was closer than anyone else, her sister Louie. Louie advised her not to marry Harry. She may have guessed that Elizabeth, when it came to it, would not have been willing to dedicate the time Harry would have needed from any wife to help him overcome the challenges of his disability.

In May 1865, Elizabeth wrote to her parents to tell them about Harry's proposal and that she had turned him down. Her letter is quoted by David Rubinstein in his biography of Millicent, 'I have not the least doubt about having been right in decidedly refusing though at the same time I know of few lives I should have liked better than being eyes and hands to a Cambridge professor and an MP.' She added, 'I wish though it had been Agnes.' Giving up marriage to Henry Fawcett allowed Elizabeth to go on dedicating her life to medicine. Once fully established as a doctor, she eventually embarked on an unconventional but immensely happy marriage at the age of thirty-four.

Harry did not give up on pursuing marriage and, if one of the Garrett daughters had rejected him, he would try another. It was not to be Agnes but Millicent. And Millicent, like Louie, was to leave home because she married. In October 1866, Harry Fawcett asked Millicent Garrett to marry him. She accepted and they became engaged. I can find no information about their courtship and how much time they had spent together before his proposal but possibly very little. Millicent was living at home in Aldeburgh and Harry was splitting his time between London and Cambridge and after earlier rejections was possibly in a hurry.

Elizabeth's reaction was one of understandable surprise and, less easy to interpret, horror. Her biographer, Jo Manton, wrote that 'pride and reticence would not allow her to speak of the offer of marriage she had received from the same man, nor what she had suffered in refusing it. Moreover, she still thought of her sister as a child.' Elizabeth immediately wrote to Millicent about Harry's unsuitability as a blind man living in poverty, who would not be able to support a family. She offered to seek the views of others, naming Jane Crow and Barbara Bodichon. She said she would come down to Aldeburgh for a family discussion if Millicent refused to change her mind. Refuse she did, and in doing so she demonstrated that she had the strength of will to match Elizabeth's powerful personality.

The route Millicent took was not to confront her directly but to enlist the support of Louie, whose judgement she trusted and who she knew could handle Elizabeth better than anyone else. Meanwhile, her father, who found it hard to reconcile himself to his daughters' marriages anyway, imposed a delay of a month before any public announcement of the engagement. Milly quickly wrote to Louie saying she had felt 'jumped on' by Elizabeth and by her parents:

> I had the most awful letter from Liz … I have not written for fear of vexing her, which I should be dreadfully sorry to do, for I know it is out of pure love for me and anxiety for my fortune that she wrote to me as she did … I believe that she would think that we were throwing ourselves away if we married the Archangel Michael with twenty thousand a year … If you see her before Saturday, giver her my love and try to talk her over or at least so far as to refrain from further jumping when she comes down here.

As so often, Louie's gentle powers of persuasion worked with Elizabeth. Having believed that a marriage between Harry and Elizabeth was not likely to have a happy outcome, two and a half years later, Louie came to a different view about Harry and Millicent. He had become an MP by then, which he combined with his academic work. Perhaps she thought that Millicent was more interested in politics than her older sister. Perhaps Louie thought that Millicent would have more time and more inclination to support Harry in a variety of ways including coping with blindness. She may also have thought that Harry would contribute successfully to the development of Millicent's growing intellectual interests, whereas he could do much less in providing the more practical backup Elizabeth needed in making decisions about how to successfully practise medicine. Whatever her reasons, Louie won Elizabeth round.

They also agreed that they would never talk about Harry's earlier proposal to Elizabeth.

In a letter to her mother, Louie was positive about the match saying, 'I do think Milly is admirably fitted to be happy as the wife of a man who is interested in public work – to enjoy the society which this state of things will bring her into and to make her husband very happy and proud too.' Sadly, Louie did not live to see just how accurate her predictions turned out to be. David Rubinstein's biography quotes from a letter Elizabeth sent to a friend a short while after Louie's intervention. She began by commenting on Henry Fawcett's good qualities, in spite of some minor faults that derived from being blind and being indulged because of it. He would not, she thought, be 'too exacting a husband'. She continued:

Millicent is rather young in years but practically she is as old as many people ten years older. She has never been unwise or flighty and she is heartily in love with him so she will not feel the service a burden. I have liked him much better than I ever did since the engagement … Mr Fawcett says frankly that Millicent is extremely like me and that is how he first thought of her, and I dare say it is so. As a matter of fact, she and I are more alike in every way than many of the others.

The comment by Elizabeth that Henry originally thought to approach Millicent because she was 'like me' seems a little self-satisfied at first sight. Nevertheless, it may have been true judging by a letter he sent to a friend the same month: 'In her whole character she bears a remarkable resemblance to Miss Elizabeth Garrett and I quite acknowledge with you that this is paying her a very high compliment.' Even more interesting is Elizabeth's view that the nineteen-year-old Millicent was more like her than any of her other sisters. Looking back over their lives much later, it is hard to dispute this. They shared a passionate belief in the potential of women to achieve great things in the wider world beyond their homes. They both dedicated their lives to women's rights, although in different spheres. Neither of them was flamboyant or charismatic, but both of them were respected and, in some ways, revered for their quiet persistence in campaigning for what they believed was needed to create a juster world for women.

Their eldest sister's commitment to feminism was unquestionably strong too. Had she lived, Louie might well have made her own contribution to reform. Only a few months after she had helped Millicent by winning over her family to the prospect of her marrying Harry, Louie fell ill. After a few days of dedicated care from Elizabeth, Louie died in early February 1867. She had appendicitis, for which surgical treatment had not yet been introduced. As she realised she was dying, she suffered greatly from the fear that her loss would be terribly hard for her four small children to bear. Elizabeth tried to console her that she would care for them, treating them as her own whether she had children of her own later or not. The loss of Louie was devastating for her whole family and especially for Elizabeth, who was so close to her.

Less than three months after her death, Henry Fawcett and Millicent Garrett were married in Aldeburgh. There is one surviving photograph of their wedding day with a few family members, although not all of them can be identified with certainty. What was most remarkable about them physically was the enormous difference in their height. He was immensely tall and she was so small. None of the Garrett sisters were as tiny as their mother, but they were all short. Other photos of Millicent show that she was particularly pretty with beautiful thick hair piled up on her head and described as the colour of amber. She had regular features with a high forehead and searching eyes. In many portraits, she is either holding or reading a book, and none shows her smiling. This is more likely a function of Victorian portraiture, in which smiles rarely featured, than of an over-serious and permanently unsmiling demeanour. On her wedding day, she was conventionally dressed in a white satin dress with a wreath of orange blossoms and tulle veil. Alice, having been sent the photograph, wrote from India that 'Millicent must have looked very pretty and nice'.

The wedding took place in the church in Aldeburgh and was officiated by the Reverend Henry Dowler, with whom Newson had quarrelled in the past and whose sermons Millicent found so tedious. Twenty years earlier, he had christened Millicent, although there is no record of whether he mentioned this at the wedding. The village celebrated the event with flags flown, according to the local newspaper, which also listed the expensive presents the couple received of silver, china, glass and books.

Like her elder sisters Louie and Alice, Millicent left home once married, but at less than twenty, she was even younger than they had been. Elizabeth never failed to take an interest in her younger sisters while they were still living at home and had encouraged them to continue to educate themselves and to consider a career. She was convinced that this would be no barrier to marriage. David Rubinstein quotes her as saying in a letter to her parents, 'They would see many more people whom they could marry, and my experience is that all men like women the better for showing that they are not *waiting* for marriage as the only object in life.' She believed that they could be happier doing something, just as she was. Early marriage precluded a career beforehand, but Millicent demonstrated the truth of another of Elizabeth's strongly held beliefs, expressed later with respect to her own marriage, that it could be combined with meaningful work beyond domesticity. Because of the kind of man Henry Fawcett was, falling in love with and then marrying him helped to make this possible for Millicent. Apparently, she did not regard his blindness as an impediment to her ambitions.

He came from a relatively conventional middle-class family, growing up in Salisbury. His father, William, was a self-made man, whose first job was an assistant to a draper. He went on to run his own business with some success and became involved in local politics as an ardent Liberal. He was elected as Mayor of Salisbury in 1832 and his son, Henry, was born the following year. Harry, as he soon became known, therefore grew up in a home where local politics affected his family life and must have been discussed frequently. He decided while still a schoolboy that he wanted to enter politics himself and studied hard, taking an interest in both politics and economics. He won a scholarship to Cambridge and after he graduated became a fellow of Trinity Hall. Harry was apparently not just respected at Cambridge but also popular. He must also have been admired after he was blinded for his determination not to let it hinder his ambitions. He was warm and witty, curious about and interested in the lives of others. He became part of a group of radicals at the university, determined to challenge orthodoxy and pursue change. The fact that he was fourteen years older than his new wife also meant that he had much more experience of the world.

After their marriage, Harry and Millicent set up homes in both London and Cambridge, as being an MP required Harry to be in London when the House of Commons was sitting from February until the autumn, and in Cambridge between October and

February to fulfil his professorial duties. He had told his father-in-law-to-be that his annual income was £800. He may well have been exaggerating in order to improve his chances of being accepted. He was paid £300 a year by the university, had royalties from his writing and an allowance from his father. However much his actual earnings were, the houses the couple rented after marrying were small and located in areas where rents were relatively low. The first London house they lived in was in Bessborough Gardens off Vauxhall Bridge Road and within walking distance from Parliament. Since his parents and his sister Maria came to stay when visiting from Salisbury, the house must have been large enough to put them up. In Cambridge, the couple had furnished lodgings in several different places, but again they were large enough for them to entertain friends. Nevertheless, Millicent claimed that she was 'a dragon over unnecessary expenditure'. Elizabeth's description of her as someone who 'has never been unwise or flighty' seems to have been apt. Millicent also devoted a great deal of time to reading a wide range of books, papers and documents to Harry. There is a touching portrait painted by Ford Madox Brown, in the National Portrait Gallery, of the young wife reading to her blind husband.

Soon after marrying, they went to Cambridge. It was a dramatic change from quiet country life in Aldeburgh for Millicent. She was thrown into the social and intellectual life of Cambridge, where Harry's genial and outgoing personality made him a frequent guest of his academic colleagues. He had a number of close friends who were drawn from those who espoused radical politics. The radicals held liberal and progressive views on a range of issues. A couple of decades earlier, they had established themselves as a group critical of mainstream Liberal thinking, espousing a reform agenda, which included extending the suffrage, in some cases to women, as well as to working-class men. Millicent was introduced by her husband to his friends and colleagues and appears to have adapted quickly to life in Cambridge, where she and Harry were entertained at the homes of their friends. Although much younger than most of them, she had enough self-confidence to hold her own in informal debates round the table. She was probably also given credit for the care she provided for Harry. Her sister-in-law, Maria Fawcett, stayed with them in Cambridge in the summer of 1867 and told Elizabeth Garrett about her visit. In a letter to her parents in Aldeburgh, Elizabeth passed on what Maria told her, writing, 'She gives a very nice account of Millicent in every way. She thinks she is filling her place in Cambridge most satisfactorily, managing the house well, doing all that Harry wants done and at the same time keeping up her own interest in things independently of him.'

'Doing what he wanted done' is not defined in this letter, but it seems Millicent could also do at least some of the things she wanted to do in her own right. Somehow, she found the time for her own interests while also acting as Harry's secretary in the first four years of their marriage, after which he employed a young man in the role. This would have required many hours of reading to him as well as writing his letters. She was already well practised in reading aloud, as she and Agnes had read to each other after they left school and returned home. Of course, the content of what she read would have been very different. It would have given her the opportunity of immersing herself in his academic work as an economist and in the political issues which engaged him as an MP. Some of the work she did independently was derived from this new knowledge that she was acquiring and probably discussed with Harry.

Very soon after her marriage, Millicent became pregnant. Her daughter was born just a year after her wedding, in April 1868. They named her Philippa. Little is known about her parents' reaction to the arrival of their first and, as it was to turn out, their only child. Did they decide not to have any more children and resort to early forms of contraception? Or were there no more pregnancies for some other reason? Millicent's reticence makes it unlikely that she would have disclosed it. There are certainly no records of her doing so, even to her sisters to whom she was so close. A letter from Alice indicates that the baby was tiny and that Millicent was unable to nurse her. By Christmas 1869, Millicent was able to write to her mother that Philippa was much better and now playing games with her aunt, Maria Fawcett. Harry also wrote to his mother-in-law with Christmas greetings and news of Philippa's improved health. He added touchingly, 'Each recurring year I seem to have more to be thankful for. The longer I live with Millicent, the more I become impressed that she is all that a wife can be.' Sometime later, Millicent comforted a friend who was finding the care of her own baby a challenge. She told her that Philippa had screamed incessantly for some months and recommended being patient. It is just possible that the prospect of another screaming baby was a risk she did not want to take.

Whatever the demands Philippa was to make, Millicent had made up her mind to continue her own education and, with Harry's encouragement, started to write. Before her daughter was born, she had attended two lecture courses in Cambridge and had written an article with the title 'The education of women of the middle and upper classes'. It was published in *Macmillan's Magazine* in April 1868. Millicent was still only twenty but already convinced that better opportunities to be educated were key to women's access to careers and to their acceptance as people with political views which should be properly considered and respected. Going to university herself was not an option, but she wasted little time after she started living in Cambridge in exploiting the opening of some lectures by individual academics to women, who were allowed to attend on an informal basis. No doubt they stimulated her and made her realise that women should be allowed far more than the part-time, unexamined and therefore limited educational experience they provided.

In her article, she argued that merely educating girls and young women to acquire accomplishments such as playing the piano, singing or learning a foreign language was far too limited. They should be able to immerse themselves in learning a range of subjects in the same way as boys and young men. She challenged prevailing views about the inferiority of women's minds, claiming that lacking the chance to develop their intellectual potential left them ill-equipped to join the professions or to debate on equal terms with their male peers. Life at home for unmarried girls was unremittingly dreary, leaving them with little rewarding activity. Millicent wanted women to be able to become graduates and the professions to be open to them. She makes no reference to Elizabeth's struggle, nor does she indicate support from Harry or other progressives, although she had no doubt absorbed their arguments. The article was good enough to get her attention and to enhance her reputation as someone who could make her case and do so persuasively. Amongst those who read it and were favourably impressed were John Stuart Mill and his stepdaughter, Helen Taylor, who read and approved another article on women's education, which was published later that year and railed against the dismissal of well-educated women as 'blue stockings' or 'strong-minded' and asked for the widening of occupations open to women.

From her earliest publications, Millicent's writing was often associated with her campaigns and had a purpose in trying to win round more people to the reforms she backed. In Cambridge, she threw herself into the campaign to admit women to the university. Emily Davies, who counted Elizabeth as one of her supporters, was the leading proponent of a new college for women. With others, Emily founded Girton College, which started as a very small residential college in Hitchin, only moving to Cambridge sometime later. Far better than nothing, however, it cannot have been anything like as rewarding as studying in Cambridge itself. Possibly for this reason, and probably because Millicent had never warmed to Emily's earnest and dour personality, Millicent backed another proposal to form an initially non-residential programme which only, sometime later, became Newnham College. In December 1869, a meeting was held at Millicent's house to initiate a project to start a course of lectures for women. Henry Sidgwick was the leading academic to back the project. He was a philosopher and political economist, a radical and widely known in the academic world. He no doubt encouraged other academics to back it, as well as the women in Millicent's circle, who were engaged from the beginning. Harry too strongly supported opening both Oxford and Cambridge to women.

Millicent helped to raise funds for the college and was one of those who persuaded John Stuart Mill and Helen Taylor to pay a subscription of £40 per annum. She believed it best to start cautiously without trying to set up a college that would give its students the right to obtain degrees. It was an early example of a view she held throughout her life that a cautious approach to change, starting slowly and in a limited way, was better than being too ambitious and risking failure. She was no revolutionary and never would be. Avoiding frightening too many people off, she focused on gentle persuasion, which may have paid dividends. Starting on a very small scale in 1871, Sidgwick rented a house accommodating five students who wanted to attend lectures but lived too far from Cambridge to do so. In 1876, a large site was acquired, and eventually in 1880, Newnham College formally came into existence with its own buildings providing accommodation for teaching and faculty as well as residences for students. Millicent sat on its executive committee for many years, generously donated money and helped to recruit students when it became residential. She got to know some of the earliest students, even taking them to the town gymnasium, where she was the best climber on the high rope. Like Elizabeth, physical fitness was an attribute she rated highly.

She had another noteworthy publication in her twenties in which Harry's encouragement had a more important role. Somewhat surprisingly, she decided to write a textbook aimed at schoolchildren and those new to the study of political economy when they were a little older. It arose from discussions with Harry when she worked with him on his revisions for a new edition of the *Manual of Political Economy*. It was published in 1870 with the title of *Political Economy for Beginners*. It was an enormous success. There must have been a market for a short book with questions for students to address at the end of each chapter, which could be used by older pupils at school, and by the Working Men's Institutes and colleges, where study in the evening was possible at the end of the working day, as well as by first-year undergraduates. It espoused a laissez-faire, free market philosophy, where competition and free trade were seen as central to economic success and to profitability. Why it ran to ten editions and was still in use in the 1920s, and why it was translated into Italian, German and several Indian languages is a puzzle. How much money it made is also not clear, but Millicent worked on revising it over many years and may have been motivated to do so by the income it provided. An attempt to capitalise on it four years later with a book entitled *Tales in Political Economy* was far less successful and never reprinted.

Because of her strong commitment to free markets, much of her analysis of the economy developed in her textbook would be seen as right-wing today. At the time, it was a simple reflection of mid-nineteenth-century liberalism. It was also tempered by views about the right of workers to be represented in trade unions, though deploring violent protest on their part. She also criticised landlords and their exploitation of tenants, even suggesting a tax on income from rents, and she wrote in favour of improving workers' education and skills. Not only would this improve productivity, but it would also reduce alcoholism, which she abhorred. In spite of coming from a family of ten children, she favoured a reduction in the growth of the population. However, her focus was not on middle-class families like her own but on the poor, where she considered a lower birth rate would be a sign of advancing civilisation. Above all, what the book showed was her confidence in pronouncing on a wide range of issues with, in the main, cogent arguments to back up her views. Sadly, this confidence could lead to assertions which were not backed up by a wider understanding and knowledge of the real world. This is exemplified in an article, in the form of a long letter, she published in *The Times* in December 1870.

This was the year of the Elementary Education Act, providing schooling for children between the ages of five and thirteen. Ten years later, in 1880, an Act was passed to make schooling compulsory for all children in this age group. Like many others with progressive views, Millicent believed in the expansion of education. What she could not accept was that it should be free. Her article was based on the theoretical assumption that anything can only be appreciated if it is paid for. To support her view, she made a series of generalisations about the behaviour and motivation of working people, which portray both ignorance and a lack of empathy. If schooling was provided without charging for it, economising would be discouraged, while early marriage and large families would be encouraged. Free education would reduce thrift and self-help, which responsible working people had pursued through friendly societies and trade unions. She even went so far as to say that because many fathers avoided drunkenness to help pay for their children's education, the motivation to avoid too much alcohol would be dented and therefore poverty brought about by drink would increase as a result of free schooling. She revealed no understanding of the difficulty working-class parents would have in finding the money to pay, nor of what it would cost to fine them if they failed to send their children to school when it became compulsory. Her obsession with temperance should perhaps have led her to a different conclusion, that inability to pay school fees might drive fathers to drink!

The fact that Millicent was only twenty-three when she wrote this piece cannot excuse her lack of judgement. Why she did not seek wiser counsel before submitting it is unclear. While her argument may have appealed to some who were totally opposed to the concept of public services, and who failed to see the wider benefit they provided to society, it was received with dismay by advocates of the expansion of education in the circles in which she mixed. There is no evidence that she was willing to retract her article in response to criticism at the time, although it may have been hard for her publicly to accept criticism. She may have feared that to be seen changing her mind could be perceived as weakness. It was also an early sign that she could be dogmatic in rejecting well-reasoned criticism. She even went ahead with the inclusion of *The Times* letter in a book entitled *Essays and Lectures*, jointly authored with Harry and published in 1872. Of the fourteen contributions, she wrote eight. They covered women's education, women's suffrage, proportional representation (which she supported) and the national debt (which she opposed). High expenditure on foreign wars, the Poor Law and the uncontrolled population increase were targets of her criticism. Harry's biographer, Leslie Stephen, wrote that the book of essays showed 'agreement of independent minds not the relation of teacher and disciple'. Nevertheless, Harry had certainly persuaded Millicent to adopt a similar approach to his own on economic questions.

The early years they spent together in Cambridge were marked by extraordinary productivity by Millicent. It is not clear how much help she had with household chores, although apparently, she had a nursemaid for Philippa. Nevertheless, she took the baby to stay with her in-laws in Salisbury and her parents in Aldeburgh, looking after her herself according to Ray Strachey's biography. However, Millicent must have employed someone to look after Philippa for most of the day while the couple were at home. While they did not have a high income and saved spending money on carriages by walking home from evening engagements, they would have been able to afford a nursemaid at the low rates of pay for young women who did this work. This was made all the more necessary given the time spent by Millicent helping Harry, her own wide reading, her writing, their enjoyment of Cambridge social life, their walking and riding and Fenland skating. To Millicent, idleness was reprehensible. Her way of life showed she was no hypocrite on this matter. She clearly enjoyed hard work, was well organised and constantly busy, and to be busy was a source of happiness, not a cause for complaint. To have achieved as much as she did in her early twenties was remarkable.

4

ENTRY INTO POLITICAL
LIFE WITH HARRY

Living part of the year in Cambridge gave Millicent the chance
to experience the academic world, to continue her self-
education and to embark on political writing. Living the rest of the
year in London allowed her to experience the political world of
the capital, including observing Parliament in action and taking her
first steps in campaigning for women's suffrage. Harry had become
the Liberal Member of Parliament for Brighton, where Millicent
was welcomed as his 'little' wife, which seemed to be a reference
to her short stature rather than her limitations as a mere woman.
Undoubtedly, Harry's role as a radical Liberal politician provided
her with contacts which were valuable and which helped to shape
her own views. Most notable amongst these contacts was John Stuart
Mill, who was an important influence on Harry's political and intellectual development. As their friendship became closer in the
1860s, Mill encouraged him and supported his election to the chair
of political economy in Cambridge, as well as in his search for a
parliamentary seat. But it was not a friendship between equals. Mill
was considerably older and already famous for his writing and for

his professional views on a range of issues. He was a mentor to Harry rather than an equal partner in the pursuit of reform. The lack of intimacy is illustrated by the fact that he heard about Harry's marriage through the newspapers.

Not long after they were married, the Fawcetts were invited to dinner with Mill and his stepdaughter Helen Taylor, which pleased Millicent as she saw it as a 'great honour'. She looked up to him; indeed, he was one of her heroes. Mill's views on Millicent were not consistently positive. Observing her at work on promoting women's interests, he described her in a letter to a colleague as having 'a prosaic literal way of looking at things' and lacking 'a speculative [and] organising intelligence'. He described her as 'quite unfit to be a leader, though an excellent guerrilla partisan'. These were harsh judgements of someone in her early twenties. Moreover, they were not consistent with the support he gave her not long after denouncing her. When asked if he would give his backing to her election to membership of the Political Economy Unit, which at that time had never had a female member, he admitted that 'she had far better claims to be a member … than many of its present members' and promised his support if her name was proposed and seconded by other leading members. In the event, despite being proposed by Charles Dilke, an eminent radical, she was not elected. Mill's verdict on her potential as a leader proved much later to be mistaken.

Two years earlier in 1869, Millicent made her first public speech on women's suffrage at a meeting in London. A few days after this first speech, she was denounced in the Commons by an MP as having disgraced herself by taking part, a classic example of the view that women should be seen but not heard. A number of eminent men were the lead speakers, including Mill, Dilke and Harry Fawcett. At the time, Mill was complimentary about the contribution of

'Mr and Mrs Fawcett' to the cause of women's suffrage. The following year, Millicent spoke in support of the trade union candidate in a by-election in Southwark. Soon after, she gave a much longer lecture to her husband's constituents in Brighton. They were her first sallies into a public speaking career, which lasted for years. The context was one in which it was considered improper for women to stand on a platform and address an audience.

Ray Strachey described the Liberals in Brighton as 'considerably alarmed' by the prospect of a woman giving a lecture on women's suffrage at a constituency event. They held that 'it was one thing for their Member to hold these odd views himself, and this might be overlooked, but for his wife to come down and gratuitously make a display of herself on a platform in support of women's rights was most unwise, and certain to do harm'. Nevertheless, the Fawcetts, with the support of three leading members of the constituency party, were determined to go ahead. Millicent spoke at great length – probably for too long – but certainly no harm was done. The response from the local newspapers was divided. The *Brighton Gazette*, a Conservative newspaper, stated, 'female orators we must regard as altogether intolerable'. Its rival, the *Brighton Daily News*, took a contrary view. It commented on how successful Millicent's speech was and that the hall was so full that many had to be turned away. The *Brighton Herald* said, 'She is a lady of short stature, and of fragile but very pleasing appearance; perfectly collected in her manner and with a very clear, distinct, emphatic delivery, not at times without a touch of humour.'

Not long after the Brighton lecture, the Fawcetts went to Ireland where Millicent spoke to a large audience in Dublin. News of this reached her sister Alice in Calcutta, who wrote back to her mother in Aldeburgh about Milly's triumph as described in the *Irish Times*.

Its leading article stated, 'Mrs Fawcett's extensive reading, her speculative power, her close reasoning, her evident aptitude for social and political discussion, do not appear to have robbed her of one natural grace, nor interfered with an exquisite feminine culture except to enhance it.' Many commentators at the time and later mentioned her speaking voice, which had unusual richness and enhanced her presentations through its clarity and easy audibility. To Victorian audiences, it was how she looked that counted too. She dressed beautifully, she was very pretty and she was demure rather than strident. She was also perceived to be a woman who fulfilled her duties as a loving wife, providing care for her disabled husband. They may not have agreed with her, but many members of the public seem to have been taken by her appearance and her sincerity.

Her first speaking tour was to the West Country. She spoke to large audiences in the cities of Bristol, Plymouth and Exeter as well as in four or five smaller towns. It took place in the spring of 1871 when she was still only twenty-three. David Rubinstein's biography quotes the local newspapers commenting on her youthful appearance and expressive voice. She was not accompanied by her husband, and Harry was thanked for generously sparing her 'to go forth and plead for her new gospel'. How this tour was organised, where she stayed and how she moved from place to place is not entirely clear. Her daughter was three at the time and may have been taken to her parents' house in Aldeburgh. Millicent makes no detailed references to Philippa's care in her autobiography, admittedly written fifty years later, although she mentions her nurse in passing.

On more than one occasion, Millicent admitted her terror of public speaking. While she clearly learnt to overcome this, she always maintained that she preferred to write and to spend time with her books than to speak. She shrank from personal publicity and hated having her photograph taken, although later in her life she often had to submit herself to the camera. The strength of her convictions about the importance of persuading people of the need to give women the rights that were denied them motivated her. She was driven to campaign, and campaigning meant speaking in public however frightening it was. In her memoir, *What I Remember*, she sets out the four routes to political and social equality for women as

a many-sided movement. Speaking generally, its most important departments dealt with (1) education, (2) an equal moral standard between men and women, (3) professional and industrial liberty, and (4) political status. My special experience and training fitted me best, as I thought, for work in the fourth of these, but I recognised that this was only one side of the whole question, and I was likewise convinced that whoever worked for any of the branches of involvement was, whether he knew it or not, really helping the other three.

While her main focus was on votes for women, she made forays into the other three areas too. Her work on helping to provide higher education for women in Cambridge described in the previous chapter is an illustration of this.

As early as 1867, soon after her marriage, she committed herself to the fourth area on her list by joining the Enfranchisement of Women Committee set up in London by Mentia Taylor, her hostess at the dinner where two years earlier she impressed Henry Fawcett for the first time with her views on Abraham Lincoln. Similar committees were set up in Birmingham, Manchester, Edinburgh and Bristol. Initially, there was no national organisation, although there was regular contact between the regional committees. Their members were mainly drawn from middle- and upper-class backgrounds, they were people of some standing within these cities and included men, although women usually took the leading roles. It is likely that Millicent's speaking tour in the West Country would have been organised by the Bristol committee, with places to stay offered by its members.

Millicent's message was disseminated more widely than to the audiences which turned up to listen to her, as these early speeches were reported on in the newspapers and often printed in full in pamphlet form. Her way of getting her points across was to list the reasons given for excluding women from voting and then to demolish them in turn. This was quite an effective way of anticipating likely opposition, only to demolish it in order to make it less likely that it would be expressed by members of her audience when she finished her speech. She identified as many as sixteen reasons its opponents cited for objecting to women's suffrage. Today, these objections seem absurd: women would neglect their families if they devoted time to voting and deciding who to vote for; women were intellectually as well as physically inferior to men and therefore would not be able to make an informed judgement about who to vote for; voting would sully their purity – little courtesies like having doors opened for them were what counted; and women far preferred not submitting themselves to boisterous electoral activity. When challenged on the biblical support for the subjection of women, she said the Bible was not a good guide to modern political behaviour. She argued that giving the vote to women was not just a matter of principle and right for its own sake – it was also an important route to correcting the many disadvantages women suffered in how they were treated. For example, husbands could deny their wives access to their children on pretexts that were laughable. In spite of the Married Women's Property Act passed in 1870, married women did not have adequate access to their earnings, and men expected to have control of any money that their wives inherited. Without the right to vote, women's power to challenge inequality and injustice was circumscribed. Just as her sister Elizabeth had said she was dedicated to improving women's lot, so was Millicent. She passionately believed that to improve the lives of women was a noble cause to which to dedicate her life. And she was optimistic that the campaigning she began in her early twenties could and would make a difference.

One of her prized possessions was a signed copy of John Stuart Mill's *The Subjection of Women*, published in 1869. One of her first experiences of parliamentary campaigning on behalf of women concerned Mill in his role as an MP. His belief that the vote was key to improvements in women's lives undoubtedly influenced Millicent's own thinking. She would have been aware of his demand for women's suffrage in his election programme in 1865 and of the petition to Parliament which Emily Davies and her sister Elizabeth had promoted in 1866 prior to the debates on the Reform Bill, which was introduced in the House of Commons to extend the franchise to working men who met certain property qualifications. Barbara Bodichon saw its introduction as an opportunity to try to persuade Mill to introduce an amendment to the Bill to allow female property owners the vote and offered to collect signatures for a petition. Mill agreed if a hundred signatures could be collected. A committee was set up in Elizabeth Garrett's dining room to work on collecting the signatures. Her elder sister Louie became its secretary. Within a few weeks, they had collected 1,498 signatures, although Millicent was too young to sign it. Elizabeth and Emily Davies took the long paper scroll to Westminster Hall to present to Mill. There they ran into Henry Fawcett, who went to find Mill. By the time he arrived, they had put the scroll under the stall of an elderly woman selling apples, leaving Mill nonplussed as to why the petitioners were meeting him without a petition. The scroll was retrieved and Mill held it up and said, 'I can brandish this with effect.'

His amendment was to change the word 'man' to 'person' in a key clause in the Bill. Henry Fawcett made a short speech supporting the amendment. Although the vote on it was lost by 198 against it and seventy-eight for it, the committee which organised the petition was pleased as the result was better than the overwhelming defeat they anticipated. They were not downhearted as they believed there would be more opportunities in the future to try to persuade Parliament to back women's suffrage.

After Millicent and Harry were married and spending half the year in London, allowing him to undertake his parliamentary work, Millicent visited the Commons frequently, listened to debates and learnt about parliamentary procedure. In *What I Remember*, she describes this new stage in her life:

My political education was just beginning … I grappled with newspapers and blue books and learnt more or less to convey their import to [Harry]. He took care that I should hear important debates in the House of Commons and the Speaker and the Sergeant-at-Arms were very kind in frequently offering me a seat in that portion of the ladies' galleries which they controlled. Of course, the heavy brass trellis which then screened off these galleries and their bad ventilation made them unnecessarily tiring and even exhausting; but the whole scene was new to me and very interesting.

She recounts hearing Mill's speech on the women's suffrage amendment. It was, she said,

> a masterpiece of close reasoning, tinged here and there by deep emotion. It thrilled me to hear my sister and her successful efforts to open the medical profession to women referred to. But perhaps what interested me most of all was the evidently powerful impression the speech made on the House.

In analysing the result, Millicent shared the views of the petitioners that it was much better than expected.

She also took comfort from the fact that the vote was not entirely on party lines and that some Conservatives had voted for the amendment. Writing her memoir in the 1920s, she said:

> From that time until our final victory in 1918 we were successful in keeping the question of women's franchise on non-party lines. Of course this had drawbacks, but these, such as they were, were greatly outweighed by advantages, especially as our chief work for many years consisted in active suffrage propaganda in the country.

What Millicent did not anticipate in the late 1860s and early 1870s was how many more times her pleas for legislative change would be rejected and how complicit in these rejections were the two great leaders of the Liberal Party, William Gladstone and Herbert Asquith. In the end, she viewed both men with utter contempt. What offended her most was the backsliding and the dishonesty of their political manoeuvring.

Millicent could, however, take comfort from one important step towards women's representation. The 1870 Elementary Education Act referred to in the previous chapter did not just set up public elementary schools. It also required the establishment of school boards to administer them. Women were allowed to vote in the election of the boards and to be candidates in these elections. A year earlier in 1869, female ratepayers in England were given the right to vote in municipal elections on the same basis as men and to stand as candidates in some cases. Given this concession, the strength of the opposition to enfranchising women in parliamentary elections is all the more puzzling. The numbers of women putting themselves forward in municipal elections remained relatively small for many years, but some of them were elected and served successfully as councillors. This was to happen in the school board elections too. The two women who were elected to the London board were Emily Davies in Greenwich and Elizabeth Garrett in Marylebone.

Elizabeth was approached to stand by the Marylebone Working Men's Association; the wives and children of the men who invited her to become a candidate were patients in her dispensary. At first, she was reluctant to accept. She was already busy in her medical practice and, like her younger sister, initially dreaded public speaking. Eventually, she accepted the petition, saying:

> I dare say when it has to be done I can do it, and it is no use asking for women to be taken into public work and yet to wish them to avoid publicity … Still, I am very sorry it is necessary, especially as I can't think of anything to say for four speeches.

James Skelton Anderson, co-founder of the Orient Line and financial adviser to the East London Hospital, organised her campaign. Amongst those he persuaded to support her were Henry Fawcett,

Barbara Bodichon, Octavia Hill, Frances Buss and Robert Browning. Her campaign was also astute in seeking positive publicity in the press. For night after night, Elizabeth spoke at public meetings acquiring confidence rapidly. Her well-organised campaign led to a magnificent outcome in which she topped the poll with a very large majority over her male competitors. There were seven candidates and she was the only woman. She was feted after her victory with positive articles in national newspapers and many invitations to dinners. In spite of this, at the first meeting of the board at the Guildhall, it was suggested that the two women elected should sit separately and not at the long table with the men. They of course resisted and took their place at the long table. Some years later and after Elizabeth had stood down, her sister Alice, having returned from India permanently, became a member of the London School Board.

One outcome of Elizabeth's campaign to be elected was that James Skelton Anderson asked her to marry him. She accepted and an unconventional but deeply happy marriage followed. Nevertheless, she and others, including her father, were fearful that her marriage might damage her medical career. Skelton, as he was known, quickly put paid to any doubts she might have about her freedom to continue to work as a doctor, and she wrote to Millicent saying:

I hope my dear that you will not think I have meanly deserted my post. I think it need not prove to be so and I believe he would repent it as much as you or I would. I am sure that the women question will never be solved in any complete way if marriage is thought to be incompatible with freedom and with an independent career, and I think there is a very good chance that we may be able to do something to discourage the notion.

There is no record of how Millicent replied, but Elizabeth's letter is revealing in two ways. First, it shows her wish to retain Millicent's respect for her as the country's first female doctor, reassuring her much younger sister that she would not let the side down. Second, it reveals Elizabeth's conviction that Millicent's marriage was no barrier to her freedom and independence either, hence her last phrase in her letter that *we* might by our example be able to discourage the idea that marriage would inevitably lead to a loss of the right to work or campaign independently.

As well as her campaigning round the country for votes for women, Millicent took an interest in some of the questions which preoccupied Harry in his parliamentary work. He was a critic of discrimination against prospective students who were barred from university for religious reasons and strongly supported the legislation to end it. The Universities Tests Act of 1871 abolished religious 'tests', which prior to the Act had prevented Roman Catholics, Nonconformists and non-Christians from holding university posts and studying in English universities. Two years later, Gladstone introduced an Irish University Bill. Although Gladstone intended to reform the system, the Bill was a muddle and failed to propose with clarity secular universities in Ireland. Harry was a leading opponent of the Bill and his opposition was effective enough to play a crucial part in its defeat. He then introduced his own Bill to secure the abolition of tests at Trinity College, Dublin, which was passed in the Commons in 1873. Millicent shared her husband's views, referring to the outrageous exclusiveness of the 'tests' in English universities, illustrated by the fact that 'when I first knew Cambridge, no honest Jew could take a degree, for it would have necessitated swearing a solemn oath in the true faith of a Christian'. She was also well aware that bringing about the defeat of the Irish University Bill was an act of rebellion that would be perceived by the government as unacceptable disloyalty, saying, 'I do not think Mr Gladstone ever forgave my husband for this defeat of his own measure and the passing into law of its rival.' There is no question that she believed Harry's independence and rebelliousness were justified.

Harry was frequently an outspoken critic of his own party and fearless in pursuing the issues that concerned him, however damaging they may have been to his reputation in government circles. He thought that Gladstone lacked the radical vision that was needed to implement change and did not hesitate to say so. Millicent was unlikely to have been a restraining influence with respect to Harry's inflexibility and sometimes dogmatic views. Although there is no evidence of her views about two of the causes he pursued as a backbencher, she is likely to have sympathised with them. The first of these was his strong opposition to the enclosure of common land. He was forthright in criticising the interests of private landlords being given precedence over the rights of the urban poor to enjoy recreational open spaces, and of the rural poor to have access to grazing land. The survival of Epping Forest, Wimbledon Common and the New Forest, to give a few illustrations, were an outcome of this campaign. His drive to improve British rule in India so that it was fairer to the Indian population, more competent and less extravagant and wasteful was likely to have appealed to her too. She hated profligacy and would have been appalled by it being committed with other people's money.

There were other feminist causes that took up parliamentary time following the failure to alter the Reform Bill. They included the repealing of the Contagious Diseases Act, the introduction of

Acts on Married Women's Property and the Factory Acts. Millicent had strong views on each of them, although her actual engagement in furthering them was not always wholehearted.

She was affronted by the Contagious Diseases Act, the first of which was passed in 1864. Prostitution was rife in the Victorian era and the legislation had been passed, in part at least, to protect women against its unpleasant consequences for their health. However, its implementation was very unsatisfactory. Working-class women were rounded up in garrison towns in particular and subjected to forced examinations, whether they were prostitutes or not, followed by treatment for venereal disease in special 'lock' hospitals. Josephine Butler founded the Ladies National Association dedicated to the repeal of the Acts in 1869. Both Agnes and Rhoda Garrett strongly supported their abolition and campaigned for the repeal of the legislation. Millicent shared most feminists' views about this question but prevaricated over personally campaigning to abolish the Acts. Her priority was always women's suffrage and she worried that any association in the public mind with prostitution would damage the cause she cared about most. Her own rather prim views about sexual morality no doubt influenced her assumption that it would be damaging if the two causes were linked.

The issue led to disagreement within the suffrage movement. Late in 1867, the Manchester suffragists proposed the establishment of the National Society for Women's Suffrage, aiming to bring together the various local societies. The proponents of a central body also backed the campaign to repeal the contagious diseases legislation. The powerful London committee of which Millicent was a member was split, although many members opposed the views of the Manchester committee and took the other side as did Mill. There was also disagreement about whether married women should be included in the campaign for formal suffrage. Today, it seems extraordinary that they should not be included. Why should a woman be denied the right to exercise her choice on who represented her in Parliament because she was married? The conventional view throughout the second half of the nineteenth century and well into the twentieth century was that their husbands, who were deemed to be the heads of their household, should vote and that wives should be represented by this means. Most suffragists thought this was unacceptable, as did Henry Fawcett, but some of them, including Millicent, thought that tactically it was better to limit the demand for the vote to single women or widows who were householders and over the age of thirty. They believed it would be far easier to obtain agreement for this as it was a smaller challenge to conventional perceptions about men's dominant role both in the public realm and at home. Moreover, the numbers of women enfranchised would be relatively small and a limited reform would be much easier to get acceptance. Millicent was a gradualist. She thought it far better to be pragmatic and start with a small-scale reform and get it through, than risk complete failure by being over-ambitious. Once the principle was established that some women could vote, she anticipated that it would only be a matter of time before all adult women would be allowed to vote. Nevertheless, the fact that the movement was split on such a fundamental issue did not augur well for the unity needed for successful campaigning.

The related issue of married women's property was another subject which gave rise to political pressure for change. Prior to 1870, on marriage, women were required by law to hand over to their husbands any money they had made from inheritance, investment or earnings from their work. This meant married women lost control over their property, and their husbands were allowed to do what they wanted with it. A wife's identity was legally absorbed into that of her husband, effectively making them one person under the law. In 1868, after a long campaign by feminists such as Barbara Bodichon, who were committed to reform, a Bill was introduced in Parliament which led to the 1870 Act, which allowed married women to have the same property rights as unmarried women. However, the Act was only a first step in that it was not retrospective, meaning that only women who married after its introduction would benefit, and it also had a number of loopholes. More campaigning was needed. Surprisingly, given its relevance to women having their own legal identity and therefore right to vote, Millicent took no part in the campaign. David Rubinstein suggests her disapproval of the secretary of the Married Women's Property Committee, who had been involved in a sexual scandal before her marriage, may have been a reason. Prudish as Millicent was, this seems rather unlikely, and Rubinstein admits to speculation about it. Another possibility was that Millicent wanted to focus on votes for women and saw it as a distraction. In any event, a further Married Women's Property Act was passed in 1882, which was a considerable improvement on the 1870 Act.

A further area of legislative change on which both Harry and Millicent had strong views were the Factory Acts. Regulation, starting as early as 1802, had been introduced to force employers to improve conditions in the cotton mills. A number of Acts were passed, focusing mainly on reducing the hours that children worked but covering women too as the century progressed. Before Harry and Millicent were married, he had supported legislation to regulate employment conditions for women. Subsequently, he modified his views, possibly as a result of Millicent's influence. In 1868, he cautioned the Social Science Association against restricting women's employment, which he believed would be unjust, and later in 1873, he fiercely attacked the Nine Hours Bill when it was introduced in the House of Commons, admitting that he had changed his mind about further restricting the hours women could work. He had indeed made clear in a later edition of his *Manual of Political Economy* that 'women should have the same opportunity as men to follow any profession, trade or employment', adding in the spirit of a believer in self-help that 'a life of dependant pauperism must be far more pernicious than honest industry'.

His change of view, which meant he no longer supported the extension of the Factory Acts, was consistent with Millicent's view that legislative prohibition on working long hours would only further impoverish women by reducing their incomes. She also thought that behind the Acts was trade union influence, since they preferred to reduce competition for jobs by driving women out of certain trades, points which she set out in a letter to *The Times*. She may have been correct in her assertions, but she may also have failed to understand the effect on women's health of long hours of heavy manual labour on top of feeding and caring for their children. However, in opposing further legislation, the Fawcetts were in complete agreement, whether reaching their opinions on it independently or whether after joint discussion in which they influenced each other.

Neither husband nor wife found compromise easy when it came to criticism of their strongly held views on many subjects. In spite of Harry's intellectual ability, his fearlessness and his hard work, it seemed unlikely that he would join any future Liberal government after the Tories won the 1874 election. His disloyalty and his refusal to be a team player were an irritant to Gladstone during the 1870s. However, when the Liberals won the 1880 election and Gladstone returned as Prime Minister, he appointed Harry Fawcett to be the

Postmaster General. This was a ministerial position outside the Cabinet, which would have contained Harry's tendency to pontificate to his ministerial colleagues on subjects which concerned him, even though they had nothing to do with his ministerial remit. Moreover, he would need to be heavily employed in managing a growing public service in need of innovation. Harry was by then forty-seven and Gladstone may have thought he had mellowed somewhat from his rebellious approach to positions taken by his party up to then. If Gladstone believed that a ministerial post would force Harry to toe the line, he was to be sorely disappointed. Harry abstained on a royal grant in 1882, displeasing the Queen, and continued to criticise the government's Egyptian policy, especially the use of Indian troops and Indian tax revenue to sustain this.

There is no record of what Millicent thought of Harry's appointment nor how she viewed the effect it might have on her life. In 1874, the Fawcetts had moved to a permanent home in Vauxhall. Although unfashionable, it was convenient and had a garden and more space than Bessborough Gardens. By today's standards, they were not short of domestic help. In asking help from a friend to find a 'promising young girl' to be a kitchen maid, Millicent revealed that they had a housemaid and a cook, whom the kitchen maid would have to help. She also noted that they kept 'no man or boy', so the new maid would also have to do the rough work such as maintaining the fires, boot cleaning and scrubbing the steps.

Some of Millicent's time was taken up with social life: they were entertained at the houses of friends, and they reciprocated by entertaining people for dinner in both London and Cambridge. There were also official engagements associated with Harry's ministerial role. As a minster's wife, Millicent was expected to be presented at court. She also accompanied her husband to events requiring his attendance, such as dinners at Marlborough House where the Prince and Princess of Wales were the hosts. Perhaps she deserved to be invited in her own right, as by then she was a well-known figure in London political life albeit without a formal role, but married women were not sufficiently emancipated in the 1880s for that to happen.

As Postmaster General, Harry was an energetic innovator, introducing the parcel post, telegrams, cheaper postal orders and better facilities for small savers and investors. His feminism also led him to expand the employment of women in the Post Office. More female clerks were appointed and he went out of his way to praise them in his annual reports. He also appointed the first female medical officer in government employment. She was one of the first University of London medical graduates and a protégé of his sister-in-law Elizabeth. This must certainly have pleased Millicent greatly, as a practical demonstration of the creation of opportunities for female employment, as well as recognition of women's ability to work in senior professional roles. While Harry was tied up with his work as a minister and precluded from the campaigning activities he pursued as a backbencher, Millicent was not inhibited from continuing to campaign and from trying to persuade her husband's boss, William Gladstone, to embrace votes for women.

In 1883, a new Reform Bill was introduced primarily to enfranchise rural male voters with property qualifications on the same basis as those in towns. When invited to contribute an article for the *Pall Mall Gazette* on female workers in the Post Office, Millicent preferred to write about votes for women. In her article, published early in 1884, she advocated a Bill which would include the enfranchisement of women with the same qualifications that were being applied to rural men. She rightly predicted that one day it would be thought incredible that giving women the parliamentary vote would be perceived as 'dangerous and revolutionary'. She urged the Liberal leadership to be more progressive, citing the municipal and school board franchises, which had been introduced without any damage to society. To illustrate her argument and presumably with the intention of reassuring conservative opinion, she claimed, 'We still like needlework; we prefer pretty gowns to ugly ones; we are interested in domestic management and economy, and are not entirely indifferent to our friends and relations.'

She also referred to the recent Liberal conference in Leeds, which had passed a women's suffrage resolution by a large majority. She was incensed when the *Pall Mall Gazette* published letters in its next edition throwing doubt on the vote's validity because many of the delegates had gone home when this debate took place and therefore the votes were unrepresentative. She asked her brother-in-law James Skelton Anderson and her brother Sam, who were both there, to challenge the editor about these one-sided letters. She wrote to Elizabeth saying, 'One longs to let out and tell these people what one thinks of them but we can't afford a good honest rage yet.' This letter illustrates her perception that the campaign had to avoid being strident or too militant. She was not afraid to be forceful but felt the need to be persuasive and take people with her without offending them.

Meanwhile, in Parliament, there was a meeting of sympathetic MPs, which included Henry Fawcett, to consider what action to take on the Reform Bill. It was agreed that an amendment should be put down to the Bill to give women the vote on the same terms as men. Soon after, a group of Liberal women, including Millicent, wrote to Gladstone proclaiming their support for the Liberal Party and asking him if he would receive a delegation. He turned them down claiming ill health but also resisting any changes to the Bill on the grounds that adding women's suffrage might endanger the measure altogether. This rejection did not deter Millicent from further campaigning. She was the main speaker at a large meeting in London in support of the amendment. She was over-optimistic in stating that she believed victory would come soon. 'But even if it should not be so near as I now believe, we must not lose heart or hope. What are five, ten, or fifteen years in a great historical movement like the one we are engaged in.' This message was one she continued to put forward to rally her troops. Even if their hopes were dashed at any particular point, as they were about to be, they must never give up because their cause was noble.

When the amendment was debated in the House of Commons, Gladstone refused to accept it, threatening that if it were passed, he would give up any responsibility for the Bill, claiming the House of Lords was likely to veto it anyway. He avoided directly revealing whether or not he was in favour of enfranchising women. In any case, the amendment was defeated by a large majority. Henry Fawcett was one of three ministers who abstained. Of the three of them, only Charles Dilke, the minister at the Local Government Board, was a member of the Cabinet. But inside or outside the Cabinet, it was expected that ministers should abide by collective responsibility and unfailingly support the government. Once again Harry was prepared to rebel. Indeed, it is hard to imagine him doing otherwise given Millicent's position and his own long-standing commitment to female suffrage. He was prepared to risk being sacked rather than abandon his principles. Gladstone wrote to him reminding him of ministers' obligations to vote with the government and that a failure to do so required them to announce their resignation. However, Gladstone added, with the agreement of the Cabinet, that on this occasion, he and his colleagues would not be sacked to avoid disruption while dealing with a foreign policy crisis. Harry replied in a letter, in Millicent's handwriting, telling the Prime Minister that when abstaining, he was perfectly aware of the consequences. Although he thanked Gladstone for his kindness at the end of the letter, he did not apologise. That Harry was not sacked did not appease Millicent. She already disliked Gladstone and had no qualms in making her views known, even though he was her husband's boss. Gladstone's speech in the Commons included the sentence, 'the cargo which the vessel carries [in the Bill] is, in our opinion, a cargo as large as she can safely carry'. Millicent's response to this political metaphor was that so far from being saved before men, women were thrown overboard. She never forgave him for his lack of leadership on the issue and did not respect the political calculations which motivated him.

Having escaped being axed, the Postmaster General returned to his desk unable to take a holiday over the summer because of complex negotiations with the private providers of telephones. In the autumn, he had to combine his ministerial work with his professorial responsibilities in Cambridge, travelling up and down from London to give his lectures. His health was not robust – less than two years earlier in December 1882, he had narrowly escaped death from diphtheria and typhoid. When it became widely known that Harry had been seriously ill for some weeks and that he might not survive, Millicent, at his bedside, felt gratitude for the many messages of sympathy and support they received. When it was apparent that he was recovering, Millicent stated that 'neither he nor I will forget the universal kindness and sympathy that were shown to us throughout his illness'. It was some months before he was able to return to full-time work and Millicent tried to shelter him from taking on extra activities likely to exhaust him.

Unfortunately, his serious illness seems to have weakened him and he fell ill again in the autumn of 1884. In October, he defiantly defended his position on the Reform Bill in a speech to his constituents, saying, 'I believe the demand of women householders to be enfranchised will not rest until it is conceded.' It was to be his last speech. At the beginning of November, in Cambridge, Millicent sent for Elizabeth, who had attended, along with several eminent physicians, during his earlier serious illness. This time none could save him. He died of pneumonia with coronary complications within a week of being taken ill, with Millicent and Philippa at his bedside. He was fifty-one, leaving Millicent a widow at thirty-seven.

There was an outpouring of public grief when Harry's death was announced. Dogmatic, loud and inflexible as he often was, he was also charming, curious about others and had a warm sense of humour. Admiration for the way he coped with blindness was widespread. He was determined that it would not stand in the way of what he wanted to do – whether that be skating on the Fens, riding on horseback or mastering a brief before making a speech. *The Times* said he had achieved a measure of national esteem not exceeded by any other public man. In the book he edited on Harry, Lawrence Goldman described reactions to his death as approaching national mourning. There were many tributes, including one from the Queen and another from the Prince of Wales. Gladstone wrote to Harry's father, who was still alive, about his extraordinary qualities. Significantly, perhaps, he did not write to Millicent. In her memoir, she stated:

A curious little sidelight of Mr Gladstone's retentive memory in some matters may be inferred from the fact that at the time of my husband's death in 1884, though I received hundreds of letters of sympathy and condolence from all sorts and conditions of people, I received not one word from the Prime Minister under whom he had served.

Amongst the most touching letters were from Post Office workers who had greatly appreciated Harry's commitment to them and his concern for improving their conditions of employment. Millicent wrote that 'the staff and employees of the Post Office made me feel that they had lost a chief that they had really loved'. A gift of silver candlesticks and an inkstand sent to her by Post Office officials, who worked closely with her husband, greatly moved her. They, like hundreds of others whose lives had been touched by Harry, attended his burial in Trumpington, a place just outside Cambridge that he and Millicent had loved. A special train was provided to take mourners to the churchyard from the funeral in Westminster Abbey.

The Victorian era was marked by building memorials to public figures and Henry Fawcett was not an exception. First and foremost was a sculptured memorial in Westminster Abbey. Leslie Stephen, his friend from his early days in Cambridge and soon to be his biographer, wrote the inscription. It ended with the sentence, 'His heroic acceptance of the calamity of blindness has left a memorable example of the power of a brave man to transmute loss into gain and wrest victory from misfortune.' There were monuments in all the places with which Harry was associated, in Salisbury, Cambridge, Aldeburgh and Trumpington. In addition, there were three others in London. By today's standards, this seems over the top, but they engaged Millicent, taking up her time as she grappled with grief and were a comfort to her.

Millicent Garrett and Henry Fawcett's marriage was extraordinarily close. It was based on nearly identical values, mutual understanding and respect, enjoyment of each other's company, shared leisure activities and a joint determination to fight for their convictions without compromise. It is difficult to know how great their physical attraction to each other was. Because of his blindness, they did not write to each other, so there are no written records of declared passion. When they were first married, Harry asked friends to describe how Millicent looked. He was interested in her clothes and asked for information about what she was wearing. She took trouble to dress to please him and was widely admired not just for her good looks but also for her beautiful clothes. At home, he often wanted to know where she was and what she was doing. 'Where are you, Milly? Are you happy?' She in turn was devoted to him and grateful for his encouragement and the independence he gave her. They were both ardent feminists. They both had little interest in grandeur and disliked snobbery. The one interest of Harry that she could not abide was fishing. When he fished in Scotland, she found other things to do, in particular mountain walking abroad, which did not appeal to him.

Their characters were similar. They were both utterly determined to pursue their beliefs and neither of them would ever be distracted, nor persuaded, to do otherwise. It is impossible to imagine that two such strong-willed people could never disagree, but if they did it was more likely to be about tactics than an issue of principle. Little is known about how Harry viewed the development of their only child, nor how much time he devoted to her. Ray Strachey refers to a shared belief in progressive childrearing, giving Philippa as much freedom as possible to think for herself. Since Millicent's father was far from absent in her own childhood, she may have expected Harry to play an active part in Philippa's development too. There are certainly one or two references to Harry and his daughter going away together without Millicent, for instance staying with the Garretts at the family home in Aldeburgh.

It is idle to speculate what would have happened had Harry lived and eventually lost his ministerial role, as was likely. But the foundations of this marriage were so strong it is unlikely to have foundered in any way. When Millicent had a riding accident when they were out together, Harry's reaction shows the strength of their devotion. Millicent was thrown from her horse and knocked out, probably suffering from concussion, although this description was not used at the time. Although he could not see what had happened, Harry would have heard the thud when she hit the ground and been terrified by her silence afterwards. He thought she must have died and wept for a long time until he was reassured that she was briefly unconscious but not dead. Millicent's later grief and suffering in her bereavement were overwhelming and required all the resilience she could muster to overcome them.

5

2 GOWER STREET — AGNES, RHODA AND PHILIPPA

The death of Harry was undoubtedly a devastating loss, which Millicent admitted altered her whole life. She wrote in her memoir:

> Left alone after seventeen years of happy active married life, having been the partner and friend of my husband in all his activities (except fishing, which I could never endure), I might have fallen into a lethargic melancholy if it had not been for the help I received from many of my husband's old friends, and also in a very high degree from all the members of my own family, father, mother, sisters, brothers and also from my own daughter. These all stood by me and helped me at every turn.

The Garrett family was unusually close in the way most of its members continued to be involved with each other throughout their adult lives. Nothing demonstrates this better than the very way they rallied round Millicent to support her after her husband's early death.

This was especially apparent when Millicent asked herself the question, 'Where am I going to live?' When Harry died, the sister she wanted with her was Agnes. Elizabeth telegraphed Agnes from Cambridge to tell her Millicent was asking for her, and Agnes came at once. She was also there to comfort and support Millicent during Harry's earlier serious illness, when it was not clear whether he would survive. The bond they had formed during their childhood was deep and lasting, although they inevitably spent less time in each other's company after they left school. After Millicent's marriage, Agnes developed a loving relationship with her distant cousin, Rhoda Garrett, who had provided Millicent with advice and companionship when she was at school.

Millicent also refers to her brother Sam becoming, amongst her brothers, her close friend and adviser. He was closest to her in age and the only one of the four brothers to have had a highly success-ful professional life: leaving Aldeburgh for Cambridge University and then working in London as a lawyer. He was clever, amusing and, unlike the other brothers, a committed feminist. But although Millicent described him as 'the first and foremost amongst my men friends', it was to Agnes that she turned to when she grieved for Harry after he died.

Although Agnes may have lacked Sam's intellectual brilliance, she was highly intelligent and remarkable in her own way. She was the only Garrett sister who never married. Instead, she formed a personal and professional partnership with Rhoda. Elizabeth, de-termined as ever in encouraging her sisters to develop their own careers, had earlier tried to suggest routes that Agnes might take to give her more fulfilling work than assisting their mother in run-ning her household. At various times Elizabeth suggested 'making [Agnes] responsible for definite and really engaging work – not make believe or useless work, not that which (as sewing) only occupies her fingers and leaves her mind at liberty'. Elizabeth proposed employment within the family business as well as outside it. In the first category was the counting house once again, where Alice had worked before her marriage and departure for India; and when nothing came of this, the malting business at Snape. This was vetoed by Edmund, her older brother, who had become their father's partner in his business and who could not conceive of 'lady maltsters'. Outside, Elizabeth suggested employment in a bank or an insurance company, presumably doing clerical work, as nothing more responsible would have been countenanced by employers in the 1860s.

In the end, Agnes realised that she would need to decide for herself what future career she should pursue. Together with Rhoda, she hatched a plan for them to work as architects or designers, and in doing so to set up their own business. They chose a field which had no relationship to the paths their sisters had taken and was largely unrelated to Newson Garrett's main business interests, although he was an active property developer in Aldeburgh and did design Alde House himself. They also had enough insight to realise that they needed to be trained if they were to be successful in fulfilling their ambition. They did not want to just dabble after attending a few terms at art school, where women were admitted as students. They wanted to be professional craftswomen with practical skills as well as creative ideas. They considered the best way to achieve this was to become apprentices and found a designer, Daniel Cottier, who would take them on. He had started life as a stained-glass artist and furniture maker and then set up a firm in London specialising in this work. After being apprenticed to him for a year and a half, they moved on to spend eighteen months' training with an architect,

John Brydon, where they learnt to draw to scale as well as various technical skills in house design. At that time, there were no formal qualifications to become an architect. Yet Agnes and Rhoda did not think that they had sufficient skills to design and build houses. The profession was in any case closed to women; professional female architects did not exist until 1898.

Agnes and Rhoda described themselves as architectural decorators and set up the firm of R. & A. Garrett House Decorators in 1874. When they embarked on their training, they had the support of Millicent and Harry, as well as Elizabeth. Harry wrote to Newson defending their decision to offer Agnes a home in London during her apprenticeship. Newson had difficulty at first in accepting that yet another daughter had challenged convention by leaving home to pursue a career, which had not until then been open to women. Harry's letter would have been agreed by Millicent, who may have encouraged him to write as he did. He said:

> I do not feel I have in any way influenced Agnes. She is old enough and has ability enough to judge for herself without interference from me. I think it is quite as laudable on her part to desire to make her own living as it was for Lizzie to do the same. Agnes was chiefly influenced in her desire to do something in London from a very proper motive that she did not want to be the cause of family disagreement, and from the tone Newson [her eldest brother] and Edmund adopted to her entering the malting business, family discord would be the inevitable result.

Thus, the Fawcetts' letter cleverly shifted the blame for Agnes's departure onto the unenlightened, conservative brothers. When

Agnes came to London to learn her chosen trade, she stayed with Harry and Millicent in Lambeth.

Once she and Rhoda finished their training, they lived together as well as working together. In the mid-1870s, soon after they set up their firm, Agnes and Rhoda took out a lease on 2 Gower Street, an eighteenth-century, white-stuccoed, five-storied house at the south end of the otherwise brick-built street, close to Bedford Square. I lived there myself a century later, from early 1988 to the summer of 1997. By then, it was owned by the University of London and leased on a peppercorn rent, as a residence for the Master of Birkbeck. Apart from the traffic, which roared down the then one-way street from north to south, it was a delightful and very convenient place to live. When the Garrett cousins moved in, the street was closed to traffic and unfashionable. Elizabeth Crawford, in her book *Enterprising Women: The Garretts and Their Circle*, said that 'late eighteenth-century brick architecture was deemed dull and monotonous when compared with the stucco splendours of Kensington'. Agnes and Rhoda preferred Bloomsbury, citing, in a book they wrote on house decoration, the solid ways in which the houses were fitted inside, and wishing that 'the fashionable world of London may one day return and live in the houses, which were built in the solid and unpretentious style' of the Georgian brick-built streets. Their wish eventually came true, although long after Millicent moved in with Agnes.

The cousins worked from 2 Gower Street and put a brass plaque outside telling those who passed the front door that it was the residence of R. & A. Garrett. The house was large enough to accommodate their office and receive their clients. What they would not have known, when they first leased it, is that it would have to become the home of Rhoda's much younger half-siblings during the school holidays after her father died in 1878 leaving them orphans. The 1881 census revealed that they also had three servants living in their house as well as a young man, who assisted them in their business as a porter, painter and decorator. Quite how they all fitted in is unclear, although the servants probably all slept in the quite large basement rooms.

The house was refurbished by Agnes and Rhoda, with specially designed fireplaces as well as new wallpaper they designed, influenced by William Morris. They also designed and built a range of furniture in the Arts and Crafts style, which was introduced in the last quarter of the nineteenth century. None of their work remained in Gower Street when I moved there, with the exception of a unique, decorated ceiling in the first-floor room at the back, which I used as my study. It was designed, and then painted, by Agnes and Rhoda apparently lying on their backs on scaffolding. A plaster frieze around the walls of the first-floor drawing room, thought to be their design, and an architrave above the door of the spare room also survived.

Their business was on a relatively small scale; there was no question of mass production. However, it was large enough for them to open a showroom, which also served as a warehouse, off Tottenham Court Road close to Gower Street and which Agnes was still maintaining into the 1890s. At the start of their collaboration, they gained publicity for their designs through writing a book, which was published by Macmillan in 1876, in which they set out the principles of their approach. It was characterised by light colours on the walls, simplicity in the use of natural materials and the avoidance of too many over-elaborate ornaments and too many patterns in the drapery. Rooms should be harmonious and restful to the eye. There was more publicity from the exhibition of their work in the 1878 Paris Exhibition and in other exhibitions in later years, including those of the Arts and Crafts Society. Some of their commissions were from their family and their friends. For example, Hubert Parry, the musician and composer, greatly appreciated the layout and the furniture they had designed for 2 Gower Street when he stayed there, so he and his wife invited them to do the interior design of their house, which they had recently purchased, in Kensington. Most of Agnes and Rhoda's work in the early years of their firm was residential and they probably gained many of their commissions by word of mouth.

Millicent identified with their strong belief that their achievements were an outcome of their training. Without it, they would not have claimed to be professional architectural decorators. Writing in 1875, Agnes claimed:

The thing which is most important to impress upon women is the necessity of a thorough and systematic training in any work they intend to do. The bête noire of women has hitherto been the idea they can do anything. Upon examination, this is generally proved to mean that they can do nothing well, not from natural incapacity, but from want of training.

Nothing in her many years of experience led her to change her views, and she claimed nearly twenty years later:

I would impress upon my readers that in order to be successful as a decorator, a woman must undertake the business seriously, and time and patience must be devoted to learning its various branches thoroughly ... What women most require as a class is

the formal business training and habits of continuous effort …
There is no way of learning the business in all its branches except
by going through a term of apprenticeship.

In today's context where too little is invested in practical training
and in apprenticeships in particular, especially for girls and young
women, her strong views more than a century ago are still pertinent.

One way in which Agnes and Rhoda took action themselves was
to take women on and train them for a fee. This opportunity would
only have been available for middle-class women, who could afford
to pay. Their numbers would also have been small because too few
well-off families would have perceived professional architectural
decoration as a suitable career for women. The Garretts undertook
all the designing themselves, but they employed men and women
to do the practical work of painting and installation, for which they
must have provided some training too, as employees rather than
pupils.

Both Agnes and particularly Rhoda were active in various roles
outside their business. Rhoda was one of only two women on the
Committee for the Preservation of Ancient Buildings and she was
a member of the Royal Archaeological Institute. She was an elo-
quent and fluent speaker and commanded a large audience when
giving a speech at the annual meeting of the National Association
for the Promotion of Social Science on the basic principles of interior design. They were also both active campaigners for women's
suffrage, and Rhoda was the most charismatic speaker, not just in
the Garrett family but amongst all the early speakers, on why giving
women the vote would emancipate them. The cousins were on the
side of including married women as well as female ratepayers, and
they were also open supporters of Josephine Butler's campaign

against the Contagious Diseases Act, so in both respects were more radical than Millicent.

Jenifer Glynn, in her book *The Pioneering Garretts*, describes how unique and special Rhoda was, quoting from her half-brother Edmund and from Ethel Smyth, the composer and supporter of the suffrage cause. They both refer to her extraordinary charm and her wit, her brilliance and her popularity. Her early death of typhoid and bronchitis in 1882 at the age of forty-one was a tragic loss. Had she lived, she might have eclipsed Millicent and Emmeline Pankhurst and her daughters, who were to emerge later, as the leaders of the suffragettes.

Millicent missed Rhoda greatly, but the person who suffered most when she died was Agnes. She loved her deeply and shared her life with her, as well as their professional work. Together, they rented a rambling house in Rustington, a village in Sussex, where they spent the weekend, whenever they could leave London. Not far from the sea, with a large garden, it was a haven for Rhoda's much younger half-siblings and for Philippa Fawcett, who played with them when she stayed there. Agnes and Rhoda were able to spend time in Rustington with friends such as Hubert Parry and his wife Maude, who built a house there, and other London friends who made Rustington their country bolthole. So shattering was Rhoda's death for Agnes that she considered giving up Rustington and closing down the firm in Gower Street.

The day after Rhoda's funeral in Rustington, Parry played Bach for Agnes to try to comfort and console her. Soon after, she wrote to Maude, saying:

> I know all she was to me, helping me perpetually from sinking into commonplace aims and low ideals. I feel as if I were an ear

of wheat that has been threshed and robbed of all living grains. It is this that has made me shrink so from going on with our work – as if I should have no freshness, no originality, no delicacy to offer people – in fact that I should be that which she hated so – a charlatan. But no one else seems to think so – they didn't know what she was so entirely as I do – and for the sake of the two boys [Rhoda's half-brothers, Edmund and John Garrett, who with Millicent's support Agnes cared for until they grew up] I have determined to go on at any rate for the present.

One of the reasons for Agnes's decision was that her earnings would allow her to keep on renting the house in Rustington, where she had such happy memories of spending time with Rhoda.

Encouraged by Millicent, Agnes quickly went back to her office in 2 Gower Street and from then on worked alone until her retirement in the early 1900s. During two decades of long professional life, she expanded the range of her firm's work from residential projects into some bigger commissions for various institutions – for example, she won a competition to do the interior design and decoration of the New Hospital for Women when it was put out for tender. She was also a key member of a small group which set up the Ladies' Residential Chambers Company to build residences for single working women.

The conception of the 'chambers' was a feminist project. When women started to be employed in a wider range of professional and administrative work and to leave their parental homes, they needed somewhere affordable to live. To rent a house or even a mansion flat was beyond their means unless they came from a relatively wealthy family and had a private income. Without a financial cushion of this kind, they were forced to rely on boarding houses or a room in a private house. Such accommodation was usually cramped and often dingy, so that the advantages of new employment opportunities for women were qualified by a miserable quality of life outside work. The *English Woman's Journal* first recognised the problem in an article on modern housebuilding in 1863, which proposed flat-living for women. In spite of more publicity about women's housing needs, it took many years for women to benefit from new types of accommodation. In the 1880s, a couple of organisations were established in London which opened for 'ladies' blocks of flats with low rents. They provided reputable accommodation in pleasant areas, with privacy and basic comforts. They were primarily designed for what were quaintly described as 'gentlewomen without means'.

In 1888, Agnes was one of five people who set up another new company with similar objectives, having found a suitable site close to Gower Street. Shares were offered and it was run on a commercial basis, therefore with higher rents than the earliest similar enterprises. The flats had two, three or four rooms and their own front doors, but residents could, if they wanted, eat in the public dining room, being provided with good food from a central kitchen. The project received the backing of both Millicent and Elizabeth Garrett Anderson, who strongly believed professional women needed a restful place to live after their long working days. Both became shareholders in the company, as did their brother Sam's wife, Clara Garrett. A number of other feminist activists with high incomes invested in it too. An architect was appointed to design the Chenies Street Chambers and Agnes was responsible for the purchase of furniture but not the decoration. In 1889, Millicent opened the building.

Just a year later, the company decided to build a second set of chambers in York Street, Marylebone. It cost more to build, resulting in higher rents and therefore a better-off clientele. Both buildings still exist today, although no longer with the same purpose as when they first opened. By coincidence, in 1961 when I first came to London to study at the London School of Economics, having failed to obtain a room in a hall of residence, my father persuaded me to live in the Club for Educated Gentlewomen in Bolsover Street, Marylebone. He knew about it because it was managed with strict regulations by one of his second cousins. I was terrified by her and frightened of transgressing the rules. There were only a small number of students who were housed on the top floor in cell-like bedrooms with communal bathrooms. The middle-aged 'Educated Gentlewomen' had better accommodation lower down. I sometimes saw them in the dining room and the communal sitting rooms, but at the age of nineteen, they seemed to me dull and dowdy. I left after nine months in search of something less institutional. I have no idea how or when it was established, but from its title, I assume it was started on similar principles to those of the Ladies' Residential Chambers Company supported by the Garrett sisters. Agnes, described by Elizabeth Crawford as a driving force in this enterprise that enabled hundreds of women to develop their professional lives from the comfort of a relatively well-managed home, attended her last directors' meeting in March 1931, having worked actively for the company for forty-three years. Crawford describes the chambers and their clientele in her excellent chapter on Agnes and Rhoda in *Enterprising Women*. In this same chapter, she also writes in detail about their work as interior designers, including many beautiful illustrations of their furniture and fireplaces, some of which she believed were in 2 Gower Street.

Millicent was close to Rhoda but only makes a passing reference to her death in her memoirs. One reason may be that Harry fell seriously ill for the first time soon after she returned from Rhoda's funeral. In contrast to Millicent's silence about Rhoda, Agnes went immediately to support Millicent, commenting, 'It was so strange to me all last night comforting Milly with my own heart bursting.' It would be unfair to Millicent to claim that she did not appreciate how solicitous Agnes was in the circumstances, since she told her husband's biographer, Leslie Stephen, that Agnes came for an hour and stayed for six weeks, by which time Harry was recovering. Putting her emotions in writing or expressing them in public, especially on the subject of grief, was avoided by Millicent. Indeed, Hubert Parry, who was greatly affected by Rhoda's death, noted how both Agnes and Millicent were very restrained after Rhoda died. Some thought Millicent cold but admitted that her unwillingness to express her feelings did not mean that she had none. It may have meant that she preferred not to share them. She would fight to hold back tears and, if unable to do so, she would leave the room, perhaps for fear of embarrassing others, perhaps because she thought it revealed weakness on her part.

Millicent's seemingly iron will certainly did not stretch to believing that she should live alone after Harry died. The solution to the loneliness which that would entail was to live with Agnes. In her memoirs, Millicent describes this as an obvious way out:

[Agnes] had lost her dearly loved friend and house-mate … We had thus each received a heavy stroke of personal sorrow, and it seemed very natural that we should henceforth live together, and make our joint home in her house. My Cambridge home was broken up, and my London home, with its pleasant garden, was only a shadow of what it had been; but I had always loved the

Gower Street house and all its associations, and so had Philippa, who had been as much devoted to Agnes and Rhoda as a child could be.

Mother and daughter moved in and Millicent lived there from the age of thirty-seven to her death in 1929. I do not know where in the house she worked, nor which was her bedroom. What is obvious is that the spaciousness I experienced would not have been available for Millicent. I shared the house just with my son and daughter-in-law and then only briefly while they were graduate students, and my daughter, away in term time as an undergraduate in Bristol but who returned for two or three years after completing her degree. There would have been more space there when Rhoda's siblings grew up and left and when Philippa went to Cambridge. However, Agnes had her office there too, and successive censuses show three servants as well as the continuing presence of Agnes's assistant, who acted as a painter and porter. He eventually married the cook; perhaps over-crowding was one of the reasons!

Just as Agnes had accepted that she should return to work after Rhoda died, so did Millicent after Harry's death, although she took around a year to start again. Even though before he died, the distractions of being a minister's wife and running two homes in two different places had meant some reduction in her writing and campaigning, she had still been quite actively engaged in various campaigns, not all of which were on enfranchisement. One of her main motives in getting back to work is that she believed this is what Harry would have wanted. She knew he was proud of her and that he would have been upset and disappointed had she relapsed into apathy and depression. In any case, her driven personality and her experience of being active throughout her life meant that she had to be employed. She had enough self-knowledge to realise that work would be a balm that would help her deal with her grief. She did not believe in an afterlife or in prayer for the dead; she did believe in celebrating in this life the memory of someone she had lost. She threw herself into pursuing the principles she shared with the husband she loved and admired, and always took pleasure after he had died in discussing his achievements with those who complimented him.

Only a few weeks after Harry's death, Millicent was asked if she would be willing to become the mistress of Girton, the Cambridge University college. This would have engaged her in an area to which she was committed: women's higher education. Nevertheless, she did not hesitate to turn down this offer. She did not think she was suited to work involving managing an institution, but she rejected it mainly because she knew that she wanted to dedicate her time to votes for women and political activism to this end. The Girton job would have provided her with accommodation and an income, but presumably she was confident that she could survive on any royalties that were still being paid from both her and Harry's publications, as well as the £9,535 (over £1.5 million in today's money) he left her in his will. The shares and property her parents later left her would have helped to ensure she could live very comfortably.

Millicent was still young and could have remarried. There is no evidence that a widower or single man ever pursued her in the hope of marriage, and it seems unlikely that she sought a second husband. She relied on the company of her sister Agnes and her daughter, her wider large family and her many female friends. The fact that she held deep emotions in an iron grip did not mean she lacked the gift of friendship. She was an interesting companion, widely read and knowledgeable about the arts as well as politics, with a sense of adventure, which she enjoyed sharing with her friends.

Her daughter was only sixteen when her father died, and without siblings, Philippa was undoubtedly dependent on her mother to share some of her leisure with her as well as to benefit from her advice and guidance. It is difficult to discover much about Philippa's personality or her interests outside her academic work. Millicent's memoirs convey little about either. She includes an affectionate description of Philippa as a quaint little girl who asked intelligent questions and challenged the replies. Philippa was dedicated to her dog after acquiring him and said, 'Now if people ask me if I have a brother, I shall say yes,' the resort perhaps of the only child who yearned for company. One of Millicent's anecdotes refers to the daily hour reserved for time with her parents before dinner and her resentment of callers who interrupted it. When Henry Sidgwick turned up, stealing her time with her parents from her, she fetched a piece of paper and a black crayon and lying on the floor wrote in large capital letters, 'WEN WILL HE EVER GO?' Their guest saw it, took the hint and laughingly left. Once the hour was over, she was returned to her nurse, as would have been typical at that time.

Millicent also refers to Philippa's precocious talent in mathematics, leading to special tutorials that she and Harry arranged for her when she was about fifteen with a fellow of Harry's college, during the months they were in Cambridge. Millicent also refers to the teaching her daughter had at University College in a small class where the other pupils were all boys, before she went to Newnham to follow the undergraduate mathematics courses at Cambridge. These arrangements reveal Millicent's commitment to developing

Philippa's considerable talent. Those who taught her, predicted that she would perform brilliantly in the mathematics tripos. What no one would have dared to predict is that she would do better than the senior wrangler, the term used to describe the top mathematics undergraduate at Cambridge. Millicent was so anxious about the outcome of the tripos examination that she decided not to go up to Cambridge to hear the results when they were read out in the Senate House. Philippa's family was represented instead by her grandfather Newson, who travelled from Aldeburgh with two of her cousins, Alice's daughters, one of whom wrote a full account of what happened:

It was a most exciting scene in the Senate this morning … The gallery was crowded with girls and a few men, and the floor of the building was thronged by undergraduates as tightly packed as they could be … All the men's names were read first, the senior wrangler was much cheered … There was such a hullaballoo that it took some time for the women's names to be read out after several requests for silence. At last [the examiner] read Philippa's name and announced she was 'above the senior wrangler'. There was great and prolonged cheering; many of the men turned towards Philippa, who was sitting in the gallery … and waved their hats … A great many people were there to cheer and congratulate Philippa when she came down into the hall … Grandpa was standing at the bottom of the stairs waiting for Philippa. He was a good bit upset.

Indeed, Newson, who was less buttoned up than his daughter, wept and was overjoyed once more when another grandchild, Alice's son, was also senior wrangler a few years later. Millicent refers in her memoirs to going to Cambridge after the announcement; in her biography, Ray Strachey says that as soon as she heard the news in a telegram, she left to take part in the celebrations later that day in Newnham. Strachey also remarked that Millicent was afraid of her own emotions when she arrived and 'tried to keep a hold upon her feelings'. Nevertheless, Millicent did enjoy witnessing the euphoria at the Newnham dinner and the fireworks in celebration that night. Back at 2 Gower Street, the telegrams and the letters of congratulations poured in. Millicent said her only regret was that Harry was not there to share her joy. In a thank-you letter to the suffragist committees for their congratulations, she drew out the political as well as the personal saying:

The news on Saturday made me very happy. You know that I care for it mainly for the sake of women; but of course I also feel especially blessed in the fact that the thing I care most of all for has been helped on in this way by my own dear child.

She also confided in her memoirs:

I always consider myself a lucky person, and this impression was confirmed by the result of Philippa's tripos examination. I should have been overjoyed if any girl, even the daughter of my dearest enemy, had gained a similar distinction. But that this great honour should come to our own child was a joy that could hardly be expressed.

In spite of excelling the following year in the second part of the tripos, Philippa, like all women, was excluded from obtaining a degree, which meant that a university lectureship was denied her.

Instead, she became a fellow and lecturer at Newnham, a post she held for the next seven years. When she was in London, her home was still at 2 Gower Street, where she was a strong supporter of her mother's suffrage work but also shared her political views, such as opposing Home Rule in Ireland. Although brought up to be independent as a child – for example, for a time when her parents were in Cambridge, she boarded with a family so that her secondary schooling at Clapham High School would not be disrupted – she did not demonstrate independence as an adult, by, for example, challenging her mother's views on political issues. She was shy and reticent. One of the letters of congratulation Millicent received after Philippa's success in Cambridge was from the Master of Trinity College, saying, 'I only wish you could have seen your dear daughter in the Senate House at the moment of her triumph. You could not have seen a more perfect picture of modest maidenly simplicity.' Others describe how calm Philippa was on this occasion.

Maude Parry, the composer's wife, kept a diary in Rustington with entries about Millicent and Agnes and one about Philippa. She recounts them all coming to tea. She said Philippa 'looked more extraordinary than ever. She munched away but never said a word.' What the reference to her looks meant is unclear. One or two photographs of her at the time reveal a neat and perhaps slightly prim Victorian young woman.

According to Ray Strachey, after Philippa's Cambridge brilliance, Millicent wanted her to pursue

some very striking career, and so carry farther the good work she had already done for the cause. She had wanted her to become in turn an astronomer, a physicist, a lighthouse designer or an engineer, or at any rate something which no woman had ever been before. When Philippa rejected these plans, her mother suggested she should train as a solicitor, or an actuary, and so force open a new calling for women; and when instead of doing any of these things her daughter went back to Newnham to teach mathematics, Millicent refused to look at this as a permanent choice, and continued to hunt for some more adventurous opening.

Well-intentioned about Philippa as she certainly was, this smacks slightly as wanting to use her daughter as a tool in women's emancipation, the cause that preoccupied Millicent above all else.

After going to South Africa with her mother, a trip which I will describe later, Philippa became interested in the expansion of education there, and with her mother's blessing, returned to help set up elementary schools. Millicent went out to South Africa again to visit her. On her return, she saw an advertisement from the London County Council (LCC) for an assistant to the Director of Education and enquired whether they would consider employing a woman. A reply in the affirmative led her to seek Philippa's permission to apply on her behalf! After Millicent did so, Philippa was appointed on the same salary as would have been given to a man, taking up the appointment in 1905. She stayed for thirty years until her retirement and held senior positions with responsibility at various times for secondary education, teacher training and county council scholarships. Although Millicent may have been a little disappointed that she did not go for one of the high-profile careers she had fantasised about, she was probably proud that her daughter was the first professional woman in the LCC education department. Moreover, the fact that a teacher training college was named after Philippa suggests that she served with some distinction, in spite of her quiet and reticent personality.

Her obituary at Newnham refers to her shyness, her almost ob-sessive tidiness and her passion for walking, an activity which she shared with her mother. To have been Millicent's daughter could not always have been easy. It would have been hard to match her mother's relentless drive and powerful personality. In contrast to her mother, others found Philippa colourless. However, maybe the fact that she was so much less forceful allowed them to live togeth-er in harmony at 2 Gower Street for so many years. The fact that Agnes was there too meant that later in her life when she was less practically active, Millicent could rely on her for companionship while Philippa was at work in County Hall.

In her memoirs, Millicent makes only one brief reference to the other occupants in the house – the servants – in an anecdote about the telegrams which arrived congratulating on Philippa's ac-ademic victory. The telegraph boy asked what was happening, was it a wedding? 'Our dear old housekeeper who was answering the door exclaimed, "Oh no! A great deal better than that."' Although Millicent does not name her housekeeper, she describes her affec-tionately. The census also reveals that at least some of the servants stayed for many years, which suggests they were content and well treated. Some of them were almost certainly related to each other. For example, in 1881 Martha Griffin, aged twenty-five, is listed as a 'servant', and in 1891, Martha reappears as well as Susannah Griffin, aged twenty-nine, who is listed as 'parlourmaid'. They were sisters. Susannah appears again in 1911 and in 1921, by which time she is listed as 'housekeeper', and, in the same year, there were two much younger women called Griffin described as 'parlourmaid' and 'housemaid'. Unrecognised as it may have been at the time, these women would have made it possible for Millicent, Agnes and Philippa to work and campaign without having to keep this large house going or cook their own meals. One way Agnes expressed her appreciation, presumably with backing from Millicent, was to give some shares in the Ladies' Residential Chambers Company to her loyal painter, who lived in 2 Gower Street for many years, and to his wife, Martha, the cook-housekeeper, and to Susannah Griffin, the parlourmaid.

According to Maude Parry, the residents of 2 Gower Street ate well. One of her diary entries on Rustington says, 'I went to dinner with Agnes and Mrs Fawcett. Such a spread. First, there was a mayonnaise of crab, then fillets of beef with peas, steamed potatoes and tomato salad. Then came grouse … We had cream and macaroni. Certainly, the Garretts know how to live.' Whether this large and elegant meal was typical is not clear. Nor is there any evidence that Millicent ever stood in the kitchen with Mrs Beeton's recipes in front of her, preparing some of the courses herself. Given her financial resources, which made employing a cook easy, and how much of her time was taken up in writing and political campaigning, it is highly unlikely.

Millicent successfully rebuilt her life as a widow, living at 2 Gower Street until she died. Although a little older, Agnes survived her for several years. They worked separately but were the closest of companions, keeping each other company at home and on their travels abroad. The fact that they worked in different spheres was a guard against rivalry. Some of Millicent's campaigns outside the suffrage movement were controversial, but there is no record of Agnes ever criticising her.

6

CAMPAIGNING WIDOW

Devastating as Henry's death was, it released Millicent from the work she undertook as his wife, giving her more time and the freedom to launch into further campaigns, not all of which were directly linked to women's suffrage. She had strong views about sexual morality and was unforgiving about infidelity and about sex before marriage. She found prostitution repellent and the exploitation of girls for the purpose of prostitution morally repugnant. She wrote at some length about how horrifying it was that girls as young as thirteen could be sold to work in brothels, without any legal restraints. Her justified indignation about this led to her involvement in the Stead case, a Victorian melodrama, which excited a great deal of publicity.

W. T. Stead was the editor of the *Pall Mall Gazette* and had published articles by Millicent on votes for women. On the back of a parliamentary victory for Josephine Butler's campaign to overturn the Contagious Diseases Acts in 1883 (although they were not repealed until 1886), the campaigners went to Stead to ask him to publicise the sale of children into prostitution. The legal position, extraordinary as it was, was based on an 1875 Act which denoted thirteen as the age of consent. Efforts to amend the Act were led by Lord Shaftesbury. He successfully took through a Bill in the Upper House in 1884, only for it to be thrown out in the House of Commons. After being approached, Stead investigated whether another attempt at legislation might be successful, given there was a new government in power. He was told by a friend, who was a member of the Liberal government, that there was not the slightest chance. He also went to the head of the Criminal Investigation Department, who confirmed that it was legal for parents to sell their thirteen-year-old daughters into prostitution and that this occurred regularly.

Convinced that there was little hope of reform through the parliamentary route, Stead decided to publicise the issue in the journal he edited and to do so in a way which would maximise publicity and support crusaders who wanted to change the law. In a series of articles in the *Pall Mall Gazette* in July 1885, under the title 'The Maiden Tribute of Modern Babylon', he exposed the horrors of child prostitution. To bolster his argument, he took the unusual step of purchasing a girl of thirteen from her mother for the purposes of prostitution. Unfortunately for Stead, in spite of the care he had taken to engage the help of the Salvation Army to support and care for the child, he was eventually arrested and charged with abducting the girl on the grounds that he had only been given the consent of the mother when the father's consent was required. Well before his arrest, his articles had led to widespread debate in which many public protests called for changes in the law; but others denounced Stead for sensationalism. Both sides could claim victory. The indignant protests rapidly led to the reintroduction of the Bill that the Commons had thrown out; it was passed within a month, raising the age of consent to sixteen. Those who resented Stead's exposure got the satisfaction of his arrest, conviction and sentence to three months' imprisonment as an ordinary criminal.

Millicent was passionate about both the necessity for reform and the need to defend Stead. She waded into the controversy by writing letters to the press and an article for the *Pall Mall Gazette*, which praised Stead's articles for their morality and the way in which they had promoted 'a deep yearning for purity', which would save young men and women 'from condemning themselves to a quagmire of vice'. In a letter to a friend, she described the attacks on Stead and his journal, which even went so far as suppressing its sale. The journal defended itself with the claim that the articles were factually true and, to verify this, it set up an independent inquiry whose members included the Archbishop of Canterbury and the Lord Mayor. Millicent implied that the opposition to the articles was part of a cover-up of the behaviour of men in high places. She ended her letter, 'I think all the deep feeling that has been aroused by a knowledge of the facts will make a great many people understand for the first time one of the reasons why women ought to have votes.'

Once Stead had been sent to prison, Millicent wrote to him expressing her admiration for what he had done and her gratitude to him for the outcome it had had in changing the law. She believed that comforting words were not enough, so set about getting his conditions in prison changed by appealing to the Home Secretary to have him treated as a 'first-class misdemeanant', which would allow him to have a cell in which he could read and wear warmer clothes. She wrote to Sir Henry Ponsonby, the Queen's private secretary, whom she knew, pleading for the monarch to intervene. Millicent claims she knew this was constitutionally impossible. Nevertheless, she deployed her usual approach to political activism, which was to build a network of influential people and to exploit it formally and informally in the hope of behind-the-scenes intervention. Her letter to Sir Henry is a good example. He politely replied that such an intervention was not possible, so he could not put her request to the Queen. However, he told her that he did telegraph the Home Secretary, whom he thought had already earlier that day issued an order to change Stead's prisoner status. The timing of the Home Secretary's decision is uncertain.

One outcome of Stead's campaign was the establishment of the National Vigilance Association (NVA). Millicent had already publicly and privately supported Stead for the honourable cause he had pursued and forcefully condemned his prosecution and conviction because he had 'unwittingly overstepped the limits of legality'. The NVA was founded to continue to campaign on the protection of girls. Millicent supported its establishment and took part in its work as a committee member or as a vice-president until three years before she died. However, she never lost her conviction that the pursuit of social improvements, including the area of sexual morality, was best addressed by giving women the vote. Indeed, in another letter, she claimed that she had not spoken before about sexual abuse because she did not believe that the law would be re-formed on this issue until women had gained the parliamentary vote. In an unusual reference to her own emotions, she continued that she could not speak in public on the way girls were abused without crying and that she had 'a morbid horror of breaking down in public', although she claimed that she now understood that if she could bring herself to do it, it would not matter if she broke down. There is no evidence of her ever doing so. She always stuck to making her case dispassionately and without demonstrations of emotion, although making her arguments forcefully and brutally dismissing opponents without hesitation. Her style contributed to a reputation, even amongst friends and admirers, of lacking warmth. David Rubinstein quotes one of her colleagues saying that 'any display of her private feeling would seem to her indecent'.

This reticence did not extend to holding back on catching out actual or potential offenders and denouncing them. This is illustrated by her participation in a 'sting' in which an army doctor, having accosted a seventeen-year-old servant girl in the street, tried to persuade her to accompany him to his home. She refused, but she was persuaded to give him her address and he pursued her by letter. She told her employers, who happened to be friends of Millicent's, and the NVA was informed and set a trap for him. When the servant met him outside the British Museum, she had a large reception committee with her, including Millicent. He was given a sound dressing down and told by Millicent that they had his letter before he made his escape. What became of him and whether he changed his behaviour is not known, but the NVA continued in identifying and campaigning against sexual immorality. Millicent took up the horrors of the white slave trade and spoke at an international conference in London in 1899, decrying the lack of any serious attempt to stop it. It was virtually impossible for girls to escape once they had been trapped and they were 'shipped from country to country like so many head of cattle', she said.

Her work for the NVA also involved another campaign which was to protect children who were employed in the theatre. Children were often used on the London stage, whether in pantomimes, melodramas or dance performances. Many of the children involved were under the age of ten and some were as young as five years old, although the numbers involved and their age distribution are unclear. Nor is there much evidence about how much they were paid, although their income would have been a handy extra for poor families. It appears that Millicent exaggerated their numbers in her campaign to prevent their employment or at least to regulate it.

Her objections were partly about these children missing out on education, which by the 1880s was compulsory, and partly about the risk of them being abused in the unregulated Victorian theatre. She chaired an NVA conference where she discussed her concerns and made her case for legislation. As a result, the NVA supported a parliamentary Bill which sought to regulate the employment of children on the stage. Millicent set out her views at greater length in an article, which reached a wider public and led to her being attacked by theatre managers. Undaunted, she followed up her article with evidence to the Royal Commission on Education, which had been appointed to examine the working of the Elementary Education Acts. She proposed that the employment of children under the age of ten should be illegal and that between the ages of ten and thirteen, they should only be allowed to appear at matinees. She cited an extension of the Factory Acts as the best route to legislative change.

Much of her evidence seems to be anecdotal, relying heavily on what teachers had told her, which may have been rather biased. She claimed that the children had poor levels of educational attainment, that their health often suffered as they were exhausted, that theatrical apprenticeships lasting for many years started at far too early an age (presumably they had little or no general educational content) and, more tendentiously, that their earnings ended up being spent in public houses by their idle and drunken fathers.

Millicent was attacked for her views not just by the theatre managers and supporters of the popular entertainment they provided but also by theatregoers who enjoyed seeing children on the stage and did not want to be deprived of the opportunity. More-over, those responsible for the care of these children while working denied that they were abused or in any moral danger. Millicent was thick-skinned enough to deal with these attacks; after all, she was used to attracting opprobrium in her suffrage campaigns. The Royal Commission appears to have accepted her argument that the children's schooling was being damaged, and it opposed the employment of children under ten 'for purposes of gain', seeing the extension of the Factory Acts to the children as a possible remedy. Millicent pursued her campaign robustly, taking on her critics. She insisted that she was not an opponent of the theatre per se, going to performances herself often accompanied by children and young people; nor did she believe they were 'dens of vice', but she did refer to the danger to which young girls were exposed at a time when juvenile prostitution was a serious social problem.

Her detractors, such as the famous impresario Augustus Harris, criticised her for 'wild, unfounded and libellous statements', re-ferring to the 'powerful imagination of this misguided lady'. Even Lewis Carroll waded in to defend a production of *Alice in Wonder-land*, in which girls aged fifteen, ten and seven had parts. He claimed all three were in 'blooming health and buoyant spirits' and that 'a taste for acting is one of the strongest passions of human nature'. As usual, Millicent was not silenced by her critics, who accused her of exaggerating the moral risks to children. Perhaps she did exag-gerate, but her concern for their lack of educational opportunities seems justified and in the end was addressed; nor did every writer in the theatre share Carroll's views. George Bernard Shaw, a music and drama critic at the time, was critical of magistrates, who did not act against the employment of children aged seven to nine in the theatre. An Act in 1899 prohibited the employment of children in places of amusement under the age of seven and required special licences for the employment of children aged seven to nine. Further campaigning led to the 1903 Employment of Children Act, which prevented children being employed under the age of ten. Millicent should take some credit for her persistence in this crusade.

Her indignation and the relentless way she took action to try to prevent child prostitution was even more admirable. The same cannot be said of her coldly vindictive actions eight years later in relation to the sins, as she saw them, of Henry Cust, a Conservative MP and the editor of the *Pall Mall Gazette*. Cust was in 1893 the MP for Stamford in Lincolnshire but fell out with the local party and was pushed out. Following his resignation, he sought the candidacy of a seat in Manchester, then held by the Liberals, but which was presumably considered winnable by the Conservatives at the next election. Cust was an upper-middle-class, handsome philanderer apt to boast about his conquests at weekend parties. When Millicent heard the Conservatives had adopted him, she set out to destroy his candidacy as she was shocked by revelations about his sexual behaviour. He was said to have fathered several children out of wedlock; he had certainly seduced a cousin from a well-established Lincolnshire family who became pregnant. Initially, he refused to marry the unfortunate young woman and made dismissive remarks about her. He was then forced to marry her, though she later miscarried. Unsurprisingly, it was an unhappy marriage.

Millicent thought this behaviour was not just unacceptable; it was immoral. Full of self-righteous indignation, she wrote in strong terms to contacts she had in Manchester, where she had done work on women's suffrage for many years. She began with the Women's Liberal Unionist Association with which she herself had been associated, but they were reluctant to get involved. Lady Frances

Balfour, another Liberal Unionist, who was the sister-in-law of Arthur Balfour, a leading Conservative politician and future Prime Minister, opposed Millicent's actions too, despite being a close friend. The other Manchester figures she wrote to may have been more responsive, although there is no clear evidence. Whatever the case, she had stirred up controversy about Cust and his suitability to be elected as an MP.

A correspondence ensued between Cust and Millicent. Cust referred to a letter signed by her 'being circulated in Manchester containing very false, libellous and damaging statements about myself and others' and asking for 'an early disclaimer'. Her reply was typically forceful:

> I am sorry to say I have nothing to withdraw; as a woman I have naturally the strongest feeling against men of known bad character being elected to the House of Commons, and as a Unionist I have special interest from the political point of view that the Conservative and Unionist Party should keep clear of the disadvantage and discredit of putting forward such men as candidates.

She added that the letters she had sent had been marked 'private' and offered to meet him if he wished. The correspondence between Cust and Millicent was also marked 'private'. Unsurprisingly, no meeting took place.

Meanwhile, Arthur Balfour asked Frances to try to persuade Millicent to give up her campaign against Cust. Instead, Millicent sent Balfour a long statement of self-justification saying that 'Cust's conduct struck at the root of everything that makes home and marriage sacred' and that to place such a man in a position of public honour and responsibility could have a very bad effect, especially on 'all young people whose character was still in the making'. In reply, Arthur Balfour sent her a five-page letter. The gist of this was that although he respected her motives in questioning the desirability of Cust's candidacy, he did not believe questions of private behaviour should become the subject of public recrimination – 'the duties of a Member of Parliament are public ones, the capacity of a candidate to perform those duties should in most cases be the sole ground of his election'. Millicent's spirited reply rebutted the case he made in another very long letter. Her case, she said, was 'that if Mr Cust persists in his candidature, the people who are asked to vote for him have a right to know what sort of man he is'. She concluded:

> On general grounds, apart from this particular case, I feel the present time to be a particularly important one in these matters. Up to our generation the whole of the social punishment in these cases has fallen on the woman and none, or next to none, on the man. But now, whether we like it or not, a movement is making itself felt towards equality.

She wanted, she said, 'to level up' and by calling them out to minimise as far as possible 'the temptation to lapses of this kind'.

In certain respects, Millicent could claim a victory, since eventually Cust withdrew, and he had to wait for six years before he found another seat. The fact that he did so meant her victory was qualified, as she wanted to drive him out of public life altogether. The story reveals the strength of her views about sexual morality as well as her view that social norms were based on inequality in perceptions of how men and women should behave. Men could get away with breaking moral codes in this sphere, but women could not. It also reveals she was not daunted by the intervention of politically important and prestigious men such as Arthur Balfour. She fought back. Unusually, she was also prepared to fight her ground, even at the expense of the suffrage cause about which she cared so much. She was told by Frances Balfour that she was widely criticised for going for Cust and she should have considered the views of her colleagues. She had certainly offended Arthur Balfour, who subsequently gave the enfranchisement of women no support. Nor was Cust her only target. The politician Charles Dilke had been the subject of sexual scandal and fell from grace as a result. Although he had been a friend as a Liberal radical, she signed a petition to stop him being selected as an alderman on the London County Council.

Millicent did more constructive work than the pursuit of these individuals, in supporting the Travellers' Aid Society, which had been set up to help young women who arrived at ports and railway stations in large cities in search of employment. She wrote articles appealing for funds to support a system to protect these young women from being conned by individuals with promises which were lies. In somewhat purple prose, she described 'a class of fiends in human form who haunt railway stations specially for the purpose of entrapping ignorant and foolish girls, often little more than children, to their ruin'. She was especially indignant about women who she referred to as 'harpies', who used all sorts of ruses to trick the girls into thinking they were respectable and were genuinely concerned to help them. One had dressed as a nurse, but Millicent was glad to say she had been caught and was now 'in temporary retirement in one of Her Majesty's Prisons; but many others are still at large'. As well as raising money for the Travellers' Aid Society through writing articles exposing the dangers to these young women who had left home, Millicent sat on its general committee.

She also did campaigning and committee work in the area of

the education and training of girls and young women, a cause she had first pursued when she was a young woman living in Cambridge, as a founder of Newnham College. Although she had never much liked Emily Davies, the founder of Girton College, she worked with her to try to secure degrees for female students at Cambridge. They tried unsuccessfully in the 1880s and again in the second half of the 1890s to secure degrees and membership of the university. When some of the female students performed so well in examinations, as in the case of Philippa, it was particularly galling that they were denied degrees. Both the women's colleges passed formal resolutions to try to persuade the university senate to accept change. The campaign was bitter, and misogyny was widespread. In spring 1897, members of the university voted 1,713 to 662 not to admit women and give them degrees. The result was not even close and from today's perspective is hard to explain. Some of the opposition was based on a refusal to contemplate greater competition for fellowships, since there were not enough to go round for the men who applied for them. Millicent reached a more brutal conclusion before the vote actually took place, referring to 'a deep-rooted belief … in the intellectual inferiority of women'.

Following their victory, some men, who wanted to keep the privilege of higher education for themselves, even proposed turning female students out of the university altogether. They suggested a separate women's university should be set up. Millicent was appalled and forcibly denounced this suggestion. In a conference speech, she said it would be the 'height of folly' for women to give up their right to study at Oxbridge for 'some fancy scheme the merits of which yet remain to be proved', for which she was applauded. Nor was there enough support in Cambridge for this backward proposal and the idea was soon dropped. Although she helped to see off segregation of this kind, she wrote, 'I am dreadfully cast down by Cambridge ... it is the worst throwback we have had for a very long time ... The most disappointing thing is the opposition of the young men, especially the younger dons – not all, of course, but a very large proportion.' She must have realised that this did not augur well for a better outcome in the near future. In fact, it was to be forty years before women were admitted as members of the university and were given Cambridge degrees.

Fortunately, Millicent did other work on education which had less depressing outcomes. It varied from supporting vocational education for women to opportunities for working women to have access to continuing education well after they had left school. In the first category, she was involved in securing training in horticulture for women through her membership of an advisory group at Swanley Horticultural College. In the second category, for more than two decades, she was a supporter of the College for Working Women and later became involved with the mixed-sex Working Men's College in Camden Town, where she sponsored its building appeal and where she also lectured occasionally. She was a governor of Bedford College and a patron of the London Pupil Teachers' Association, serving as its president and giving them money and books. Somehow, she also found time to give lecture series, for example at King's College's department for ladies and for the university extension movement, which provided part-time evening courses. She was generous with her time in giving occasional talks at girls' schools as well. Without using the term, she was in fact an early proponent of lifelong learning, saying that once women had the vote, she would become a student herself in order to, in her words, 'secure herself a "happy old age"'. The reason this never materialised was that she had to go on devoting herself to the cause of women's suffrage well into old age.

Millicent was, however, recognised for her work in education by the University of St Andrews. Having been a professor at Cambridge and the founder of the university extension movement, John Stuart Mill became the rector at St Andrews and got the university to award Millicent an honorary doctorate of law in recognition of her work for education. He told her he particularly wanted to honour a woman; very few women had been given this distinction at the time. The award delighted her colleagues in the women's movement, and she was inordinately proud of her honorary doctorate, quite often wearing her gown and hood at formal occasions and much later for a portrait. I did not know Millicent had preceded me by nearly a hundred years when I was given an honorary degree for my educational work by St Andrews. If only I had known, I would have tried to find a copy of her acceptance speech and quoted from it in mine.

Millicent also became peripherally involved in causes relating to the employment of working-class women during the 1880s and 1890s. She was not in favour of equal pay for women, as she thought this would limit their opportunities for jobs in many areas, but she did advocate more training and skills for women, opening occupations to them that so far they had been denied. She was critical of the trade unions and, as I described earlier, of parliamentary intervention in employment conditions for women. Her obsession was with the right to work, and because of that she was inclined to ignore questions of pay and conditions, although she did support the role of trade unions in supporting employees against their exploitation by ruthless employers who had no regard for health and safety.

For example, although earlier legislation had excluded women working underground in coal mines, these women were given jobs doing heavy manual work above ground at the entrance to the pits. They were known as pit brow workers, whose main task was to sort the coal, removing the stones, when it came to the surface at the shaft top. They were dressed in red scarves tied round their heads to keep the coal dust out of their hair, heavy jackets, trousers with a skirt or apron over them and clogs. Their 'uniform' was the subject of criticism, since wearing trousers offended Victorian norms on women's dress and was considered unfeminine – or even indecent! They worked long hours and were only paid half of male surface workers' earnings. Opposition to their employment at the collieries gathered some momentum in the 1880s. True to her principles that women had the same right to work as men regardless of lower pay, Millicent fought to prevent their exclusion. Rather oddly, she claimed that the women were cleaner than men who did similar work and compared them with chimney sweeps who always washed on Sundays whether their faces were dirty or not. She also defended the right of women chain makers in the Midlands to work in spite of their very poor conditions and low pay. Two decades later, in 1910, after a ten-week strike supported by Mary Macarthur, the leader of the National Federation of Women Workers, the Cradley Heath chain workers won a famous victory and secured an improvement in their conditions and higher pay. There is no record of Millicent's position, but by then, public opinion had shifted strongly towards forcing employers to be more enlightened in a case of this kind.

The matchgirls' strike at Bryant & May in the East End of

London in 1888, following the public exposure of the use of white phosphorus in the manufacture of matches, was championed by Annie Besant, the social reformer and social activist. The company was exposed for its failure to protect the health of its young female employees who suffered from the horrible disease of necrosis of the jaw as a result of being exposed to white phosphorus. They also worked in wretched conditions and were paid a pittance. External investigations led to confirmation by the girls of the existence of 'phossy jaw' and a refusal to cover up for their employers. As a result, one of the matchgirls was unfairly dismissed, leading to their decision to strike. There was widespread public support for the strikers and Bryant & May were forced to climb down and improve working conditions. Millicent also supported it, saying, 'It is not often that I find myself in agreement with Mrs Besant, so I more gladly take the opportunity of saying how much working women owe to her for the courage with which she conducted the Match Strike to a successful termination.' It seems that her views on protecting the health of workers were more progressive than on equal pay or regulating the hours of work.

Unfortunately, any improvements made by Bryant & May after the strike did not lead to the long-term removal of white phosphorus from the manufacture of their matches. There was another public row in 1893, when the factory inspectorate revealed that the company had failed to report eighteen cases of necrosis, including six deaths. Millicent had recently become a small shareholder and she wrote to the firm's managing director asking for more information. She said she did not wish 'to pocket dividend warrants reeking of phosphorus'. At his invitation, she visited the factory. She also met workers at a local girls' club who praised the company and were indignant when she told them there was an outcry suggesting women and girls should not be employed where phosphorus was used. They asked where else they could earn the money they needed to support their families. This was an argument that would always appeal to her. Moreover, she also had the wool pulled over her eyes by the company which showed her happy workers and told her how much they had spent on ventilation and on medical treatment if a worker became ill. Her conviction that all was well led her to a vicious attack on the well-heeled philanthropists who were campaigning for action to prevent further wrongdoing by Bryant & May. David Rubinstein, in his biography, put it well, 'she was blinded by faith in self-help and belief in the importance of women's employment to the possibility that even "professional philanthropists" were sometimes right and that publicity often led to reform', as it eventually did in this case.

In spite of Millicent's involvement in so many different issues, which took up her time and engaged her emotionally, she never abandoned her suffrage campaigning, although the two decades after the failure of the Reform Bill in 1884 were marked by little progress in gaining votes for women. There was little or no support in Parliament for another Bill and the movement outside Parliament was split. In Chapter 4, I described splits on issues such as whether or not married women should be included in the campaign or whether to focus only on female householders. For the next fifteen years, until the turn of the twentieth century, the movement remained divided. The most important dispute was over whether political parties should be admitted to suffragist organisations. The split within the Liberal Party between those who favoured Home Rule for Ireland and the Unionists, who were strongly opposed to it, complicated matters. Conservative men were much more likely to oppose votes for women than the Liberals, although the Primrose

League, formed to promote Conservative ideals, allowed female members who were able to become active politically. However, it was never a proponent of women's suffrage.

Millicent was a leading member of the National Society for Women's Suffrage (NSWS) in late 1888, when the issue of admitting political organisations was debated. She was strongly opposed to changing the rules to allow this. Since there was no support from the Conservatives for enfranchisement, why admit them but why preclude individual Conservatives or Primrose League members who did support it from taking part? She had lost faith with the Liberal leadership over Home Rule and over Gladstone's manoeuvrings in 1884. She believed that if he and others had kept their word, women would already have the vote. She claimed to have lost respect for political parties and believed that accepting the new rules would endanger the movement by over-politicising it when it might be close to success. She was certainly over-optimistic about the latter and possibly wrong about the former. She lost, as there was a majority in favour of admitting political bodies. The result of the vote led to those in favour of change setting up a new organisation named the Central National Society for Women's Suffrage. The minority continued as the NSWS with strong Unionist leanings and with Millicent as its honorary secretary, a position she held until the two bodies eventually merged at the turn of the century.

That the split lasted so long was absurd and must have led to some confusion and uncertainty about which side to join amongst young women, who came forward wanting to support the campaign. It was also an excuse for parliamentary inaction. A Women's Suffrage Bill in 1891, introduced by a Liberal MP, William Woodall, was talked out. A great deal of energy was wasted by Millicent and others in trying to promote it, leading to misery and despair when it made no progress. Millicent was told by Woodall and his Conservative supporter Edward Cotton-Jodrell that the split between the societies 'has greatly injured us for the present'.

Nevertheless, campaigning round the country continued, with Millicent speaking quite often, and the two separate organisations seem to have cooperated without rancour, although the split meant there was no formally appointed leader of the movement. Yet informally, Millicent increasingly occupied this role. It was she who led the opposition to those who denounced women's suffrage in newspapers and journals. She used her intellectual ability to take apart their arguments and wrote cogently and forcefully. A good example was the appeal against women's suffrage published in the journal *Nineteenth Century* in 1889. This was signed by over a hundred women, many of whom were the wives of prominent men, rather than women known in their own right, but it included Beatrice Potter, later to become Beatrice Webb, who eventually abandoned her anti-suffrage views, and it was organised by Mary Ward, who was usually known, as was typical of the time, by her husband's name: Mrs Humphry Ward. The article appealed for more support and in little time another 1,800 women had signed up. Millicent wrote a powerful rebuttal and helped to organise a counter-appeal, which attracted signatures from over 2,000 suffragists, many of whom were professional women and social activists. A second article was published, preceding this list, on why women should be enfranchised.

After nearly twenty years of facing down misogynistic prejudice from opponents of women's suffrage, Millicent had carefully honed her arguments, so taking them on was relatively easy. Nevertheless, it was particularly galling when women themselves advocated maintaining the status quo, clinging to the view that a woman's place is in the home and jeering at 'advanced women'. In doing so, they had absorbed Victorian views about women's roles and the necessary limitations of any contributions to public life that they might make. From today's perspective, such views seem defeatist and conservative. Yet it should not be forgotten that they were still common seventy years later in the 1950s. I seethed with outrage when asked to write an essay on 'Women's Place Is in the Home' in the sixth form of my girls' grammar school in 1959. I would have benefited from some quotes from Millicent Fawcett in my efforts to rebut this notion. She replied to one Liberal MP who promoted the women-in-the-home argument in a pamphlet, saying there was a 'curious mixture' in his mind of 'sentimental homage' and 'practical contempt' for women. Another denouncer of women's suffrage was derided by Millicent for relying 'on his memory for his eloquence and on his imagination for his facts'.

During the 1890s, Millicent's activism in promoting the emancipation of women established her as the best-known advocate of the cause. To describe her as a household name would perhaps be an exaggeration, but in political circles, she began to be perceived as the movement's leader. This was enhanced in 1893 when she became the president of a committee under the auspices of the Central Committee of the NSWS to launch a national appeal for women's suffrage. For a year or two, she travelled round the country, speaking at events to build the numbers needed for a national petition as well as continuing to write letters and articles in newspapers and journals. She and others succeeded in obtaining 258,000 signatures, which were eventually presented to Parliament in a petition. She never abandoned a focus on mainstream politics, and after the 1892 election, she urged people to support political candidates who supported suffrage and withheld support from those who opposed it.

She was delighted when another Private Members' Bill on votes for women was lost by only twenty-three votes; and she used it as an opportunity to attack Gladstone, her old enemy, who she continued to deplore, particularly for his advocacy of Home Rule in Ireland. There was even greater parliamentary progress when Faithfull Begg's Suffrage Bill won a comfortable majority of seventy-one in its second reading in the Commons; a sign that the views of those opposing women's suffrage were beginning to be discredited. However, further time to complete the Bill was not allocated, so it went no further. Millicent was abroad at the time and therefore unable to capitalise immediately on this moral victory.

Within the movement, she engaged in work to promote the unification of the split organisation, moving motions calling for greater cooperation between the different societies. In late 1897, it was agreed that a national union should be created. However, it had no money and not much power. It was essentially a liaison committee and for a time Millicent was its treasurer but, as she put it, 'with few treasures'. It was another ten years before the National Union of Women Suffrage Societies was reconstituted with an elected executive and a president. By now, Millicent was the undisputed leader of the suffragist movement. From then on, her participation in other areas of the kind of crusades which she had mounted in her early widowhood became less frequent. Meanwhile, at the end of the nineteenth century, her active campaigning for votes for women did not end but was somewhat disrupted by the war in South Africa. Millicent was a partisan supporter of the government's rationale for the war and a strong opponent of the Boers. This led to work of a kind that she had not done before, which tested her in new and challenging ways.

7

THE LIBERAL IMPERIALIST

Millicent's opposition to Home Rule for Ireland was based on her patriotism and her belief in the empire and the benevolent effects that British rule delivered. These beliefs applied not just to Ireland but to everywhere that had been colonised by Britain. Like many Victorians, she was an imperialist who strongly resisted claims for Irish independence and did not question Britain's right to govern in Asia or Africa. Millicent's patriotic views continued throughout her life and she justified her country's wars by defending their legitimacy.

Her work on women's suffrage had to compete with her dedication to the cause of union with Ireland during the 1880s and 1890s. She believed that British involvement in Ireland was marked by its civilising mission. She was contemptuous about the Irish, deriding them for being idle, shiftless and priest-ridden. In a speech at a Liberal Unionist meeting summarised by David Rubinstein, she said the Irish had 'many attractive and charming qualities' but that the concessions won by Irish tenants were not based on skill or honesty but on political agitation and that the concessions had tended to 'weaken the honesty, the industry, the self-reliance upon which alone any permanent economic well-being must be grounded'. She denounced Irish nationalism for being fixed on a hatred of England, a sentiment Millicent found abhorrent and which she could not conceive of being remotely justifiable. Her hatred of Gladstone was reinforced by his conversion to Irish Home Rule. Despairing of the Liberal Party's position, she advocated the Irish problem being dealt with on non-party lines by a national body, which should have for its aim 'the Unity of the Empire'. This proposal mustered little support. English–Irish relations had to be resolved through mainstream party politics.

When Millicent first became engaged in political activity, she was, like her husband, a Liberal radical. Over the years, her loyalty to the Liberal Party declined; it was tested mainly by the failure of the party wholeheartedly to adopt a feminist commitment to votes for women. Once Home Rule became such a dominant issue and the Liberal Party split over it, she abandoned the party of Gladstone and became a Liberal Unionist. This decision would not have caused her distress, so certain was she that Home Rule for Ireland was mistaken. At an early meeting of Liberal Unionist women, she stated that Home Rule would not just be a disaster for Ireland; it would also be 'a blow to the prosperity and greatness of England'. She never appeared to be plagued by any doubts on this issue. As one well-known Irish nationalist said at the time of her death, she was 'more bitter and more tenacious against Home Rule than even the original Tory … She was virulent in her attacks on my unfortunate party and policy.'

Millicent played a part in the Women's Liberal Unionist Association for nearly a decade between 1886, the year when the first Home Rule Bill was defeated until 1895 when the Conservative government led by Lord Salisbury included Liberal Unionists. Her activism was greatest in the 1880s, when she spoke frequently at meetings round the country. She was even asked by Lord Hartington, a Unionist leader, to join the platform at the very first large public meeting which launched the campaign. According to Ray Strachey, Millicent was intimidated by this invitation but accepted it partly because it pleased her hugely that a female speaker was included on the platform. In doing so, she enhanced her political reputation as a speaker who could escape from being a single-issue activist to become involved in wider political issues. It was a step forward, however small, in women being publicly recognised as legitimate contributors to topical debates. In many of her appearances in pursuit of the Unionist cause, she used the opportunity to underline the valuable contribution women were making to it and how much more valuable it would be if only they were enfranchised.

Millicent had spent time in Ireland previously, mainly in pursuit of the suffragist cause. During this period, she did take the trouble to revisit Ireland and meet Irish women, although they would not have included Irish Nationalists. Given how often she denounced them, it was unlikely that they would have wished to spend time with her. In a letter to *The Times*, she said, 'I am one of those who think that those who kill or shoot their neighbours, maim cattle, cut off the hair of girls and pour tar over their heads, ought to be punished whether they live in Ireland or in England.' As she saw it, enduring political institutions could not be built on crime and intimidation.

Although Millicent was especially passionate about Ireland, she was also interested in India. Since the mid-eighteenth century, when the East India Company established itself in Bengal, eventually extending its power and influence over much of the subcontinent, India had been perceived as one of the most important parts of the

British Empire. Following the Indian Mutiny in 1857, when locally recruited Indian soldiers, known as sepoys, attacked British officers at military garrisons, the British government intervened. The East India Company, which was blamed for the mutiny, was eventually dissolved and the British government imposed direct rule. A new Cabinet post of Secretary of State for India was set up as British power over India was transferred from the company to the Crown.

When I first became a member of the House of Lords in 1987, I shared a room with five other Labour peers, all of whom were much older than me and most had been in the Lords for many years. One of them was the 5th Earl of Listowel, by then in his eighties, who had been in Clement Attlee's Cabinet as the last Secretary of State for India. He was teased for his forgetfulness by the Cambridge ladies in the room led by Pat Llewelyn-Davies, the former Chief Whip in Harold Wilson's and James Callaghan's governments in the 1970s. I felt sorry for him but did not know how to reach out to him. I greatly regret my failure and that I did not ask him to tell me about his experiences in his role leading up to Indian independence in 1947.

Following the transfer of power to the Crown in the late 1850s, the British viceroys appointed in London ruled India from Calcutta until 1911, when Delhi became the capital. They were supported by the Indian civil service, which, though formally open to Indians, consisted almost entirely of British officials, posted across India and supported by 65,000 troops by the end of the 1860s. Under the Raj, as it became known, the British did not mix with the 'natives', as they were known, and kept to their private clubs and their own, separate leisure activities.

Many middle- and upper-class families had members posted to India and, through them, direct connections with Raj India. In

Millicent's case, her older brother Newson and her sister Alice both lived there for some time. Alice was an intelligent woman who kept up with what was happening in her home country through regular newspaper reading and frequent letters to and from her family. She did charitable work in Calcutta yet was nevertheless dismissive about the 'natives'. Writing to her mother, she thought it

> right to show them all kindness and hospitality if they wish to go into English society and conform to the manners of it, but I think generations ought to pass for them to increase in purity and manliness before any English women ought to marry even the best of them. Trottie [a family nickname for Millicent] would say that is because I am in a 'slough of conservatism'.

Whether Millicent would have reacted in their defence is perhaps debatable, but it is interesting that her sister thought she would. Like most of her contemporaries, Millicent did little to challenge Victorian racist attitudes and she fervently believed in the superiority of the British.

She never visited India, although late in her life she went with Agnes to Ceylon, where there was some support for women's suffrage, which she encouraged. In the case of India, her main intervention was a forceful condemnation of child marriage and the demand that it should be made illegal. British rule did in fact lead to a change in the law, making it illegal under the age of fourteen. In practice, however, it made little or no difference. The law was never upheld, and girls continued to be married at a very young age.

Millicent also railed against the lack of medical care for women in a country where there were no locally trained female doctors, but the treatment of women by male doctors was not accepted in traditional families. She shared with her sister Elizabeth concern about the consequences for women's health. She backed finding ways to alleviate the suffering of Indian women in this respect by, for example, British female doctors practising in India. Since their numbers would not be large enough to make much of an inroad into this problem, providing opportunities for Indian women to come to Britain to train as doctors would have been an additional way of addressing the lack of access to medical care for women in purdah, but it was not an option at the time. Money had been raised in India earlier for Henry Fawcett's election expenses in London. Presumably, this was in recognition of his parliamentary campaigns, described in Chapter 4, to prevent extravagant spending on British interests at the expense of the Indian population. Millicent and Philippa decided to allocate the unspent money of £400 for two Henry Fawcett prizes for Indian female medical students. In this respect, Millicent's feminism prevailed over any negative views she might have had towards Indians.

Moreover, Millicent's convictions about the need to expand educational opportunities for girls and women in England were just as powerful with respect to India. Although she believed British rule in the empire was largely benign, it ought to have occurred to her that there were large gaps in this benevolence given that it totally neglected to address many areas where reform was desperately needed. Girls' education was one such case, and in campaigning about it, she did go as far as lobbying Edwin Montagu, the Secretary of State for India, about it and, later in the 1920s, she led a deputation to Lord Lytton, when he became Governor of Bengal, on the need for educational opportunities for women in India.

Just as Millicent was justifiably shocked by child prostitution in England, so she was when it took place in India. She devoted time and energy to the individual case of an eleven-year-old girl who was bought by a British planter in Burma, which was illustrative of the exploitation of children for sexual purposes, which was all too common there. The purchase of Aina for ten rupees was exposed in a Burmese newspaper by an English journalist named Channing Arnold. His efforts were rewarded by his prosecution for defamation, and he was imprisoned for a year. This caused outrage amongst feminists as well as amongst Arnold's fellow journalists. Millicent commented, 'While we feel most the intolerable degradation & ruin of childhood and the flimsy hypocrisy of passing "White Slave Traffic" Acts here, while in British dominions in the East men are allowed to purchase openly and without shame young children.'

Millicent lobbied the India Office about this case and met the Secretary of State for India. She said that the purchase of Aina meant not only ruin to the child herself but also degradation of the British flag and the empire. Failure to protect children would lead to British rule being 'identified with sexual abominations lower than anything which either West or East had separately touched'. The case combined issues of sexual morality, which concerned her greatly, with her belief in the empire to which she was devoted and whose reputation she hated to see tarnished.

It was not in India, however, that Millicent's passionate and fervent patriotism found the most important expression, but in South Africa. Her knowledge of the country was enhanced by the fact that Rhoda's much younger half-brother Edmund, for whom after Rhoda died, Agnes became almost a surrogate mother, lived in Cape Town. After studying at Cambridge, he had become a journalist working on the *Pall Mall Gazette*. Sadly, his health deteriorated with the onset of tuberculosis and his editor sent him as a correspondent to South Africa, where the climate might mitigate its impact. Edmund became wholly engaged with political and social issues in the country and regularly wrote back describing them to Agnes and Millicent in 2 Gower Street, where he had spent a lot of time as a young adult. He described South Africa as 'the workshop of our Empire just now', alluding to diamond fields and gold mines, including the fact that English miners outnumbered Boers. After two years, he came back to London continuing to write, although before long he was advised to spend time in a sanatorium in Germany. Eventually, his continuing interest in South Africa led to his appointment as the editor of the *Cape Times*. His views on the black population were paternalist, but unlike the prevailing attitudes of the time, he was in favour of social reform which would help black South Africans escape from dire poverty, be better housed and have access to education with the aim 'to educate but not assimilate'. Jenifer Glynn comments that in welcoming movement by the British in the Cape Colony northwards into the Transvaal, Edmund wanted to spread the benefits of British civilisation as far as possible.

His letters back to Gower Street gave plenty of material for Millicent to ponder. She was not especially concerned about the poverty and powerlessness of the black population. What did concern her was the grave injustice, as she saw it, of the Boers' treatment in the Transvaal of British settlers known as 'Uitlanders'. Edmund himself had influenced her views by his partial support for the Jameson Raid, whereby the British tried to invade the Transvaal and abet an uprising against the Boer government. Edmund's letter to Agnes about this instructed her to 'tell Milly I look to her to put the right head on this in England and the Liberal press especially'. Millicent hardly needed Edmund's encouragement. Her chauvinist views led to her aggressive denunciation of the Boers for denying the British in the Transvaal citizenship rights. She could not accept that her countrymen in Johannesburg had to pay taxes yet did not have the vote. Of course, she had made the 'no taxation without representation' argument about women in England hundreds of times. She thought it was just as wrong in the case of the Uitlanders as it was for women.

Relations between Britain and South Africa were more complex than the question of allowing British settlers to vote. By the 1880s, Britain had only partially colonised South Africa. Cape Colony and Natal were British. The Boers, farmers originating from Holland, had trekked north from the Cape in the 1830s and occupied the vast open spaces to the north of the Vaal River, which became known as the Transvaal and the Orange Free State and, eventually, formed the South African Republic, where the Afrikaners (Boers) were largely independent from Britain. In 1886, vast deposits of gold were discovered in the Transvaal with fortune seekers flocking from Britain to profit from gold mining. Britain's wish to unite its South African territories with the Boer republics then became far more pressing than before. When Britain sent large numbers of troops to Cape Colony, stationing them along the border with the Boer territories, it led to war. Most historians describe what followed as a colonial war in which Britain wished to expand its control over all of South Africa, strongly motivated by economic interests.

After the government embarked on war with the Boers, Millicent, as an imperialist, was vociferous in supporting the war. She had no time for the argument that a great power was taking its imperialist objectives out on a small nation in the interests of a group of wealthy immigrants exploiting the natural resources of this nation as they mined for gold and diamonds. The war was controversial and had many critics. To the government, support for it from well-known figures such as Millicent was a godsend.

At the start of the war, the hugely outnumbered but more agile Boer troops, who were familiar with the territory, were winning the conflict, successfully besieging a number of key towns. Following large British reinforcements and the relief of the besieged towns, the tide began to turn. To counter Boer guerrilla tactics, the British instituted a scorched-earth policy of burning crops and torching farmhouses, which left many families of Boer soldiers homeless and without food. As a result, over 100,000 women and children were swept up and placed in forty-five camps in late 1900; the term 'concentration camp' entered the English lexicon. In late 1900, Emily Hobhouse visited some of the camps. She was from a well-known Liberal family in Bristol and, through her connections, was able to get permission from Alfred Milner, the British High Commissioner in South Africa, to take supplies in a railway truck to the camps in the Cape and Orange River colonies.

Hobhouse wrote a report on what she had seen, which was published in June 1901 in London after her return. She did not mince her words. She portrayed horrific conditions in the camps, with starvation diets, wholly inadequate accommodation with severe overcrowding, contaminated water, a lack of fuel so that boiling water was difficult and very poor, if any, medical facilities. The death toll that resulted was enormous, especially amongst children, who died mainly of measles and typhoid. Of the 100,000 white women and children who were rounded up, 26,000 died. The report attracted a great deal of adverse publicity and led to questions in the House of Lords and a decline in public support for the war. As a result, the British War Office set up a commission to visit South Africa to report on the conditions in the camps. Meanwhile, Millicent had been quick to publish a riposte to Hobhouse's report by suggesting that those who staffed the camps worked hard to do their best for their inmates in difficult circumstances. She also pointed out that the Boer farms were used to store and supply ammunition to Boer soldiers and were the source of misinformation to British troops.

Given that the government decided that the Commission of Inquiry should be made up of women, Millicent Fawcett must have seemed a safe choice to take part in it. She supported the war and she had publicly qualified the conclusions of Hobhouse's report. The *Daily News*, a Liberal paper, did cast aspersions on her appointment on the grounds that her article on the report was not impartial, and asked that if she was to be on the committee, why was Emily Hobhouse not appointed too? The government's reply was that they were not sending anyone out who was identified with a particular opinion. Yet one of the two women to accompany Millicent was the wife of a British general in South Africa and, as such, was unlikely to be unbiased. The other, the first female factory inspector, was not known to have publicly supported the war but was the daughter of a soldier and, as a government employee, was probably thought to be a safe choice. The other three members were living in South Africa, two of whom were doctors, the other a nurse. Dr Jane Waterston ought to have been ruled out, having had a letter published in the *Cape Times* denouncing criticism of the camps in colourful terms. Before leaving for South Africa, the three London-based commissioners failed to agree a time to meet Emily Hobhouse and hear her account, which did not augur well for an open-minded approach to the commission.

Travelling by ship, on a voyage that lasted for three weeks, Millicent found the journey difficult as she suffered from seasickness. However, Philippa left Newnham College to accompany her mother, and her companionship would likely have helped Millicent cope with the journey. Never indolent, Millicent used her time on board to try with her colleagues to learn some Afrikaans, so they could greet the Boer women they would meet in their own language. She devoted time to reading background papers provided by the War Office, as well as preparing the index for one of her books. She also managed to take part in leisure activities provided on board, such as egg and spoon races, while Philippa excelled at hopscotch. The stupendous view of Table Mountain as the ship approached Cape Town led Millicent to write, 'It looks like a country worth fighting for.' Soon after their arrival, a telegram arrived from the War Office appointing her as president of the commission. The commissioners set off by train and were vigorous in covering as many as thirty-five camps, half of which were in the Transvaal and most of the rest in the Orange River Colony. Their report was long – 208 pages – and detailed. Completed before the end of 1901, it was published by the government in February 1902, but families were not repatriated to their homes until June 1902, after the war had ended with the defeat of the Boers.

The commission report started with the supposition that the camps were an unfortunate consequence of war and that it was inevitable that women and children in rural areas would be rounded up and that many of the children would have died anyway if they had remained at home in Boer farmhouses. With this as a starting point, the report could well have been a complete whitewash, but in spite of its overriding patriotic tone, the commissioners did list many detailed criticisms of the way the camps were run, offering constructive proposals on how improvements should be made. They included recommendations to dismiss some of the men in charge of the camps for incompetence, which had serious consequences for the inmates. Even though these failures might have led to neglect and even cruelty, the report argued that the staff, who had been appointed by the British Army, were mainly well-intentioned and humane, even if disorganised and inefficient. They accepted that the food provided for children was often inadequate and made recommendations for improvements. They praised the educational provision and put down a lack of cleanliness, at least in part, to the supposed unhygienic habits of Boer women. Clearly, the camps varied, and the commissioners found that some were much better than others. They revisited the worst camps, such as Mafeking and Kimberley, at the end of their travels, to check whether the improvements they had recommended had been implemented.

The commission could not be criticised for failing to collect the evidence needed to reach well-informed conclusions; the commissioners spent four months visiting the camps and no stone was left unturned. The report commented on the appropriateness of their locations, on details about the kitchens, the quality of the food and its preparation, the availability of fuel, the water supply, the medical facilities, the classrooms, bedding and the tents themselves. It also revealed plenty of failures in many of these respects as well as praising the good intentions of the staff in the camps. Asking whether 'our officials were exerting themselves to make the conditions of the camps as little oppressive as possible', Millicent claimed they were, but the strength of her patriotism would have made it difficult for her to conclude otherwise. Similarly, her conclusion that much of the squalor in the camps could be blamed on the Boer women suggests she was prejudiced. Nevertheless, the fact that she and her team of female commissioners asked for substantial improvements, especially in the supply of nutritional food, did lead to a decline in the death rates in the camps. Yet in her memoir, Millicent is guilty of complacency in the surprisingly rosy picture she gave of the camps, focusing on the fact that their inmates were supplied with food, clothing, medical care and schooling free of charge but making no mention of how many children died.

The reception of the report when it was published was mixed. Its general fervour concerning the British administration's justified decision to set up the camps meant it found favour in government circles. However, the fact that it found so many failings, which were set out in detail, meant that even those opposed to the war and sympathetic to the Boers recognised that it led to improvements. Emily Hobhouse herself admitted this, although she remained critical of its tone and refuted the view that the Boer children would have died anyway if they had stayed at home. Those who, like Emily, opposed the war, including some of Millicent's friends and acquaintances, were directly hostile to Millicent. She complained that 'several pro-Boer people who used to be quite good friends of mine now cut me dead and turn their backs if I am coming towards them; but I try to bear it with patience'. Millicent had learnt to be resilient in her many years of political campaigning. Undoubtedly, the strength of her patriotism was unappealing to many progressives in the women's movement and outside it. It was her prevailing views about the empire and her unquestioning support of the war against the Boers that caused offence rather than her findings on the camps.

Although the commissioners were well looked after – with a sleeping compartment for each of them, a large saloon for their meals with a travelling kitchen attached and a Portuguese cook to prepare their meals – five months on the move was a substantial commitment and the work was tiring. In the long chapter in her memoirs about her experiences in South Africa, Millicent wrote enthusiastically about the challenges and without complaint. One of the bonuses, when their work was completed, was the journey home. They went by ship from Durban up the East African coast and across the Mediterranean to Naples. As I will describe in a later chapter, travel away from England was one of Millicent's greatest pleasures; and to be able to put in at Mozambique, Zanzibar, Dar es Salaam and Aden allowed her to learn a little about a part of the world she did not know. Another bonus of the role she played in South Africa was that it was the first time the British government had given the task of an inquiry of this kind to a small team of women only, including a female leader. Millicent makes no specific mention of this in her memoir, but it was a 'first' about which she could have been deservedly proud.

The South African visit made a big enough impression on Philippa for her to leave Newnham and return to the Transvaal to organise the development of elementary education there, having discovered that more was being done in the camps to provide schooling than was usually the case outside. Her mother returned to South Africa to visit her in 1903, where she saw early signs of some reconciliation between the Boers and the British and believed that 'a great united nation' would follow as a result of the complete colonisation of the country. Millicent believed until the end of her life that the British Army had done a splendid job in South Africa. As Emily Hobhouse's brother commented, in spite of the thorough work Millicent had done on the commission, it was a pity she was unable 'to understand that one may do a far greater service to one's country by withstanding its errors than by accepting all its doings without criticism'. Millicent's fierce patriotism made it difficult for her to do so. She could not conceive of any other nationality or race being anything other than inferior to the British. Her unswerving support for Britain's role in the First World War is another illustration of the hold her patriotism had over her. The Boer War and her sojourn in South Africa had led to a temporary halt to her campaign for women's suffrage. As we shall see later, the Great War of 1914–18 also led to her abandoning her suffrage work on the grounds that nothing should be done to distract from the fight for British victory against the Germans.

In the late 1890s, Millicent wrote two books which, in different ways, demonstrated her love of empire and her interest in colonialism. The first was a biography of Queen Victoria, published to coincide with her Diamond Jubilee in 1897. Given Victoria's anti-feminist views and denunciation of female suffrage, she is a surprising subject for a cloying volume of praise for the great achievements of her reign. The Queen's decision to accept her Prime Minister Benjamin Disraeli's suggestion that she should take the title of Empress of India undoubtedly pleased Millicent. Ray Strachey praises the biography for being very readable and 'full of shrewd observations' but admitted that Millicent was 'over-enthusiastic about the Queen'. Strachey also notes that the author's deep love of England appears in this book. As a patriot, Millicent identified with a female monarch, who was revered across a vast empire.

Millicent praised Victoria for her ability to undertake demanding political work as well as being a devoted wife, with many children, and an exemplar of all the domestic virtues. Given what we know about Victoria's limitations as a mother, about the way she shut herself away from public life for some years after her husband's death and her denunciation of 'this mad, wicked folly of women's rights', Millicent's book is surprisingly unbalanced in its assessment of the Queen. She praised the British constitution for allowing a woman to sit on the throne in contrast to Germany, which was true although hardly noteworthy given it had been the constitutional position since the Tudors.

Victoria's stand against the 'loose morals of the previous reign' appealed to Millicent's somewhat prudish attitude towards sexual infidelity. Both George IV and William IV, Victoria's uncles and predecessors as Kings, could hardly have been worse models for high standards in personal behaviour. The contrast between them and their niece Victoria could not have been greater. Millicent appreciated this and referred to 'the magnificent example of her own life and character'. The celebration of her Jubilee filled Millicent with patriotic pride. Somehow, she turned a blind eye to her anti-feminist views because Victoria had accomplished what was required of her as the longest-living female monarch at that time.

Millicent's biography of Sir William Molesworth, a long-forgotten mid-Victorian Liberal politician and founder of the Reform Club, is a better book. She wrote it when she halted the campaign for votes for women because of the war in South Africa. Consequently, she had enough time to produce a serious biography. Her reasons for choosing him as a subject for a long book are based on the high regard her husband had for him – he had helped to shape Harry's views in several areas – and because of his convictions about colonisation, which was of some relevance to political issues in South Africa. After studying at Cambridge and travelling in Europe, Molesworth returned to London and his family's estate in Cornwall. He co-edited the *Westminster Review* with John Stuart Mill and developed his radical views, becoming an MP at the time of the Great Reform Act in 1832.

Millicent sympathised with his views on most subjects, including, as listed by her, 'the ballot, free trade, national education, religious equality, household suffrage, and better government of Ireland'. His views on many of these issues were progressive and made him ahead of his time. His belief in the expansion of British colonies and in the benefits that British rule could bring were what especially appealed to Millicent. In some respects, they were more conventional than his convictions in other areas: the benefits of colonisation in pursuit of increasing trade were widely accepted. What was more unusual was his strong belief in colonial self-government, whereby the colonies could develop their own representative institutions rather than keep being ruled from Britain, in spite of being under British sovereignty. Millicent shared his view that this was the form the empire should take.

Molesworth was briefly the Secretary of State for the Colonies in 1855, but his early death a few months after he was appointed meant he had little time to develop his views in practice. The biography was published by Macmillan in 1901 and was picked up for favourable reviews by a few journals such as *The Spectator*, but it seems unlikely to have attracted a large readership, except perhaps from adherents of Thomas Hobbes, whose works Molesworth had edited. Jenifer Glynn, in her book on the Garretts, described Millicent as using her book 'as a platform for an outburst of patriotism'. She goes on to quote Millicent, who, referring to the rescue of British hostages in Abyssinia in 1868, states:

Who is there who does not think that it is worth something to be a British subject. That if he is wronged anywhere in the ends of the earth, Great Britain will see him righted … every Briton repays the debt he owes his country with love and gratitude, and with his life if need be.

For these views, some branded Millicent as a Conservative. In fact, once she had parted company from the Liberals, she was aligned with no political party and was willing to work with any party in power to pursue what was on her agenda.

Millicent Garrett Fawcett's parents, Newson and Louisa Garrett, in their old age. Newson was a determined businessman and a leading figure in the local community in Aldeburgh, Suffolk, while Louisa organised the busy household, buying provisions and teaching their ten children to read and write. Source: Wikimedia Commons

Millicent and Agnes, one of her older sisters, in their teens. The two girls attended boarding school together and formed a close bond that was to last throughout their lives.
Source: Women's Library, LSE Library

A postcard of the Garrett family home, Alde House in Aldeburgh, which Newson built. It had a large conservatory, many rooms and extensive grounds.

Elizabeth Garrett, Newson and Louisa's second child, painted soon after she qualified as a doctor in 1865, the first woman in Britian to do so. She was a role model to Millicent.
Source: LSE Library via Flickr Commons

Millicent Garrett and Henry Fawcett on their wedding day in 1867, pictured with Newson and Louisa Garrett and William and Mary Fawcett. Milly and Harry, as their friends called them, were drawn to each other's passion for politics and women's suffrage.

Millicent and Harry one year after their wedding, photographed by Henry Joseph Whitlock.

Source: LSE Library via Flickr Commons

Harry had been blinded in a shooting accident as a young man, but his loss of sight was no impediment to his success as a scholar and politician. Millicent devoted a great deal of time to reading to Harry and writing his letters, as captured here by Ford Madox Brown.

© National Portrait Gallery, London

LEFT Agnes and her cousin Rhoda leased 2 Gower Street, London, in the mid-1870s, when they opened their interior design company. After Harry's early death in 1884, Millicent and her daughter Philippa also moved in. Source: Wikimedia Commons

BELOW Agnes and Rhoda completely refurbished 2 Gower Street, using wallpaper and furniture that they had designed themselves. They also decorated the ceiling in one room, lying on their backs on scaffolding to paint it. © Lloyd Sturdy

ABOVE Rhoda (*left*) and Agnes (*right*) lived and worked together until Rhoda's untimely death in 1882.

LEFT In the 1890s, Millicent's activism in promoting the emancipation of women established her as the best-known advocate of the cause. She frequently travelled the country on speaking tours.

Source: Wikimedia Commons

LEFT Millicent's daughter Philippa was a talented mathematician. But despite her near-perfect examination scores, Philippa was denied a degree because she was a woman. She persevered in academia for a time and became a fellow at Newnham College, Cambridge, which had been co-founded by her mother. Source: Wikimedia Commons

BELOW Thousands of marchers joined a procession led by Millicent and the National Union of Women's Suffrage Societies (NUWSS) in June 1908, demonstrating to the new Liberal Prime Minister Herbert Asquith that there was mass support for women's suffrage. From front left: Lady Frances Balfour, Millicent Fawcett and Emily Davies, in the foreground. Source: LSE Library via Flickr Commons

LEFT Millicent busy working at her desk, photographed by Olive Edis. © National Portrait Gallery, London

Suffragists from across the country marched to London in 1913. Following a successful rally in Hyde Park, Millicent led an NUWSS deputation to Asquith. He was not enthused, and she was deeply disappointed.

Millicent photographed outside her home at 2 Gower Street, on the day she was created a Dame Grand Cross of the Order of the British Empire in 1925, seven years after securing women the right to vote.

Millicent and Agnes taking flowers to the statue of John Stuart Mill in May 1927. He had been one of Millicent and Harry's political heroes. Source: LSE Library via Flickr Commons

In 2018, 100 years after some women were given the vote, a statue of Millicent Garrett Fawcett was unveiled in Parliament Square. Source: Wikimedia Commons

8

NEW APPROACHES IN THE CAMPAIGN FOR WOMEN'S VOTES

After she came home from South Africa, and once the war was over, Millicent returned to her suffrage work, although as so often, she found time to pursue other interests too. One example was her support of a project devised by her friend and neighbour in Gower Street, Dr Jane Walker, who set up and ran a sanatorium near Nayland, on the Suffolk and Essex border, mainly to treat people with long-term chronic illnesses such as tuberculosis. It was the first hospital entirely run by women and Millicent's cousin Edmund spent some time there after he left South Africa, in the hope that it might alleviate his tuberculosis. Her deep affection for Edmund was an added reason for her commitment to Jane Walker's project; Millicent became the chairman of the board of management and for three decades undertook fundraising for the East Anglian Sanatorium, as it was then known. It still exists under its founder's name, Jane Walker Hospital, and I see the signs for it when driving along the road from Nayland to Bures, where my Suffolk cottage is located.

Even though the South African war and the particular role Millicent played in it distracted her from suffrage activities, this boosted her commitment to them. Some years later she put it this way:

> After thinking of the war and its causes the first thing in the morning and the last thing at night for nearly three years, there were many thousands of Englishwomen who asked themselves why, if the vote of Englishmen in the Transvaal was worth £200,000,000 of money and some 30,000 lives, it was not also of great value and significance to women at home? Why, they said to themselves and others, are we to be treated as perpetual 'uitlanders' in the country of our birth?

During the early years of the twentieth century, Millicent reached out to women who wanted answers to this question, by speaking publicly round the country, although it did not match the frequency of her speaking engagements in the mid-1890s, after the National Union of Women's Suffrage Societies (NUWSS) had launched a national appeal for women's suffrage, and she had been elected as its president. The NUWSS was established in sixteen cities by the end of the 1890s. Its membership consisted mostly of middle-class, educated women already converted to the cause. What was needed in the new century was more recruits drawn from a wider range of backgrounds and more publicity than could be extracted from the public meetings the societies held from time to time, the petitions sent to MPs (who did nothing with them) and the letters to newspapers (which seemed to have little impact). The reasoned arguments Millicent and her colleagues used, however justified, were not inspiring a popular movement. They were politely listened to by men in power but easily swatted away.

The care Millicent had made to appeal to mainstream opinion about the role of women had not really brought the dividends she sought. She accepted the view that women were different to men and claimed that she was not trying to turn them into men. In saying this, she was trying to comfort those opposed to women having the vote on the grounds that it would 'unsex' them and destroy their womanly qualities. She went as far as arguing that women were often a conservative force in valuing order but that order was essential to liberty. The logical but convoluted conclusion to her argument, put in a pamphlet in the mid-1890s, was that 'the representation of man would represent us, but not being alike, that wherein we differ is unrepresented under the present system'. She passionately believed in widening women's horizons, hence her commitment to both better educational opportunities and an increase in women's employment outside the home. Although she never dismissed the importance of the home, she claimed that being confined to creating domestic comfort for their families limited women's lives. To have the vote would bring 'the ennobling influence of national responsibility'. Above all, she wanted to promote women's rights in general, and optimistically, she believed that enfranchisement would bring this about. The law as it existed was unjust in its treatment of women in so many different spheres: from access to divorce and access to their children following divorce to the banning of their employment in many occupations to denying them the award of university degrees.

The turn of the century marked little progress in acceptance of the case that Millicent had been making for more than thirty years. Yet however frustrated she felt herself, she never stopped extorting her followers to keep fighting, and she encouraged them to believe that they would eventually win, even though there was little evidence to support her optimism. The Conservatives had been in power for more than a decade and were highly unlikely to introduce legislation giving women the vote, even though a few Conservative MPs were sympathetic. However, the Conservatives were to be swept aside in the election of 1906, when the Liberals were returned to power with a large majority.

Henry Campbell-Bannerman became the new Prime Minister, and not long after he took office, he was asked to receive a deputation of MPs, female leaders and suffragists. Under pressure, he agreed. While not opposed to the enfranchisement of women, he did not attach any priority to it, as was revealed when he met this very large delegation in May 1906. At the time, Millicent was away on holiday in Sicily and contemplated returning so that she could take part, but she found that the timetable of available boats made this difficult. Although widely recognised as the suffragists' leader, Millicent was not formally elected as their president until the following year, in 1907, after which time her absence from a deputation to the Prime Minister would have been unthinkable. In the event, she probably concluded that she had not missed very much. Campbell-Bannerman admitted that the suffragists had an irrefutable case. Nevertheless, he told them that they should continue to campaign so that even more people around the country were persuaded, which was reported as 'go on pestering'. His sympathetic views were not supported by everyone in his party and he was not prepared to invest time and effort in persuading them to change their minds. Millicent could be forgiven for thinking that he was only a little better than Gladstone. At least he did not make any promises only to renege later, as happened in Gladstone's case.

After Millicent became the President of the NUWSS in its new, more formal structure, which replaced a loosely built group of separate societies, the campaign became more rigorous and organised. This was undoubtedly stimulated by the arrival of militancy and the setting up of a rival organisation, the Women's Social and Political Union (WSPU), which was founded in Manchester in 1903 by Emmeline Pankhurst and her eldest daughter Christabel, with the support of her younger daughters Sylvia and Adela too. The Pankhursts had been members of the NUWSS Manchester Society and started the WSPU there, as a breakaway local body in search of new members and new approaches to campaigning, but without, in Millicent's words, 'any trace of intentional violence or non-constitutional action'.

An example of their orthodox campaigning was to ask questions of senior politicians at public meetings, as happened at a meeting in Manchester Free Trade Hall, where a Liberal Party event took place in late 1905. The Liberal politician Edward Grey was the main speaker and he was asked by Christabel Pankhurst and a young working-class feminist, Annie Kenney, whether the Liberal government, which by then seemed likely to be elected, would give votes to working women. Just putting the question led to an angry outburst in which some of the audience shouted, 'Be quiet' and others countered, 'Let them be heard.' The stewards then roughly forced the two young women to sit down. They were asked by the Chief Constable of Manchester to write their question down, so that he could take it to the platform, ensuring they would have a reply. They complied and it was passed to each speaker in turn, but neither Sir Edward Grey nor any of the other speakers answered it, much to the fury of the two women and others in the audience. During the uproar that followed, the questioners were dragged by the stewards into the street, where they called a meeting and refused to disperse when the police asked them to do so. Meanwhile, back in the hall, Grey got up saying he had unwittingly caused a disturbance and that he *was* in favour of women's suffrage but did not think it was a fitting subject that evening as it was not a party question. He typified politicians who try to avoid answering tricky questions, however legitimate.

The outcome was not happy for Christabel Pankhurst and Annie Kenney. In court the next day, they were given the choice of paying a fine or going to prison for seven days in one case and three in the other. They chose to go to prison. Millicent's views about it are notable and worth quoting in full, as they show strong sympathy at the outset for the forceful interventions of Mrs Pankhurst's supporters:

Nothing could have been more inept than the official conduct of this whole episode. If Sir Edward had replied that the Liberal Government not being formed he could not say what it would do on the subject of women's votes, but that he himself was favourable to the inclusion of women in the next Reform Bill, no one could have complained, but to howl the questioners down and knock them about, then to charge them with obstruction and to fine them and, in default of payment, to imprison them, was a course more worthy of a Czardom than a free country. It put the whole question in a false position: the only thing that was some consolation was that the Press, which, with few exceptions, was very chary of admitting that there was any demand on the part of women for political freedom, now blazoned forth with tremendous energy the enormity of two young women rising in a public meeting to inquire of a Liberal leader what his party intended to do for the unenfranchised masses of women.

We had become quite accustomed to holding magnificent meetings in support of women's franchise with every evidence of public sympathy and support, and to receive from the Anti-Suffrage Press either no notice at all or only a small paragraph tucked away in an inconspicuous corner. The sensation caused by the action of the Women's Social and Political Union suddenly changed all this. Instead of the withering contempt of silence, the Anti-Suffrage papers came out day after day with columns of hysterical verbiage directed against our movement. At the outset the directors of these papers made the mistake of supposing that the Suffrage movement was capable of being killed by the batteries which were opened against it. If abuse and misrepresentation could have killed it, it most assuredly would have died in the early years of the twentieth century.

She continued:

After this … the whole country … rang with the doings of the Suffragettes, as the violent Suffragists came to be called. I would point out, however, that for the first five years of their existence, while they suffered extraordinary acts of physical violence, they used none … If there was great vehemence in their demonstrations, there was also great restraint.

Public demonstrations became more frequent, replacing the more genteel meetings where the arguments for votes for women were put to well-behaved audiences, whose convictions may have been strengthened but who went quietly home without taking further actions to push their case. For example, in the summer of 1906, a number of young militants, including Annie Kenney, besieged the London home of Herbert Asquith, the Chancellor of the Exchequer, who had become known as one of the Liberal leaders who vociferously opposed votes for women. Arrests and imprisonment followed. Millicent immediately wrote an article defending them. They may have been 'excitable', as she put it, but she recognised that the extension of the franchise for men had nearly always been introduced as a result of militancy. Pamphlets needed to be written to set out the case, but more militant methods often gained the attention needed if change was to happen.

A few months later, there was a WSPU demonstration carrying flags and making speeches in the lobby of the House of Commons, which was out of bounds to protesters. This time, as many as ten women were arrested, some of whom were sentenced to two months, including the daughter of the radical Liberal politician Richard Cobden. Anne Cobden-Sanderson was in her fifties when she was sent to Holloway Prison and was a well-known campaigner for various causes, including vegetarianism and the Women's Tax Resistance League, which she had helped to found. Millicent had known her since childhood and refused to believe stories in the newspapers that she and the other women had bitten the police. She decided to ask if she could visit Mrs Cobden-Sanderson in Holloway and was granted permission to do so. She described what she saw at some length in her memoirs: the tiny narrow cell, the small window so high up that nothing could be seen out of it, no chair to sit on and the coarse material of the prison uniform in which her friend was dressed. As a vegetarian, Anne was given three potatoes for dinner, but she bravely told Millicent how an order from the doctor for the supply of two ounces of butter a day had made a big difference. She did not complain as, in Millicent's words, 'she was sustained by her belief that what she was enduring would hasten the day of women's freedoms'. After what Millicent had seen and heard, she wanted to find some way to recognise the sacrifice of the militants, particularly as in her view they had done nothing immoral. She began by writing to *The Times*, admitting that nearly fifty years of work for women's suffrage had led nowhere, which had persuaded campaigners to adopt more sensational methods. She asked that those of her colleagues in the movement, who were critical of the new militancy, should think again, saying that 'far from having injured the movement, they have done more in the last twelve months to bring it within the region of practical politics than we have been able to accomplish in the same number of years'. It was brave of her to admit this and revealed that she was capable of flexibility in accepting that different means could be deployed to achieve the end that both organisations wanted. While their methods might be different, there was room for various approaches, so Millicent thought there should be no denunciation by one side of the other. All their efforts should be focused on their anti-votes for women enemies. David Rubinstein reports on a speech she made the day after the women were jailed to the National Union of Women Workers, of which she was vice-president. In chairing a session on women's franchise, she 'rose to the drama of the occasion', according to Evelyn Sharp, who was there to report on the meeting for the *Manchester Guardian* and who revealed that Millicent's speech led her to join the militant movement.

Millicent's conclusion that 'we have plenty of enemies outside, let us hold together' led to a conviction that a way should be found to thank the prisoners on their release and, in so doing, to demonstrate unity in the suffrage movement. Her first idea was to hold a large public demonstration on the streets of London. This was dropped in favour of a different approach, which was the organisation of a banquet at the Savoy Hotel to welcome them when they came out of prison. In her memoirs, she reproduces the letter she sent out 'on her personal responsibility', describing her proposal and her reasons for it and asking for volunteers to serve on a general committee to promote the project. In an attempt to assuage the concerns of her colleagues who opposed the new militancy, she stated:

> I need hardly say that I am convinced that the work of quiet persuasion and argument form the solid foundation on which the success of the women's suffrage movement will be reared, and I and the great majority of suffrage workers wish to continue the agitation on constitutional lines; yet we feel that the action of the prisoners has touched the imagination of the country in a manner which quieter methods did not succeed in doing.

The public demonstration of support she proposed was partly motivated by what she described as 'the unscrupulous abuse and misrepresentation to which they had been subjected in the Press'.

Millicent was criticised for taking this decision personally without adequate consultation in the NUWSS. Nevertheless, the dinner went ahead. She addressed the diners, applauding the courage and self-sacrifice of the recently released women, saying that women had been driven to more drastic action in the face of indifference from the politicians who had the power to introduce reforms. One article about the event at the Savoy praised her logic, humour and enthusiasm, another described her appearance, portraying her as 'a dignified old-time lady with lilies of the valley in her dress and diamonds on her neck'. Whether Millicent, who was fifty-nine at the time, would have appreciated this description is a little doubtful. What would have pleased her was the comment that an alliance between the conservative and militant suffragists 'was sanctioned with her unrivalled authority'.

She used her authority in her role as President of the NUWSS to promote more public campaigning than in the past. It was undoubtedly a consequence of her perception that greater militancy on the part of the rival WSPU was successfully raising the profile of the cause and attracting new participants to the movement. Early in 1907, she organised a march from Hyde Park to the Albert Hall. To move on from meeting rooms and public halls to take to the streets marked an important addition to their tactics and it was one which many old hands in the suffragist societies found difficult to embrace. Lady Frances Balfour, a long-standing colleague and close friend of Millicent, admitted that she was a reluctant participant, as was the headmistress of a well-known girls' school and a strong supporter of the movement. When asked by Millicent whether she was going to join the procession, she said that she hated and loathed the very thought of it but that of course she would be there. From today's perspective, it is hard to understand this reluctance, but marching was not part of the repertoire of genteel women, who would have to put up with being jeered at as well as cheered. However, Millicent herself did not fear bystanders' hostility. She marched at the head of the column, apparently far too fast for many of the 3,000 women who followed her. In the words of Frances Balfour, she 'pirouetted through her part as leader with the step of a girl of seventeen'. In spite of the pouring rain, she thoroughly enjoyed herself in what became known as the Mud March, and shared a platform with Keir Hardie, the leader of the Labour Party and the novelist Israel Zangwill at the rally when the march reached its destination. A month later, another big event took place in London – a mass meeting at the Queen's Hall where Bernard Shaw was the main speaker – but without Millicent, who had to miss it to go to her mother-in-law's funeral. The following year, a big procession was organised in June when the weather was fine and around 15,000 marchers took part. They walked from the Embankment to the Albert Hall with banners and flags in the distinctive colours of the movement. Again Millicent led the march, having emphasised its purpose of drawing attention to a constitutional approach to reform when it had been announced a month earlier. When they arrived at their destination, she was visibly moved by the presentation of thirty bouquets of flowers from representatives of the marchers. In her speech which followed, she urged them all to dedicate their lives to the success of the cause that was as great as any the world had seen. Just a week later, the WSPU held a vast rally in Hyde Park attracting between a quarter and half a million participants and spectators. One journalist described it as a 'vast democratic assembly' compared to the 'cultured procession' of the week before. Undoubtedly, the militant movement within five years of its establishment had been able to recruit far more active supporters than the constitutionalists. Nevertheless, the fact that the two peaceful events took place within a week of each other and were conducted without acrimony between the two sides led to considerable coverage, giving the cause of votes for women the publicity it needed.

One result of the rise of the militant wing was a paradoxically rapid increase in the size of the NUWSS. From fewer than twenty societies in 1903, it grew to seventy by 1909 and 308 by 1911. The wider backing that this growth represented with a large increase in members led to much more activity. Millicent was greatly in demand as a speaker and decided to cut back on other commitments, so she resigned from the court of Newnham College, Cambridge, and did far less work for the East Anglian Sanatorium, as well as turning down new offers such as membership of the Royal Commission on Venereal Diseases.

She also welcomed the establishment of various specialist women's suffrage societies such as the Artists', the Actresses' and the Jewish Leagues and the Catholic Society. As the public face of the constitutional movement, she needed to encourage donations, welcome distinguished converts, thank donors, as well as keep up the work she had begun nearly forty years earlier in writing regularly to the press to try to persuade their leaders to support the cause. Her speaking tours required tiring travel and moving from hotel to hotel. Genteel drawing room meetings belonged to the past, and although most of her speaking engagements went off peacefully, some were disrupted, usually as a result of misconceptions that they were part of the militant movement. Even when shouted down or when the meeting became so rowdy that the platform was charged, she never seemed to lose her composure. She was tough and dismissed as greatly exaggerated the fears of her close colleagues after such an event that she must have been in terrible danger.

In 1908, Millicent became the first woman to address the Oxford Union in a debate on women's suffrage when she spoke in support of a twenty-year-old undergraduate called Ronnie Knox, who was later to become a well-known author, wit and Roman Catholic priest. In the debate, she poured scorn on the frequent complaint that women were too ignorant to vote, pointing out that at elections, candidates sought the help of these 'peculiarly ignorant people' to persuade others how to vote, yet they were denied the right to vote themselves. In her memoirs, Millicent expresses her gratitude to the young men who invited her, given that she was neither a resident, a graduate nor an undergraduate and of the wrong sex! The motion that the electoral disabilities of women should be removed was lost by 329 to 360, a better result than she had anticipated. Moreover, she was told the outcome would have been different if only undergraduates had voted and older members of the university had not turned out to defeat the motion. She was relieved to hear that youth was on her side.

Another more novel speaking engagement she took on at this time was a debate with the Women's National Anti-Suffrage League led by Mary Ward who, many years earlier, in 1889, had organised a national appeal against women's suffrage (see Chapter 6). Twenty years later, she had not given up and helped to found a women's anti-suffrage society which within two years joined a similar group formed by the Conservative peers Lord Curzon and Lord Cromer. Before the merger, a public debate was arranged between Millicent and Mary Ward in front of an audience of several hundred. Millicent had little difficulty in destroying Mary's arguments and won the vote decisively, much to Mary's discomfort, who said she would never take part in a debate with Millicent again. When not debating with her, Millicent was more generous about her opponent than might be expected. She respected her other public work, notably in adult education, and thought that unlike some of the other anti-suffragists, she had integrity and was honest, but she was dismissive about her views on votes for women, which she thought were not just silly but absurd in arguing that women were by nature politically ignorant. She did not blame Mary herself for the innuendo spread by the anti-suffragists that those backing votes for women were in favour of free love and that they had even published an obscene pamphlet. Nevertheless, charges of immorality infuriated Millicent and she indignantly dismissed them as unfounded and threatened to sue them.

The increased campaigning that was taking place around the country by the law-abiding constitutionalists was accompanied by continuing efforts to engage political leaders and Parliament. After the Liberal victory in 1906, they remained in power throughout the years leading up to the First World War, although with changes in the party's leadership. Henry Campbell-Bannerman was replaced by Herbert Asquith in 1908. One leading suffragist described this as a change from 'weak support' for the cause to 'determined opposition'. After Asquith became Prime Minister, David Lloyd George became an increasingly powerful and influential member of the government and was much more sympathetic towards votes for women. Millicent's own political affiliations were complex. Although certainly a Liberal as a young woman, she had parted company with mainstream Liberalism over Home Rule for Ireland. Although her enthusiasm for unionism began to wane by the early twentieth century and she abandoned the organised Liberal Unionists, it never disappeared completely. Nevertheless, from then on, she wanted to devote all her political energy to the suffragist cause.

A far higher proportion of Liberal MPs than Conservative MPs supported female enfranchisement but not all did. The arrival of thirty-three Labour MPs in 1906, all of whom were committed to greater enfranchisement under Keir Hardie's enthusiastic and active endorsement of it, was a new factor in her certainty that it would be best not to return to the Liberals and to remain unaffiliated. Indeed, thirty years later in her memoirs, she revealed the depth of her disappointment at the Liberals' failure to deliver and her admiration of the Labour Party for its consistent and unanimous endorsement of votes for women. Yet she continued to prefer the movement to remain publicly detached from any one party, so that it would be free to work with a wider range of politicians who pledged their support, including pro-suffragist candidates at by-elections. One unusual example was the well-known philosopher Bertrand Russell, who was on the executive of the NUWSS and stood in a by-election in Wimbledon in 1907 as a women's suffrage candidate and unofficial Liberal in a hopeless seat. Millicent strongly supported him, spoke in his election campaign and donated money. Although the publicity gained was helpful, the effort involved was too great to repeat this experiment elsewhere when defeat was a certain outcome. Nevertheless, the NUWSS tried to provide some support at by-elections to pro-suffragist candidates from various parties, as their victory would add to the numbers they needed to get legislative change through the House of Commons.

The big policy question which divided the suffragists at this time was whether to stick to fighting for the right to vote for female property owners alone rather than for all women or indeed for all men too. It was hotly debated within the movement, but in the end, Millicent's long-standing cautious approach to back what she, and many of her colleagues, believed to be the most modest and therefore least threatening change with the best chance of winning approval was the one that prevailed. They believed that once the 2 million women in this category could vote, further enfranchisement could later be introduced successfully. Unsurprisingly, it was too unambitious for the suffragettes, who wanted all women to have the vote, and it was too unambitious for the Labour Party, who wanted the vote to be universal for all men and women. In the end, Millicent won the argument in the NUWSS. Though many agreed reluctantly, they bowed to this which allowed her views to prevail. Over the years, she had acquired huge respect and greater authority. Her leadership skills were based on avoiding being dragged down by disputes about less important matters, of which there were many. She rose above them and carried her members along with her enthusiasm and optimism. She knew how to deflect argument with humour and wit and by moving the agenda on. These were political skills she had honed over many decades.

In spite of these skills, and the fact that she had become a national figure, she continued to be thwarted in her pursuit of victory in Westminster. In the past, so many Private Members' Bills had been introduced and got nowhere, mainly because the government never gave them the parliamentary time they needed, as happened in the case of two Bills introduced in 1907 and 1908. It was not a tactic worth pursuing any longer. She did back a novel idea, which was to ask permission for five women, herself included, to plead in support of a petition to remove the political disabilities of women. As they expected, the request was turned down, but it provided some more positive publicity which contrasted with the suffragettes' rule-breaking demonstrations at Westminster. However, gestures of this sort were only of limited value and Millicent realised that direct pressure needed to be put on the government through requesting delegations to Cabinet ministers and to the Prime Minister himself. Requests from the suffragists for meetings with political leaders were accepted on more occasions than might have been expected given how little priority these powerful men tended to attach to female enfranchisement. In the years between 1906 and the onset of the First World War in 1914, Millicent had consolidated her position as a public figure and was adept at using the newspapers to promote her campaign. Presumably, the Prime Minister and the Chancellor thought it was safer to open their doors to her than to shut her out. They may also have reckoned that they could fob her off with promises, which they need not necessarily keep. On the whole, this was the tactic Asquith adopted, as did Lloyd George initially.

Millicent was fearless and utterly unintimidated when she met them as the leader of these delegations. She forcibly set out her arguments to the men in power and did not hesitate to dispute with them when they failed to respond positively. She was confident of her case and unwilling to be put down by them. A precis of her own account of a meeting with Lloyd George in 1910 when he was Chancellor of the Exchequer minutes the way she handled these occasions. It took place at his official residence at 11 Downing Street and her purpose was to reinforce the necessity for government support for women's enfranchisement. He told her that this was impossible because of 'militancy' and asked her as President of the NUWSS to put a stop to it. 'Impossible,' she told him, asking how he imagined that she could achieve this when the government had had no success in doing so:

> You have the whole resources of the Government behind you: a
> police force of many thousands at your beck and call: a bottom-
> less purse to draw upon: but you have not succeeded in stopping
> it, and why should you expect us to succeed when you, with these
> enormous advantages have failed? There is only one way of stop-
> ping militancy, and that is to grant the justice of the claim of
> women to representation and to give facilities for a Suffrage Bill.

Lloyd George was irritated and repeated that militancy was seriously alienating her cause, citing his wife who had warmly supported women's suffrage earlier and now no longer did so. In these circumstances, the government could do nothing, he claimed.

Millicent then resorted to an anecdote about a recent visit to his constituency for a suffrage meeting which had been very successful, describing her surprise the next morning to pass a handsome house, all of whose windows had been smashed. She was told it housed the offices of the local Conservative Association and that the windows had been broken by Lloyd George's supporters celebrating his victory in the recent election. Although the ring leaders were arrested and charged, they were let off because the magistrate said allowance must be made for 'political excitability'. Millicent asked:

> Why is allowance made for political excitement in the case of men who can and do express their feelings at the ballot box, but no allowance is made in the case of women where they are excited by political injustice and are driven to express their indignation by acts of violence?

Lloyd George gave no answer, deftly moving on with the suggestion that he would introduce Millicent to his wife.

Of course, Lloyd George knew perfectly well that Millicent led the anti-militant wing of the campaign for votes for women, so his request to her was disingenuous, but he must have wanted to convey to her his view as a politician, who was sympathetic to giving women the vote, that violence, which at that time was focused on damaging property by smashing windows, was making this more difficult. More cynically, he may also have been using it as an excuse for government inaction. In the chapter that follows, I will examine similarities and contrasts between the suffragists and the suffragettes and how Millicent's own views about the militant wing of the campaign began to change as violence became their dominant tactic. Before doing so, I want to describe the impact of Herbert Asquith becoming the Prime Minister in the spring of 1908. As a long-standing opponent of women being given the vote, his promotion was a huge setback, which led Millicent's biographer

David Rubinstein to say, 'In retrospect it seems that suffragists should have taken up some other issue until he left office, for it seems inconceivable that any suffrage bill would have been passed during his tenure whatever the behaviour of its advocates.'

This judgement may have been correct, but Millicent was determined to continue the campaign. The organisation she led was sharpened by its growing membership and the dedicated work of a number of talented women, who volunteered, many of them working full-time on the cause. In 1909, the NUWSS benefited from joining with the *Common Cause*, an impressive weekly magazine edited by a professional journalist. It was able to keep in touch with local branches and individual members ensuring they were aware of any new developments in the campaign. It is also unlikely Millicent would have wanted to abandon the battlefield, allowing Emmeline Pankhurst and the suffragettes to take it over.

It would be unfair to accuse Millicent of being naïve in deciding to take the fight to Asquith. She knew what she was up against. Soon after he became Prime Minister in 1908, he promised a deputation of suffragist MPs that his proposal for an Electoral Reform Bill would be drafted in a way which would allow an amendment to include women. When Bertrand Russell expressed his pleasure about this apparent concession, Millicent wrote to him saying:

We must remember that he has always been and remains an enemy of the movement and looks to me now very much as if he were heading us off (or trying to do so) with the Adult Suffrage trap ... I have as a suffragist suffered too much from the political tricks of official liberalism for the past thirty years, not to be on my guard against them now.

Her perception that Reform Bills, which enfranchised most adult men but not women, were a trap, because amendments to them to include women could not be guaranteed, was justified. Nevertheless, she was determined to confront Asquith directly.

She had already taken a deputation to him when he was Chancellor of the Exchequer. In her book *The Women's Victory and After*, published some years later, she revealed what she and her colleagues were up against. While they were in the waiting room, Asquith's private secretary asked to see her alone. The agitated young man's purpose was to ask her to guarantee that there would be no physical violence when they met the Chancellor. She told him that she was astonished he would be so frightened, but she guaranteed that 'no member of my deputation will either employ or threaten violence. The idea of it considering who they were entertained me and I took no pains to conceal my amusement.' They were a group of highly respectable older women who were part of the long-established suffragist leadership. When they went into the reception room, there was a young woman sitting in the corner. Millicent teasingly told the private secretary that as she did not know who she was, she could not guarantee that this woman would not be violent. His agitated reply was that this was Mr Asquith's daughter.

Asquith bristled with hostility. He claimed that he was unaware of any wish for enfranchisement amongst women themselves. When a delegate offered the opportunity to him to attend a meeting in Yorkshire, where he would find many working women who passionately wanted the vote, he replied, 'The prospect does not greatly attract me.' Millicent's tart comment made later about this interview was that 'it was our lot to taste the insolence of office and the proud man's contumely. It was part of our job.' Because she saw it as a duty to continue promoting the cause, however disagreeable, she took several deputations to Asquith over the years when he was Prime Minister. He never relented from his belief that women should not be given the vote, although his manner became less hostile. Towards the end of his time in office, Millicent even told him cheekily that she had never seen a man so improved. Before reaching this point, she observed that there were many political hurdles that Asquith placed in her way, which related mainly to the political tactics he deployed.

Asquith was not so much deeply hostile to women being able to vote as utterly indifferent. As his remark to the deputation when he was Chancellor of the Exchequer suggested, he did not think it was an issue which engaged the public much nor could he conceive it as a matter of fundamental rights but merely as an issue about good governance, which he did not think would necessarily be improved if women had the vote. He was certainly not a misogynist; indeed, he enjoyed the company of intelligent women. Roy Jenkins ascribed it to a lack of imagination in his biography of Asquith. As a man whose views were relatively progressive on most social issues by the standards of his time, his indifference is nevertheless puzzling.

The rest of the chapter will cover the Conciliation Bills, which were introduced in the House of Commons on a cross-party basis to try to make progress on votes for women. The 1910 election resulted in a hung parliament but left the Liberals in power with the support of the Irish Nationalists and the Labour Party. Henry Brailsford, a political journalist, suggested that the best way to get votes for women onto the Statute Book was to form a cross-party conciliation committee to take forward a Bill limiting the vote to female property holders, which would have the greatest chance of success as it would attract support from both Liberal and

Conservative MPs. When consulted, Millicent supported it on the grounds that she would support any Bill with a good chance of success. A cross-party committee of thirty-six members was formed, led by the Liberal Lord Lytton, whose sister Constance Lytton was a militant suffragette. The Bill was carried by a large majority but fell because time was not provided for the next steps before a general election was called by Asquith on the Parliament Bill to curb the powers of the House of Lords with respect to Finance Bills.

The Conciliation Bill was reintroduced after the election and again had a majority at second reading, but it was without the support of some Liberal leaders including Lloyd George, who preferred a Bill that would lead to a much wider enfranchisement than just propertied women. Winston Churchill also opposed it on the same grounds, although he had anyway long been opposed to women having the vote, unlike Lloyd George who was in favour. Again, it went no further because it was denied the time needed for it to go through. In 1912, a third attempt was made to get the Bill on the Statute Book. This time it lost by twelve votes at second reading. It was rumoured before the vote that if it went through, Asquith would resign, then the Liberal Party would fall apart so Home Rule would be jeopardised. This led the Irish Nationalists to vote against it, leading Millicent to complain that typically the Irish had 'ratted'. Prior to the Bill's defeat, Asquith had told a delegation in 1911, when cross-questioned by Millicent, that he would introduce his own Reform Bill that would give the franchise to almost all men and repeated his earlier promise that his Bill could be framed in such a way that it could be amended to include women – and that the government would not oppose such an amendment. In 1913, the Speaker refused to allow such an amendment on the grounds it would fundamentally change the nature of the Bill. It became known as the 'government fiasco', as the Speaker's ruling killed the Bill, but Asquith had got his way and had out-manoeuvred Millicent and the suffragists.

Meanwhile, the NUWSS had begun to consider looking elsewhere for political support. Pledges from Asquith were worthless and the suffragists concluded that he never intended to do anything to advance political rights for women. They then started to consider modifying their position that they should remain independent of any party affiliation in favour of greater collaboration with the Labour Party, all of whose MPs were committed to widening the franchise to include women. As a consequence, the case was made to support Labour candidates standing in by-elections by working in their constituencies to encourage the electorate to vote for them. However, many of Millicent's NUWSS colleagues were apprehensive about this and clung to their long-established position to be free of attachment to any political party. The politically independent Eleanor Rathbone, a leading feminist and social reformer, was one of them. Millicent gave reassurances to the doubters that they would not altogether abandon the non-party character of the NUWSS, but she herself favoured a shift in the direction of actions which would take into account Labour's clearly expressed commitment to women's suffrage. The main mechanism for doing so was to develop an Election Fighting Fund to promote the resources needed in by-elections. The Labour leaders were hesitant about accepting this offer. Ramsay MacDonald and Arthur Henderson had doubts about formally accepting funds from a non-Labour source, and MacDonald was suspicious of what he perceived to be a primarily middle-class movement. He was also hostile to militancy. Millicent, with the help of others, eventually convinced Labour to accept the proposal; and she also prevailed in the NUWSS where she angrily denounced members of the executive, who had formed a pressure group publicly to campaign for the status quo, for threatening the very survival of the organisation. Eleanor Rathbone's comment that the executive's victory was no more than 'one long series of votes of confidence in Mrs Fawcett' is revealing about the tactics Millicent used to get her way.

An earlier by-election in which the Election Fighting Fund played no part was in Bow and Bromley late in 1912. George Lansbury, then a rebellious backbencher but later to become leader of the Labour Party, resigned his seat and fought the by-election that followed on the suffrage issue. Millicent spoke on his behalf at an eve of poll meeting as well as issuing an appeal to electors. After he lost, she wrote a fulsome letter thanking him for his efforts on behalf of women, which, she said, had not been wasted and telling him that she knew his great work would continue.

It was not unusual for the movement she led to invite political speakers to the large rallies that they now organised. At one such occasion in 1911 at the Albert Hall, the volatile and rather unreliable Lloyd George was a speaker. This took place not long after a very public spat between him and Millicent in which they had exchanged insults. In a letter to *The Times* about his failure to vote for the Conciliation Bill, she denounced him as a Celt, stating that 'the political genius of the Celt is for destruction. He can destroy but he can never create.' This was a silly generalisation and Lloyd George got his own back by denouncing it as an 'ill-natured, ill-conditioned and fatuous observation' in a speech to Welsh female Liberals. Yet as Rubinstein comments, both contenders had more to gain from cooperation than continuing the insults. Then, at the NUWSS meeting in the Albert Hall, Millicent introduced Lloyd George as 'the strongest and most forceful personality in the present Government' and he referred to her as 'a leader worthy of the dignity and greatness of the women's movement'. Over time, her respect for him grew.

At another Albert Hall meeting a couple of years later, the NUWSS invited Arthur Henderson, one of the leading Labour politicians, to speak. As he rose to his feet, a militant suffragette instigated an uproar in an attempt to drown him out. Millicent was unclear why the militants had a vendetta against him and why they therefore disapproved of the invitation to him to speak. Her decision to invite him proved wholly justified, as this quotation from her memoirs indicates:

> Mr Henderson held his own splendidly. He has at command a gigantic voice, and as the shrill cries of the suffragettes rose, he first changed his pitch, drew out another stop, as it were, from the big organ of his vocal chords, flung out his voice at its loudest and went on undisturbed, unhurried, without ever losing the thread of his argument or taking the slightest notice of the riot. He never lost his temper nor his nerve, and the consequence was that instead of overwhelming him in confusion, exactly the contrary effect was produced: everyone in the hall became aware that they were witnessing the pluckiest performance that they had ever seen at a public meeting.

Millicent's admiration for Henderson extended to other Labour leaders, in particular Philip Snowden. She was delighted by the way in which he helped to take through a resolution at the Labour Party conference in 1913 to oppose any Franchise Bill in which women were not included. At a time when the movement despaired of progress being made in Parliament after the collapse of the Reform

Bill, it renewed hopes that all was not lost, since it made any re-introduction of a Bill which was confined to extending the suffrage to men alone impossible. There was further consolation from the Trades Union Congress; at its conference later that year, it censured the government for its failure to fulfil its promises to the women's movement and passed a resolution which demanded a Government Reform Bill that included women.

While the political advance of the Labour movement gave rise to renewed optimism, Millicent's endless campaigning in the five years leading up to the First World War did not produce the tangible victory of the passing of parliamentary legislation enfranchising women. The suffragists battled against a background of growing violence from the suffragettes throughout this period. More needs to be said in the next chapter about what Emmeline Pankhurst and her followers did, what impact they had and how Millicent and her supporters reacted to it.

9

THE SUFFRAGETTES AND THE RESORT TO VIOLENCE

The journalist Mary Stocks recalled that 'never were two women who served the cause so wholly unlike one another' as Emmeline Pankhurst and Millicent Garrett Fawcett. This is only partially true. While they did have different approaches to how to campaign and to what they saw as legitimate actions to further their cause, there were more similarities than seem to have been recognised, particularly in their backgrounds.

Emmeline was born in Manchester in 1858, so she was eleven years younger than Millicent. Her father, Robert Goulden, started life as an errand boy. Like Newson Garrett, he worked his way up to be a successful entrepreneur who became a factory owner and was able to provide his growing family with a prosperous lifestyle, moving to a large house with a big garden on the edge of Salford during Emmeline's childhood. Her mother, a teacher, came from the Isle of Man, where the family spent their holidays. Like Louisa Garrett, she had ten children, of whom Emmeline was the eldest. Both her parents were committed to the anti-slavery movement and her father was on the side of the abolitionists in the American

Civil War. Her mother took Emmeline at the age of five to a bazaar held to collect money for emancipated black slaves, an experience she did not forget. Her father was a member of the Liberal Party and played a part in developing his eldest daughter's political awareness by asking her to read the newspapers to him while he had his breakfast. Millicent too benefited from being a member of a family where politics were discussed, sometimes with her family but mainly through the Sunday evening debates masterminded by her elder sister Elizabeth.

Even though in both families, the education of the sons was given greater attention than that of the daughters, Emmeline, like Millicent, was sent to a small boarding school for girls, where she was joined by her younger sister Mary. Both her parents were also in favour of women being given the vote. Emmeline was undoubtedly exposed to discussions about this, as Millicent was through her older sisters Louie and Elizabeth. Both girls read a great deal from an early age and were intellectually precocious, although Emmeline eventually confined her reading to novels in contrast to Millicent's wider reading. Unlike Millicent, who was brought home from school in her mid-teens, Emmeline had the advantage of being sent to school in Paris where she became fluent in French and an ardent Francophile, whereas Millicent relied on the French she had learnt at her English school.

Both girls were required to help their mothers with housekeeping and the care of the younger children when they left school, although in Emmeline's case, as the eldest in the family compared to Millicent as the seventh child, it was probably more arduous. Their escape was to marry and to do so when they were young; Millicent was just under twenty, Emmeline was just over twenty-one. Both fell in love with men who were considerably older and already established in their professional lives. Neither of the young women saw marriage as a substitute for being able to work outside the home. Emmeline said later that she 'felt strongly the necessity of women being trained to some profession or business which should enable them to be self-supporting ... Women are the better and happier for occupation, it raises them socially and intellectually.' This closely matched Millicent's views, as we have seen, in her work to open further education to women and the arguments she promoted about the necessity for women to have employment, which would provide them with an income and allow them some independence.

Both women attached importance to how they dressed. Emmeline in particular was exceptionally elegant. They also both had excellent speaking voices, which helped to hold their audiences. Their husbands were unusually interesting men with similar connections. Neither of the husbands they chose were conventionally handsome, although Emmeline was petite, slender and beautiful, and Millicent was small, slight and pretty. Richard Pankhurst grew up in Manchester as a Baptist Dissenter and an evangelical liberal. Although brilliant, he was denied a place at Oxford as a Nonconformist, going instead to Owens College, Manchester, and then the University of London, where he studied law proceeding to a doctorate. After working as a solicitor, he was called to the Bar at Lincoln's Inn and then returned to practise in Manchester. Henry Fawcett, as we have seen, was an intellectual too and a Liberal radical with strong anti-establishment views on a range of issues. Pankhurst leaned further to the left and was devoted to fighting injustice wherever he saw it. Both of them wanted a wife who would be their partner in their public work, which probably was what most attracted Millicent and Emmeline to them. Their marriages to the 'Red Doctor', as Pankhurst was known in Manchester, and the blind professor, who was an MP too, were intensely happy.

Both women became pregnant soon after they married and each of them had a daughter, although for reasons that have never been explained, Millicent had no more children while Emmeline went on to have two more daughters and two sons, one of whom died at the age of four, and the other at the age of twenty. In both marriages, there was mutual support: the husbands providing advice and encouragement to their wives' campaigning work, and in Millicent's case, her writing too; and their wives providing back-up to their husbands in their political work inside and outside Parliament. Richard Pankhurst was an unsuccessful parliamentary candidate on three occasions, twice for the Independent Labour Party. Both couples had a circle of friends who were active in public life and entertained them at home together. The Pankhursts divided their time between London and Manchester and the Fawcetts between London and Cambridge. For several years, the Pankhursts had a house in Russell Square, a stone's throw away from Millicent, by then widowed and living in 2 Gower Street. Did they ever run into each other as neighbours? There is no record of them doing so.

Just as Henry Fawcett suffered from ill-health when he reached his fifties, so did Richard Pankhurst, who eventually succumbed to a gastric ulcer and death in his early sixties. He had been married to Emmeline for nineteen years and she was left a widow at the age of forty. Millicent was widowed at the age of thirty-seven after seventeen years of marriage. The deaths of their husbands devastated both women. Emmeline was so heartbroken that she could not find the motivation needed to continue her public work for some months, just as Millicent had abandoned her campaigning work for some time after Henry's death. As new widows, both of them were supported by siblings after losing their husbands. Emmeline's sister Mary and an unmarried brother lived with her for a period, then her eldest daughter Christabel became her closest companion, later sharing the direction of the suffragette movement with her. Like Philippa, Christabel was academically able and did not enjoy helping her mother run the shop she established after Richard's death. Christabel sought more intellectual challenges and decided to follow in her father's footsteps to become a lawyer, while at the same time taking part in the Manchester Society of the NUWSS. She completed a law degree at Owens College, which later became Manchester University, and was awarded first-class honours, but she was refused admission to Lincoln's Inn, which would not accept women as the legal profession was barred to them. Instead, she threw herself into suffrage activities in London. Meanwhile, her mother's grief became less all-encompassing and Emmeline took on a new role as a registrar of births and deaths, which was paid and provided her with an income she desperately needed. She was also elected under the auspices of the Independent Labour Party to the Manchester School Board. The outbreak of the Boer War rekindled her interest in national politics. She was even more passionately opposed to the Boer War than Millicent was in favour of it. Emmeline denounced Britain as an imperialist aggressor. However, it was the position of women that was preoccupying her; her experiences on the school board and as a registrar revealed discrimination against female teachers in the first case and the grinding poverty of working-class women who came to her to register the births of their children or the deaths of their husbands in the second case. Emmeline, like Millicent before her, believed that equality for women could not be successfully pursued unless women were able to vote in national elections, thereby forcing MPs to consider the position of women.

Christabel was a key influence on her mother when they discussed how to approach women's suffrage in the early 1900s. Impatient for action and disappointed by both the suffragists' cautious constitutional approach and her perception of the lack of priority given to it by the Labour Party in spite of Keir Hardie's support, Christabel argued for a radical rethink. She and her mother plotted a new approach in which the slogan 'deeds not words' would be adopted and new, younger recruits would be sought out to refresh the movement. Rather than trying to reform the NUWSS, they decided to set up a new organisation. At a meeting of left-wing suffragists at Emmeline's home, they decided to call it the Women's Social and Political Union (WSPU). Like the NUWSS, they determined it should not be affiliated to any party, but unlike the NUWSS, it would be a woman-only organisation. Set up in 1903, it operated in Manchester and one of its first interventions leading to widespread publicity was the interruption of a Liberal Party meeting, where Sir Edward Grey was the main speaker, followed by Christabel's brief imprisonment (see Chapter 8). The intention was not to replace the NUWSS but to run the new organisation alongside it. As described earlier, Millicent was phlegmatic about it and recognised its success in attracting new members to the movement and noted that, because of its militancy, it was making a significant contribution to gaining a higher public profile for the campaign.

This was Millicent's view for several years and she only changed it when violent tactics by the WSPU became commonplace, which she believed damaged the cause in the eyes of the public and made politicians more wary of making any parliamentary concessions on votes for women. She was frequently told by politicians in favour of reform that violent militancy made progress more difficult. While critical of the violent battles with the police, the smashing of shop windows, the throwing of bricks through the windows of Cabinet ministers' houses, the flinging of burning tapers into letter boxes and the even more serious forms of arson, Millicent never retreated from expressing the view that all forms of violence committed by the suffragettes derived from the failure of political leaders to take action to enfranchise women. She was also outspoken about the violence of the authorities towards the suffragettes, especially in the early years of the WSPU. Later, she deplored the treatment of suffragettes in prison, especially the horrific practice of force-feeding when they went on hunger strike. She also showed considerable insight on the effects of the authorities' refusal to accommodate protest. In the *Common Cause*, she wrote in 1910:

> This movement will not be put down by persecution and punishment … The more the women suffragists are persecuted either by prison, or by other forms of suffering … the more determined they are to go on until they have succeeded in their work. It is hardship and persecution that rouse heroism in the heart of man, yes and women too.

In Millicent's memoirs, she reflects on why she did not leave the constitutional movement to become a militant. She was clear, she said, that

> we should keep our artillery for our opponents and not turn it on one another: on the other hand, I could not support a revolutionary movement, especially as it was ruled autocratically, at first,

by a small group of four persons, and latterly by one person only … In 1908, this despotism decreed that the policy of suffering violence but using none, was to be abandoned.

This decision convinced Millicent of the 'principle of supporting our movement only by argument, based on common sense and experience and not by personal violence or lawbreaking of any kind'. However, she conceded that, at this time, the suffragettes suffered from more violence than they ever inflicted and cited, as an example, prison officers turning a hose on a suffrage prisoner in Strangeways jail on a midwinter's night as 'disgraceful torture'. Moreover, she frequently referred to the remarkable and moving courage of the militants.

Her denunciation of the despotic leadership of the WSPU refers to Emmeline Pankhurst. Whether this was fair is debatable. Certainly, Emmeline was dismissive about the need for rules on how the WSPU should be organised. The one occasion when her leadership was seriously challenged was in 1907, when disaffected colleagues planned a coup. Emmeline was ruthless in putting down the dissent. The way she asserted her authority was to annul the organisational aspects of the constitution, to cancel the annual conference and to have an election of a new committee not by the membership but simply by those present at the meeting, where she sought loyalty from those attending. As her biographer June Purvis wrote, Emmeline offered no apology for the autocratic structure of the union, adding the following quote from Emmeline's own later account of the organisation:

The WSPU is not hampered by a complexity of rules. We have no constitution and by-laws; nothing to be amended or tinkered with or quarrelled over at an annual meeting. In fact, we have no annual meeting, no business sessions, no election of officers. The WSPU is simply a suffrage army in the field. It is purely a volunteer army, and no one is obliged to remain in it.

This supports Millicent's criticism that the way the WSPU was run was autocratic, compared with the more conventional and democratic NUWSS over which Millicent presided. However, Emmeline herself was not much involved in the organisation of the WSPU's work. This was left to a triumvirate consisting of her daughter Christabel, who was paid to work full-time for the union, and by Emmeline and Frederick Pethick-Lawrence, wealthy suffragists who devoted much of their time to the WSPU, each acting at different times as the treasurer. Emmeline Pankhurst had no interest in the minutiae of administration and she wanted to be free of it to campaign ceaselessly around the country, including speaking at every by-election she could to draw attention to women's exclusion from the vote and to denounce the government candidate. Although she was consulted on policy issues from 1907 to 1912, the direction of the union was left to the triumvirate, so describing her as a dictator was perhaps an exaggeration. Towards the end of this five-year period, there was growing evidence that Millicent's opposition to violence in principle, and misgivings about its effects on public opinion in practice, were justified. Public opposition to damage to private property was growing, but it did not deter Emmeline and Christabel from a decision in 1912 to increase violence, which was in their view the only way to force the government to concede. The Pethick-Lawrences disagreed, but Emmeline would not entertain any opposition. In consequence, while the Pethick-Lawrences were on holiday in Canada, the Pankhursts arbitrarily removed them from their roles in the WSPU. They were devastated but were shown no mercy by either mother or daughter. Five years earlier, they had encouraged Emmeline to abandon any semblance of democratic governance. Now they were the victims of this, as they had no way of appealing against autocratic decision-making.

There was only one attempt to unite the two wings of the movement. During the autumn of 1909, Maud Arncliffe Sennett, a leading suffragette, rather than Emmeline Pankhurst herself, appealed to Millicent for an amalgamation and, at the very least, cooperation between them. Millicent was adamant that the NUWSS could not accept this proposal. At a meeting of its council soon after the appeal for amalgamation, a long discussion took place, after which a resolution strongly condemning 'the use of violence in political propaganda' was passed by a large majority. The gap between the two organisations on tactics was just too great for them to cooperate, let alone merge, so they remained divided.

There was, however, a short period while the suffrage movement was trying to get the Conciliation Bills through Parliament when the militant movement was persuaded to desist from violence. The longer prison sentences for suffragettes damaging property or disrupting meetings by howling down speakers in demonstrations of uncontrolled anger led to hunger strikes. Force-feeding by the authorities involved horrific violence towards female prisoners. Emmeline worried about the long-term physical and mental effects on these women, which meant the short truce focusing on peaceful protest gave her and other militant leaders some relief. The only event in which both sides of the suffragist movement took part together was during the period when the Conciliation Bills were being debated. The Women's Coronation Procession took place in

June 1911 and was a response to the Royal Coronation Processions planned for a few days later, which were to represent 'the manhood of the Empire' with no place for women. On the day of the Women's Coronation Procession, between 40,000 and 50,000 marched from the Embankment to the Albert Hall. A year earlier, there had been an attempt to stage a joint suffrage event, but it failed to take place mainly because of the refusal of the WSPU to abstain from militancy until it was over. Consequently, the NUWSS and the WSPU held separate demonstrations in the same month. When a year later, the executive of the NUWSS debated whether to take part in the Coronation March, there was hesitancy about it because of earlier militant insurgence. Millicent was in favour, which was consistent with her opinion that it was wise to limit where possible the breach between the constitutionalists and the militants. Her view prevailed but left some members of the NUWSS unhappy with the decision to join in. She confronted the doubters in an article in the *Common Cause*, noting that the NUWSS had clearly and publicly criticised the WSPU for violence and writing that 'this seems no reason for refusing to cooperate with them when they are acting on lines which we heartily approve', i.e. non-violence.

The Coronation March was a great success: seventy bands played; the women walked five abreast carrying banners and pennants in the June sunshine; it was seven miles long; it had empire and international contingents; and there was an atmosphere of harmony and optimism. Millicent led the NUWSS contingent, which the press suggested attracted more marchers than the other groups. Millicent wrote to Maud Arncliffe Sennett, one of the suffragette organisers of the march, saying, 'I was delighted with the procession and I was never surer of anything in my life than that it was the right policy for the Cause, for the [NUWSS] to cooperate in it.' Emmeline Pankhurst was equally jubilant and told a meeting in the Albert Hall afterwards:

What does this demonstration of ours mean? It means Victory! ... We have proved that we can combine, we have proved that we can put aside all personal beliefs, and all personal objects for a common end; we have proved that women have great powers of organisation ... We have shown that women, alongside with men, are worthy to build up a humanity that men can never make without our help.

Sadly, this was to be the only time that the two sides of the suffrage movement cooperated to take part in an event together. The failure of the Third Conciliation Bill was seen by both sides as treachery on the part of Asquith. They were not just disappointed that all their optimism was unfounded; they were outraged. The WSPU's truce was ended and violent militancy began again. Millicent was deeply depressed by the demise of the Conciliation Bills. She said, 'I felt that what I had been working for for forty years had been destroyed at a blow; but I also felt what beavers feel when their dam has been destroyed, namely, that they must begin all over again and build it up once more from the beginning.' Where others might have abandoned the struggle, she resolutely returned to the campaign. One action she took was to renew her opposition to violence as the suffragettes' militancy became more extreme. Unannounced window-smashing on a vast scale became frequent. A little later, they resorted to arson, setting pillar boxes on fire and burning down an orchid house in Kew Gardens; telegraph and telephone wires were cut; railway carriages and empty churches were set on fire; and a bomb was planted in a railway station which exploded. But no life was to be lost, meaning that buildings should only be set on fire when empty. Emmeline frequently insisted on this.

There was no difference between the two leaders of the movement in their passionate commitment to fighting on. They shared throughout their lives of campaigning the determination not to be beaten and they both had remarkable energy in pursuing their goals. Although both had the ability to inspire loyalty in their followers, undoubtedly Emmeline was the greater public speaker. Her way with words and her charisma were spellbinding. She roused and inspired her audiences in ways that Millicent, who made her case through reasoned and carefully constructed arguments, could not match. Nevertheless, the criticism sometimes made that Millicent was cold and dry seems harsh and contradicts the evidence of the warm reception that she had from her audiences. Christabel Pankhurst described her as 'trim and prim' after attending one of her speeches. There may have been an element of truth in this, but Christabel was biased. Millicent's sister Alice wrote to her in 1910 telling her:

> I felt dear sister that the cause is to you what religion was to dear mother. Of course we all know this, but you are speaking so much more now that I think you must be glad to know that you can touch other people with the flame that burns in your own heart.

But Alice was biased too and her reference to Millicent's 'impassioned fervour' seems a more apt description of Emmeline's public speaking.

After the demise of the Conciliation Bills, the suffrage groups took different routes when they returned to the fray. Emmeline had endorsed violent militancy but agreed to retreat from her position following Millicent's plea to suspend violence to give a better chance to the amendments to include women in Asquith's Manhood Suffrage Bill. As we have already seen, the Speaker's intervention prevented the requisite amendments anyway, so the brief suspension did not lead to Millicent and the NUWSS's hoped-for outcome. Emmeline then urged her supporters to increase their militancy, telling them it was their duty to pursue violent action. The day after one of these speeches, an empty house which was being built for Lloyd George was blown up. Emmeline was then arrested for procuring and inciting women to commit offences, and she was eventually convicted and sentenced to three years' penal servitude. It was not the first time she had been imprisoned, but this was a far longer sentence than she had had before. In Holloway jail, she embarked on a hunger strike, which lasted for nine days when her rapidly deteriorating health led to her release.

To deal with suffragettes on hunger strike, the government passed the Prisoners (Temporary Discharge for Ill-Health) Act, which became known as the Cat and Mouse Act. This provided for those on hunger strike (the mice) to be released on licence to recuperate only to be reimprisoned by the authorities (the cat) to complete their sentence. Emmeline spent the summer of 1913 in and out of prison, a victim of this legislation. By then in her fifties, repeated hunger strikes took a huge toll on her health, leaving long-lasting damage. In the autumn, she escaped to the United States for a fundraising speaking tour, only to be arrested again on her return. When out on licence, she bravely spoke at meetings in London and elsewhere, but her campaigning was limited by the threat of rearrest as soon as her period out on licence was over. To ward off rearrest, she escaped for short periods to France and went into hiding when back in the United Kingdom. This pattern continued through the first half of 1914 against a background of increasingly public anger against the WSPU's violence.

Meanwhile, Millicent returned to peaceful campaigning, which included delegations to political leaders, marches and open-air demonstrations and a prolific output of articles for a wide range of journals and newspapers. She aimed to try to capitalise on public sympathy for the cause following its rejection by Parliament, which she believed was perceived to be unfair by the public.

In support of her optimism, she cited in her memoirs a series of articles in the *Manchester Guardian* 'which struck blow by blow, telling and well directed, in our support'. She noted that 'the drama also was a great ally' in that a number of plays, such as Bernard Shaw's *Androcles and the Lion* and James Barrie's *What Every Woman Knows*, 'were immeasurably helpful to us'. One way the NUWSS devised to build on public support and gain national publicity was to organise what they called the 'Pilgrimage'. This was a march to London in July 1913 along eight different routes from all over the country, converging on London on a given day with a huge rally in Hyde Park. Initially sceptical about how walking would help getting the vote, walk Millicent did, joining the East Anglian route with the friends and neighbours of her childhood, although she left it from time to time to join other routes and be present at some of the larger demonstrations that took place on the way. Although there were occasional incidents when the marchers were subjected to violence, the reception they received was mainly warm and enthusiastic. Millicent wrote in her memoirs, 'The whole thing caught on to a tremendous extent; villagers ran out to meet us, begging us to stop and give them a meeting; all kinds of hospitality were offered and gratefully accepted.' She was also euphoric about the Hyde Park rally and a service the next day in St Paul's Cathedral.

It was an opportune moment to take a deputation to Asquith, which took place a few days later. It demonstrated to the Prime Minister, who in the past claimed there was no public enthusiasm for women's suffrage, that across the country, the marching suffragists were well received. This did not prevent him from stating before the meeting, 'I feel bound to warn you that I do not see any way to add anything material to what I have lately said in the House of Commons as to the intentions and policy of the Government.' At the meeting, while polite, he was true to his word, and Millicent wrote to Lloyd George afterwards expressing her disappointment with its outcome, in spite of some improvement in the Prime Minister's language and attitude. Earlier private meetings with suffragist sympathisers such as Sir Edward Grey and Lloyd George himself, as well as a subsequent meeting with Andrew Bonar Law, the Unionist leader, were also without positive outcomes. The leading politicians continued to reject overtures to them.

The exception to this was the leadership of the Labour Party, with whom Millicent had become closer, following the decision described in the previous chapter to support Labour candidates at by-elections. Some Liberals did lose their seats to Conservative candidates when Labour candidates stood too, although it is difficult to estimate whether the NUWSS's support made much difference. The next general election was not to take place until 1915 and it is hard to predict whether Millicent would have successfully proposed that the NUWSS should back Labour. Because of the war, the election never took place anyway. During the two years leading up to the war, Labour figures endorsed what they called the 'women's agitation' for getting onto the political agenda not just votes for women but the wider question of the franchise for men too.

Violence by the militants and disturbances at their meetings led the police to discourage open-air meetings. Nevertheless, the NUWSS continued to hold them and Millicent spoke regularly at venues such as Hyde Park. She stood on the back of a cart determined to defend free speech and the right to appeal for justice for women. Without the microphones available today for outside speaking, she struggled to make herself heard in the open air but persevered in speaking at these events. She never wavered in her criticism of the suffragettes' tactics. Sensationalism offended her; she thought it damaged the cause greatly and that protest should abide by the law. Nevertheless, she never wavered either from saying that the blame for violence lay as much with the government as with the militants. The remedy was to do what women deserved and respect their rights as citizens by giving them the vote. She was also acutely aware of the sacrifices of the suffragettes given the harsh coercion they suffered at the hands of the government. She privately admired Emily Wilding Davison, who, at the 1913 Derby, ran out onto the track during the race and grabbed the reins of the King's horse and as a result died. Millicent refused to join in the public criticism of Davison by many law-abiding suffragists.

The campaign for women's suffrage was not confined to Britain. Women clamoured for the vote in many European countries and in the United States and Canada. The first countries to enfranchise women were New Zealand in 1893 and Australia in 1902, followed by the Scandinavian countries of Finland in 1906, Norway in 1913 and Denmark in 1915. During the 1899 International Congress of Women meeting in London, which was devoted to improving the position of women in a variety of areas, Millicent chaired a meeting focusing on international women's suffrage. Three years later in 1902, the International Women's Suffrage Alliance (IWSA), a new organisation dedicated to the subject, was founded and had its first meeting in the United States' capital. This was followed by a meeting in Berlin, which Millicent did not attend, although her presence would have been entirely appropriate as she had been reaching out to female campaigners round the world for many years. She was convinced that women from different countries should support each other across country boundaries, at first informally and subsequently in an international movement. At the Berlin meeting, she was made vice-president. Meetings then took place every two years: in Copenhagen; in Amsterdam; then, at Millicent's invitation, in London in 1909, where she was involved in organising the event and obtaining good press coverage of it. Her patriotic nationalism did not preclude an internationalist perspective, which she believed would benefit the English movement just as much as the global one. From small beginnings with just six delegates attending the first meeting in Washington DC, by the time of the Budapest meeting in 1913, there were twenty-nine delegations. By then, London had become its headquarters, where a monthly paper was produced reporting on international developments. Millicent also established close, long-term friendships with leaders from other countries, of whom Susan B. Anthony from the United States was the closest.

In spite of frequent invitations, Millicent never visited North America. The reasons for this are not clear. It seems unlikely that her severe seasickness alone could have been the cause, since she overcame it to go to South Africa on more than one occasion, as well as to Palestine and Ceylon much later in her life. She certainly cared about what she called 'the uplifting of our entire sex all over the world'. The invitations to the United States came over a 25-year period and included offers to pay all her expenses but still she turned them down. One American feminist, perhaps a little unfairly, alleged that Millicent thought the United States was 'on some other planet'. In contrast, Emmeline Pankhurst embarked on several lecture tours to the United States and Canada and spoke in many locations to huge audiences of up to as many as 3,000 people. Always short of money, unlike the comfortably off Millicent, Emmeline used the tours not just to inspire her audiences to join the fight, which she did with great success – they were mesmerised by her – but also to earn quite large sums of money to take home. Had Millicent ventured across the Atlantic to undertake a speaking tour, it seems likely that she too would have attracted large audiences, although without Emmeline's powers of oratory, she is unlikely to have matched the extraordinary impact Emmeline had as she travelled from city to city across the United States.

Emmeline shared Millicent's views on the importance of international links. The WSPU, probably at her instigation, applied to be a member of the IWSA in 1906, although this was opposed by Millicent and was turned down anyway as the policy of the IWSA was to permit only one organisation per country to play a part in its meetings. Thus, members of the WSPU could only be admitted as 'fraternal delegates'. Since Emmeline believed strongly in international links and that the fight was not just for women in Britain but for 'the womankind of the world', she was determined to get into the act during the IWSA conference in London in 1909. She also wanted to convince the international delegates of the need for militancy. The clever idea she came up with was to invite them to take part in an event at the Albert Hall to celebrate the release of suffragettes from prison. One by one, as an acknowledgement of their self-sacrifice, they were presented with a Holloway brooch and an illuminated scroll signed by Emmeline who, along with Christabel, spoke powerfully on the need for militancy. Whether the event persuaded many of the audience members to back it is questionable, if the views of one of the Americans were widely held. According to June Purvis, this overseas participant ridiculed the seemingly manufactured 'here, heres' and 'shame, shames' shouted out as approving or disapproving responses to the speeches, claiming 'it is a ridiculous way ... Everybody who at first thought they like the work of the suffragettes changed their opinion after that evening ... They do no end of harm by the way they act and go about in their noisy ways.' Emmeline's magic did not work on everyone.

She did, however, convince Elizabeth Garrett Anderson, who supported the WSPU in the early years of the militants' campaign. Families were split on which route to follow in the fight for women's suffrage – for example, Lady Constance Lytton was a militant suffragette, who was sent to prison, while her brother Lord Lytton was one of the organisers of the Conciliation Bills and was strongly opposed to violence, fearing its negative effect on parliamentary opinion. The Garrett family was far from unique. In spite of her sister Millicent's reluctance to endorse WSPU actions, Elizabeth took part in one of their early lawbreaking demonstrations in Parliament. When Millicent learnt that her sister, by then aged seventy, was going to the House of Commons to demonstrate, she became worried about her safety. This led to one of Millicent's best-connected colleagues informing the Home Secretary who made it clear that Elizabeth would not be arrested. Millicent was relieved but saw it as a further demonstration of the unequal treatment dished out to the privileged and well-connected compared with working-class women as happened in the way suffragettes were treated in prison. Millicent was deeply offended by the injustice of these disparities.

Parting company with Elizabeth was painful for Millicent and, in late 1911, she wrote to her sister, whom she had always admired and respected, to tell her of her wish to disown the WSPU. In her letter she said, 'I hope we shan't drift apart over this, but I think the chances of this misfortune (which would be very great to me) are less likely if we are quite frank with one another.' Elizabeth replied the next day, 'Dearest Milly, I am quite with you about the WSPU, I think they are quite wrong.' She continued that she had already written to Christabel Pankhurst saying she wished to cut her ties with the WSPU but had received no reply.

In earlier years, Elizabeth had probably been influenced by her much-loved daughter Louisa, a practising doctor, who was a committed militant and was imprisoned for a short time in Holloway in 1912. At this time, Elizabeth had some correspondence with Millicent about her daughter, telling her that Louisa had managed to send her a couple of notes from prison in which she did not grumble or complain about her treatment and said that it was great to have twelve hours in bed! Elizabeth also expressed the hope that she would take her punishment wisely and that the enforced solitude will help her to 'see more in focus than she always does'. The sentiment behind Elizabeth's maternal judgement is explained in another letter to Millicent three days later, where she pointed out, 'I don't think Louie [as she was known in the family] has the least insight into the feeling of the general public and of their wrath.' At the same time, Elizabeth stated that it would have been better not to sentence those convicted to terms in prison but instead to issue large fines. This was a naïve proposal, since the suffragettes' usual policy was not to pay fines and to accept that imprisonment would follow. Moreover, Louisa, who was strong-willed and resilient like her mother, was more likely to respond to imprisonment with a determination to continue violent resistance than to change her mind. But at least, as this correspondence shows, Millicent and Elizabeth were reunited, which meant a great deal to both of them.

I started this chapter by describing some of the similarities between Emmeline Pankhurst and Millicent Garrett Fawcett, which have not often been acknowledged. Of course, there were substantial differences too. Millicent invested a great deal of effort into writing, whereas Emmeline had difficulty in using a pen to promote her cause beyond letter-writing to friends. In contrast, during her lifetime, Millicent wrote a dozen books, a number of which I have referred to earlier, around twenty pamphlets, some of which were reproductions of her speeches, and well over a hundred articles for magazines and newspapers, as well as many letters for publication. It was a prodigious output, which would have required self-discipline and determination to complete. Indeed, she made by far the greatest contribution to written propaganda for the cause. A different kind of self-discipline and determination were needed from Emmeline to take on several energy-sapping lecture tours in North America, in which she travelled thousands of miles to make rousing speeches and having to relate to different hosts in each city she visited. I once gave twenty-five talks in twenty-one days, all over New Zealand, a relatively small country, and was exhausted by the end of it. How did Emmeline do it? Both women travelled all over Britain to speak, although Emmeline's speaking programme, including all the by-elections she covered, was probably more demanding than Millicent's. Moreover, she lived out of a suitcase for some years without a home of her own to which she could return.

Millicent had the great advantage of returning to 2 Gower Street, the home she loved for more than forty years, and where she could enjoy the quiet companionship of her sister Agnes and her daughter Philippa.

Emmeline went to prison on eleven separate occasions, although always for a short time as hunger strikes forced the prison authorities to release her. The only time they tried to force-feed her, she resisted so fiercely they gave up and never tried again. Nevertheless, her health was damaged and, in this sense, her sacrifice was greater than Millicent's.

However, the number of years Millicent devoted to the cause of votes for women was much greater than in Emmeline's case. She spent nearly fifty-five years involved in the campaign compared to Emmeline's eleven, admittedly more intense, years of campaigning.

Much of what I have said so far dwells on their similarities, nevertheless there were notable and obvious differences between them in their tactics. Emmeline's approach was characterised by dramatic and impetuous onslaughts on conventional rules about how to behave in pursuing a political goal. She was impervious to acquiring notoriety through breaking the law. Indeed, she welcomed notoriety as a valuable route to publicising her cause. When she spoke, it was to the heart. In contrast, Millicent was cautious, rational and rigorous in assembling evidence, and when she spoke, she appealed as much to the head as to the heart.

The onset in 1914 of what was known at the time as the Great War was to unite the two female leaders of the movement to acquire votes for women in a decision to suspend the campaign. In the next chapter, I will describe how this happened and the impact it had on their supporters, as well as how Millicent Garrett Fawcett and Emmeline Pankhurst contributed to the war effort.

10

THE FIRST WORLD WAR AND VOTES FOR WOMEN AT LAST

On the evening of 4 August 1914, Great Britain entered the war, which had just started between Germany and Austria–Hungary on one side, and France and Russia on the other. Britain's entry was triggered by Germany's invasion of neutral Belgium, from which the German Army swiftly moved into France, with whom Britain was allied. In London, as the prospect of war seemed increasingly likely, Millicent followed events closely and with growing trepidation. On 4 August, she walked from a meeting in the Strand and then down Whitehall to Parliament Square where many people had gathered waiting for news from the House of Commons. The decision to declare war was announced and Millicent trudged slowly back to 2 Gower Street on foot, worrying about what was to come.

In the days leading up to Britain's entry into the war, the NUWSS executive committee met, spending the whole of 2 and 3 August trying to decide what to do. Millicent herself thought that the war was inevitable and that decisions needed to be taken about how to consult the 500 societies on the actions the NUWSS should take.

The committee agreed that suffrage work should be suspended in the national emergency entailed in Britain's participation in the war. However, decisions were needed on what to do about the NU-WSS's organisation, including its paid staff and its friends. How, if at all, could the organisation be used to support the nation's war effort? The decision to stop 'political propaganda' was conveyed by post to the NUWSS societies and, at the same time, they were consulted about what role they could play in the national emergency. The executive met again on 6 August. The replies they had received by then supported their decision and agreed that the organisation should be used to undertake war work.

Before that, on 4 August, Millicent represented the NUWSS at a women's meeting in London called by various bodies representing women in the labour movement to discuss the threat of war. Representatives of the International Women's Suffrage Alliance, who happened to be in London, also took part. The intention of many who attended was to plead for peace and to call statesmen 'to leave untried no method of conciliation and arbitration', and many of the speakers made passionate protests against war. Millicent, who was presiding, told them it was too late to call for peace, although she sympathised with their horror of war. She said, 'We who are voteless are not responsible for the complicated series of political events which have led up to war, we could neither permit it nor prevent it.' Indeed, she said, 'War was insensate devilry ... The highest and most precious of national and international aspirations and hopes will have to be set aside, but we as citizens have our duty to perform.' The strength of feeling at this meeting about the over-riding need for peace anticipated what happened in the women's movement during 1915.

Meanwhile, Millicent continued to secure the support she

needed in the NUWSS to end political campaigning and instead resorted to mobilising women to undertake new roles to help the war effort. Emmeline Pankhurst, who was a Francophile and a long-standing critic of Germany, was in St Malo, Brittany, when Germany declared war against France. Almost immediately, she decided militant campaigning should end during the crisis. When Britain declared war on Germany, the WSPU announced a truce in their campaign against the government. The government then declared the unconditional release of the suffragettes who were in jail and Emmeline and Christabel were free to return to England without the threat of being imprisoned. Emmeline was even fiercer than Millicent in speaking out on the righteousness of the war and campaigned for rapid action to mobilise women, especially to fill the vacancies created by men joining up.

The more formal structure of the NUWSS compared to the WSPU made it a rather better vehicle for organising war work. It kept in post all its staff and organisers round the country, and in David Rubinstein's words, Millicent was 'the standard bearer' in promoting relief work. The message she sent out on the outbreak of war was 'women, your country needs you … Let us show ourselves worthy of citizenship whether our claim to it be recognised or not.' The response to this call for action was rapid. One of the first tasks was to find work for unemployed women, whose numbers initially increased after war was declared. Workshops were opened and training was provided, notably in basic engineering skills since women were needed to work in munitions factories. Day nurseries were opened to help care for children. Hospitality centres for Belgian refugees were set up. Services for military camps were provided, such as canteens and rest rooms for soldiers in training. Efforts were also made to prevent young girls from hanging around outside the camps, with a system of female patrols, in a context where there were calls for the Contagious Diseases Acts to be reintroduced. Some forty-five NUWSS societies became Red Cross Centres, and the care of pregnant women and babies was supported by the creation of clinics.

One request made to the NUWSS was firmly turned down by Millicent. She believed the promotion of military recruitment should not be a role it should accept; 'it was not its function to lecture men on their duty but to encourage women to do theirs.' In contrast, the Pankhursts did exhort men to join up until conscription was eventually introduced in 1916. Millicent also argued that female doctors and nurses should stay at home caring for the medical needs of the civilian population rather than going to war. It did not take her long to retract this advice. Indeed, in her memoirs, she wrote about the work of Dr Elsie Inglis of the Edinburgh Society, praising her for founding hospital units entirely staffed by women who were sent to the front to treat soldiers in France as well as in Serbia. Millicent describes Dr Inglis's experience when she offered her help to the head of the Royal Army Medical Department in Scotland, who told her, 'Dear lady, go home and keep quiet.' Millicent's niece Louisa Garrett Anderson, a surgeon, and Dr Flora Murray were also rebuffed at first when they offered to take staff and equipment to set up a hospital as near the front as possible. Both they and Dr Inglis resorted to working with the French Red Cross until the British military authorities changed their minds. Later in the war, at the invitation of the War Office, Louisa Garrett Anderson and Flora Murray took over the Endell Street Military Hospital, which was housed in an old workhouse in Covent Garden. It was entirely staffed by women who treated severely injured soldiers brought back from the front. A recently published book describes the life-saving surgery they undertook, as well as the soldiers' recognition of the skills of these female doctors and their gratitude for the care they received from them and the nurses. Millicent was justifiably proud of Louisa for continuing the Garrett family's pioneering tradition.

During the early months of the war, Millicent's patriotism, which she had exhibited in the Boer War too, motivated her to undertake non-stop work to encourage as many women as possible to work for victory, although she never doubted that Prussian militarism, as she described it, would be defeated eventually. At the same time, she denounced crude forms of promoting patriotism by, for example, lurid press reports about German atrocities. She protested that 'it is surely no part of patriotism to stir up by speech or writing un-governable rage and fury against the whole German people'. She also greatly disliked the white feather movement, where unenlisted men, considered to be cowards, were presented with white feathers. She wrote to the *Manchester Guardian* that 'I do not think it is the function of men and women to lecture each other on the special duties of the opposite sex.' She also recognised the enormous sac-rifice and suffering of men in military conflicts, where inevitably death and destruction were central to their experience, whereas women were fortunate in their role 'to serve the state by saving life rather than destroying it'.

As it became increasingly obvious that early hopes for a short war were to be dashed and that the conflict was likely to continue for months if not years, dissent began to develop within the NUWSS executive. Many of Millicent's key colleagues with whom she had worked closely in pursuit of the franchise did not share her patriotic views on the war. While the goal of achieving votes for women was put on hold, feminist pacifism replaced it amongst the membership of the executive. Late in 1914, a dispute about whether to hold a congress of the IWSA triggered a deeper split amongst the leadership of the NUWSS. A proposal was made by the Dutch women's suffrage leader to hold an international congress in a neutral country during 1915. Millicent was adamantly opposed on the grounds that a peace congress involving female representatives of the belligerent countries could lead to strong disagreements amongst them and was therefore wholly inappropriate in a wartime context. She went over the heads of her executive, many of whom did not share her views, and approached Carrie Chapman Catt, President of the IWSA, who was American, to express her strong opposition, telling her that if it went ahead, she would refuse to attend and might even resign her position as first vice-president of the alliance. In the end, it did not take place, but Millicent had offended her executive, most of whom supported the congress as a means for women from different countries to come together to discuss peace.

At the NUWSS council in February, there was fractious debate and a range of resolutions, many in conflict with each other. A number of speakers opposed Millicent's patriotic position, arguing instead that the union should not engage in activities which might promote the continuation of the war. Rather, they should accept that peace was in the interest of the nation and promote debate about the ethics of war and how to work for a peaceful settlement. Others wanted an expression of international goodwill between women of all nations and education on the causes of war with a view to preventing them in future. On the other side, the endorsement of work to sustain the nation in the absence of suffrage campaigning was expressed, with admiration of the heroism of those serving the country in defence of the nation. What all this demonstrated was that once the unifying cause of fighting for votes for women was put on the back burner, fundamental disagreement about how to fill the gap had emerged.

Millicent was not in the chair, but there is little evidence to suggest she would have used the skills she had so often demonstrated in the past to bring members back to some resolution of their differences or at least to identify areas where they could agree and move on. On the contrary, in her presidential address to the council, she had already hammered home her strong message with no attempt to find ways of nuancing it. 'I am heart and soul for the cause of Great Britain in this war,' she said, claiming that if Prussian militarism was victorious, it would be a blow to women's suffrage. Moreover, in a speech at the council, she discussed the resolutions which promoted a pacifist approach claiming that it was a national duty to remove German troops from France and Belgium. She asserted that 'until that is done, it is akin to treason to talk of peace'. Her inability to compromise in any way was a failure of leadership and led to the resignation of half of her executive. The split was irrevocable, and she lost some of her most dedicated, intelligent and committed colleagues. All the officers left with the exception of the treasurer. Undoubtedly, Millicent was deeply wounded. She had been used to winning people round and, on this occasion, had failed, partly because she had not tried hard enough.

Nevertheless, many of the ordinary members of the NUWSS stuck by her, as she reflected the predominantly pro-war views of the population. The pro-peace group was perhaps over-idealistic without any plan on how to pursue peace. Others, who had some sympathy with the call for peace, did not believe the NUWSS was the right vehicle for pursuing it. There was a danger that pursuing peace might damage the cause of female suffrage in the longer term, since it was out of kilter with popular sentiment and, however unfairly, the union might be perceived to be pro-German. Indeed, there were articles in the press later describing those who had resigned as German sympathisers, which Millicent and others forcibly repudiated. Yet for some of the women involved, their pacifism overrode their feminism.

Later, Millicent was to describe the rift in the NUWSS as the worst experience of her life. Yet as so often, she had the resilience to overcome the loss of close colleagues, whom she liked and respected. Soon after their departure, a special council was held in June 1915 before which there had been a rejection anyway by the IWSA of the proposal for an international congress on peace. Millicent certainly still had the support of members, who had accepted her patriotic appeals to undertake war work, and she received an ovation. None of the executive who had resigned decided to stand again and new candidates came forward and were elected. One of them was Ray Strachey, later to be Millicent's biographer. Those who had left were thanked for their service to the NUWSS, but Millicent continued to feel bitter and could never bring herself to forgive several of them. In other cases, she buried the hatchet and saw them on friendly terms, even nominating one of them to speak at the NUWSS victory rally in 1918.

Once the NUWSS was back on an even keel, Millicent was able to focus much of her attention on the employment of women to fill the vacancies left by men at the front. The huge number of men who had enlisted was further increased when conscription was introduced. Millicent's old Liberal views about freedom of the individual made her a little hesitant about endorsing conscription, but she backed it as a necessity to maximise the number of fighting men whom she thought were needed to secure victory. She also refused to sign a petition against the imprisonment of conscientious objectors. She wrote:

No State could carry on especially in the crisis of a world war like this, if men were allowed to be the judges in their own case and defy on their own responsibility the law of the land. Every Government must under circumstances such as the present consider the effect not only on the little handful of conscientious objectors at present defying the law, but on the great body of men throughout the country to whom for various reasons the giving of personal military service is irksome and repugnant to the last degree.

Although Millicent had no sons, she had many nephews and younger cousins who lost their lives or were badly injured during the course of the war. As many as twenty-nine members of her extended family were killed, including one of her sister Alice's sons; her brother Sam's son Henry Fawcett Garrett, who was her godson and named after her husband; and one of her elder sister Louie's sons. She grieved over these young men's deaths, and the sacrifices they and others made probably influenced her views about 'the sacrifice which the conscientious objectors decline to share'.

To replace the huge numbers of men who were no longer in the existing workforce was an enormous task, but Millicent was confident that women could take on many jobs which would have been seen as inappropriate for them before the war, a point of view supported by both employers and the trade unions. In the early months of the war, she began a series of articles exhorting women to enlist, which she continued throughout the course of the conflict. The need to increase the output of the armament factories was paramount, but many other sections of industry needed workers. In March 1915, the government issued a circular announcing a new Register of Women for War Service. Its aim was to build the recruitment of women on a large scale to work not just in manufacturing but also in other sectors such as transport, the civil service and local government. Women responded with, in Millicent's words, 'magnificent adaptability' and 'industrial efficiency' and she was convinced that the output of female industrial workers was often higher than that of skilled men, although it is not clear on what evidence she based this claim. But perhaps it was the sort of propaganda women needed if they were not to be taken for granted.

The extent of women's mobilisation is borne out by the statistics. In industry as a whole, the total employment of women and girls increased by about 800,000 from 2,179,000 to 2,971,000. Transport saw the greatest proportionate increase in women's employment from 18,000 in 1914 to 117,000 in 1917. In the now vanished occupation of bus conductor, there were 2,500 women, many of whom were recruited from domestic service. The number of women working in munitions increased from 212,000 in 1914 to 819,000 in 1917. Woolwich Arsenal, the largest armament factory, employed 25,000 women by 1918.

One of Millicent's concerns was that women were not being paid enough for their patriotic work. She wanted women to be paid the same wages as men for the same work. This was in contrast to the position she had taken twenty-five years earlier, when she believed that demands for equal pay would have the effect of reducing job opportunities for women and that actually to be employed was of paramount importance. The circumstances of war allowed her to drop this somewhat defeatist line. The need for women in the labour force was such that, in principle, equal pay was more attainable than ever before. In securing recognition of women's contribution to the war effort, which went way beyond knitting and nursing, Millicent was trying to establish a cultural change where the range of jobs thought possible for women would continue to be much wider once the war ended. She did not want them to be excluded from skilled work in the future and she railed against the injustice of refusing to embrace equal pay then. She was highly critical of the government for excluding women from the higher grades of the civil service and deplored their poor representation in the commercial world. Sadly, it was to be many years before her views about women in economic life were to be widely accepted. The Great War did not bring an end to prejudice against women in employment, although it gave credence to the view that women were capable of doing many different jobs.

One area of suffrage activities which continued to occupy Millicent during the war was international work. Her main purpose as the first Vice-President of the IWSA was to keep the alliance alive, which had the support of most British suffragists, but also to ensure that it did not become dominated by pacifists promoting peace. Having successfully fought to prevent the Hague congress, mentioned earlier, from taking place, she was determined to stop the IWSA from using its organisational structure to propagate a debate about peace, mainly through articles in its journal. In this, she was supported by the French vice-president, who shared her opposition to articles emanating from the IWSA which could be perceived as pacifist propaganda. The IWSA's American president was justifiably annoyed that she had not been properly consulted before correspondence discussing the merits or otherwise of the journal debating war and peace was published. She herself was sympathetic to discussion of peace, as were one or two other vice-presidents, but they gave way in the interest of keeping the IWSA unified. Millicent skilfully patched up her disagreement with the president, but the story demonstrates her somewhat narrow-minded patriotism and her willingness to sacrifice free speech in her pursuit of it. Behind it lay her fear that a German victory would lead to the loss of any chance of female enfranchisement, but this does not excuse her high-handedness.

When the war broke out, Millicent was deeply depressed about its likely impact on votes for women, worrying that their introduction could be delayed by many years. By the second half of the war, despite the misery caused by carnage at the front, her depression lifted and she became more optimistic. She started to increase her political work to keep reminding her readers or her audiences that any Reform Bill that might be introduced should include women. She took a deputation to Conservative leaders in London and toured the country visiting local groups giving them an optimistic message about the likelihood at last of a successful Franchise Bill. She believed that the role women had played in supporting the war effort would be crucial in any new debates about their political status as voters.

Millicent was buoyed by a change in coverage of the movement in the press. Even *The Times*, which had been an inveterate enemy of the suffrage cause, began to support it. In line with newspaper coverage, public opinion was shifting too. It was also apparent that before the war ended, a Reform Bill would be needed to ensure that returning troops would be able to vote. A new electoral register was required as many men in the armed forces had been disenfranchised as a result of the requirement that occupiers had lived for a minimum of twelve months at the same address preceding the register. Such a Bill provided an opportunity for women to be included as voters too.

The creation of a coalition government in 1915 was a further boost to Millicent's morale. A number of old anti-suffragists were removed from the Cabinet and replaced by pro-suffragists, such as the Conservative peer Lord Robert Cecil, the Labour MP Arthur Henderson and Sir John Simon, who was to be Home Secretary. Millicent knew them all well, as friends and supporters. Asquith remained Prime Minister and Millicent decided she should write to him in May 1916, making the case for the inclusion of women if, and when, a Reform Bill was introduced. He replied that at the time, no such legislation was being contemplated, but if it were, her letter would 'be fully and impartially weighed'. In fact, it was very soon being contemplated in Parliament and was the subject of questions and debate, but Asquith was playing for time and proposing simply tinkering with the register rather than going for a wholesale change in the franchise, which would allow all men returning from military service to vote. However, he was soon persuaded that large-scale franchise reform was needed and even admitted in the House of Commons that he had changed his mind about including women, at least in part because of their war service.

By the end of 1916, Asquith had been replaced as Prime Minister by Lloyd George. Millicent was delighted. Her old enemy, who had caused her so much anger and such distress over the years, had been ousted and replaced by a man with more progressive views about emancipating women. Before Asquith's resignation, a momentous decision was taken by the government to set up a Speaker's Conference to consider the contents of a Reform Bill. The cross-party committee undertook this task in late 1916 and reported in January 1917. The report unanimously recommended adult male suffrage for all men over twenty-one and also included a proposal, supported by the majority, to give the vote to women who were over the age of thirty or thirty-five and either householders or the wives of householders.

Millicent had been extraordinarily consistent in her views on the subject for most of the fifty years she had been campaigning for women's votes. It was better to move step by step than to ask for too much and lose everything. The verdict of the Speaker's Conference fell short of equality between men and women; it aimed at an electorate in which the proportion of women to men would be approximately two to three. If its proposals were adopted by Parliament, it would produce a far greater addition to the electorate than any previous change to the franchise. Had women been given the vote on the same terms as men, there would have been more female voters than male voters in the demographic circumstances at the time when as many as 880,000 men had lost their lives on the battlefield. Some supporters of the suffragist cause, including members of the Speaker's Conference Committee, worried that this could jeopardise reform, leading cautious Members of Parliament to vote against it. Nevertheless, Millicent was all too well aware of how many NUWSS members by now favoured equal adult suffrage. As ever, she was committed to proper consultation within the movement and was aware of the need for unity if the proposals were to be accepted in Parliament. At times like this, she led from the front and although admitting that the proposals did not go as far as she would have liked, she noted that compromise was necessary. She won over the NUWSS executive when she spoke to the motion to support the Speaker's Conference proposals. Emmeline Pankhurst also favoured accepting them as the best that could be expected in the context of war.

With the movement behind her, Millicent turned next to the task of making sure that Parliament would vote for the proposals. Her past experience of being let down by parliamentary indifference leading to inaction was such that she was determined to lobby as many MPs as possible. First, she wrote to the Prime Minister. She asked him to receive a deputation of women to enable them to put the case to him in person for the inclusion of women in the forthcoming Bill. She flattered him by telling him that 'we know you are our friend, as no previous Prime Minister has been' and that he understood how, during the war, 'the suffragists had considered the claims of their country before their own immediate demands'. Lloyd George agreed to meet Millicent and the large representative group she led. Just before the scheduled day, 10 Downing Street told the NUWSS secretary, Ray Strachey, that Emmeline Pankhurst could attend too. This was badly received by the constitutional suffragists. What transpired was that Ray Strachey went to Emmeline to tell her that she could attend but not be formally part of the delegation. This reaction was petty but indicates the distrust of the past militant leader still felt by those who had opposed lawbreaking and violence. Surprisingly, Emmeline accepted the restriction imposed on her and turned up and spoke compellingly about the need for speedy action in passing the new legislation without dispute and differences of opinion, telling Lloyd George, 'Whatever you think can be passed ... we are ready to accept.' Moreover, after the meeting with Lloyd George, Emmeline told audiences that she accepted the legislative proposals and that in spite of their limitations, it was right to compromise, referring to the recognition women now had of the contribution they had made to the war, thereby deserving the right of citizenship. By then, the views of Millicent and Emmeline were more or less identical, although their tactics varied somewhat.

Lloyd George was already won over before receiving the deputation, telling it that a Bill had already been drafted including votes for women. However, he did not commit the government on women's suffrage, saying it was a matter for the House, although he claimed most members of the government would vote for it. Whereas Emmeline followed up with moving speeches saying that victory was nigh, Millicent devoted much of her time to lobbying as many MPs individually as she could, starting with ministers. As usual, she deployed the quiet reasoning that marked her style, although when faced with doubters, she reminded them that if women were failed again, a return to militancy might happen after the war ended. She also insisted that the age of thirty, not thirty-five, should be adopted. When meeting her supporters in Parliament, she sought their advice about tactics. The Labour Party had decided to support the recommendations of the Speaker's Conference even though equal adult suffrage, which they favoured, had not been proposed. Millicent assured them that she thought what was being proposed was only a first instalment and that in future the suffragists would campaign for a democratic extension of the vote so that women would be treated equally with men. She was convincing, but in any case, most Labour MPs realised that to pursue equal adult suffrage in 1917 would be doomed to failure.

The only rally of any size held before the key votes on the Bill in the Commons was held in the Queen's Hall in London in the late spring of 1917. This was partly to placate Lord Northcliffe, an anti-suffragist, who was under the delusion that there was no widespread public clamour for women's suffrage, which needled Millicent. The rally took the form of a war workers' demonstration. A wide range of occupations were represented, from lamp lighters, bus conductors and railway engine cleaners to chemists, bacteriologists and factory workers – all of whom demanded the vote. Millicent also undertook a speaking tour round the country, travelling to the Midlands and the north, but it was disrupted when she succumbed to bronchitis and had to go home to bed. She wrote to a friend saying, 'I never had a week in bed before, since Philippa was born,' but at least it gave her more time for reading than was usual, she said.

By the time the Bill was introduced in the Commons, Millicent was confident that it would succeed, but she wanted the size of the majority to be as large as possible to help its progress through the House of Lords, whose leader, Lord Curzon, was an arch-reactionary on this as on so many other matters. As she had done many times before, Millicent followed the second reading debate in the Commons. She was pleased that all three party leaders' speeches were supportive and that even Asquith had, as she put it, confessed his errors, saying that some of his friends might think that his 'eyes, which for years in this matter have been clouded by fallacies, and sealed by illusions, at last have been opened to the truth'. This was a resounding, if flowery, confession from the old enemy. The second reading was carried by a massive majority of 359 to forty, a hugely gratifying result for Millicent. What mattered just as much to her was the outcome of the debate on the clause to include women. She sat in the Speaker's Gallery looking down on the benches below on a very hot day, and by the early evening, the air was stifling. She listened attentively to all the old arguments: there was little new in what was said on either side, yet the atmosphere was quite different without the sneering or vitriol that occurred during debates in the past and instead there was much warm approval of the clause.

When it came to the vote, there was a majority of seven to one for the inclusion of women's suffrage in the Representation of the People Bill.

Although victory seemed almost certain, there was one more barrier to be surmounted: the House of Lords. No Bill could be enacted before going through both Houses. Cautious as ever, Millicent decided there should be no celebrations until that had taken place. What she could not prevent was the celebration by her friends and supporters of her seventieth birthday. A special public number of their paper was produced and letters of congratulation and banks of flowers were sent to 2 Gower Street. She looked considerably younger than she was and had seemingly undiminished energy. Some of her energy was applied to securing a further amendment to the Reform Bill in the Commons to extend the rights of women to vote in local elections. She worked with the Labour Party to try to change the law, so that in local elections, not only the women who were already on the register but the wives of men who were on it could also vote, applying the same principle as had already been agreed in the Bill for parliamentary elections. She went on a deputation to the Home Secretary, and she promoted a mass lobby round the country by NUWSS members. Snowed under by letters demanding that the same principle should be applied locally as nationally, the President of the Local Government Board conceded.

After this victory, Millicent turned her attention to the House of Lords. In her memoirs, she listed the important peers who were friends of the movement for women's suffrage, including, she claimed, the Archbishops of Canterbury and York and most of the bishops too. The debate on the key clause lasted over two days. She sat throughout, squashed in a small space close to the bar allocated for visitors and found herself sitting next to her old adversary, Mary Ward. There were plenty of speeches from reactionary peers to keep Mary happy. Millicent sat through them all listening, as she had in the Commons, to the same old arguments being trotted out again with elderly men solemnly declaring that the right place for women was the home and that women were politically untrustworthy, but she was cheered by the speeches made with passionate conviction by friends of the movement such as Lord Selborne. When Lord Curzon, the Leader of the House and Millicent's most powerful adversary, rose to speak, she was unsurprised by his claim that women's suffrage would be a disaster and would ruin the country, but this hyperbole was followed by his admission that it was inevitable. As I have so often heard decades later in the House of Lords, Curzon had to admit that the size of the majority in the House of Commons was so large in favour of the clause that it would be inadvisable to vote against it. To do so would discredit the Lords and lead to a struggle between the two Houses if the Lords overturned it; therefore, Curzon would abstain. He said it was the best he could do and advised others who shared his opposition to the clause to do the same. One hundred and thirty-four peers voted for the clause to include women, and seventy-one voted against it.

Mary Ward, who during the debate had asked Millicent if she would join in an 'agitation' for a referendum on votes for women, went home angry and disillusioned by her former comrade Curzon. Millicent went home triumphant and happy. Although she had dismissively told Mary there were no circumstances that would lead her to support a referendum and lectured her on the fallibility of referenda as a means of decision-making, Millicent claimed that she could not help feeling sorry for the dejected Mary, whom she still believed honourable if delusional. Perhaps it was easy to be magnanimous in the circumstances, but it showed that Millicent was capable of sympathy towards opponents who had lost.

After congratulations by friendly peers and MPs when she left the chamber as well as by suffragists waiting outside, Millicent went back to 2 Gower Street to face demands for interviews from journalists. Her main message to them was that the fifty years of campaigning had consisted mainly of 'ups' rather than 'downs'. In an article she wrote, she said she

> sometimes compared it, in its slowness, to the movement of a glacier; but like a glacier it was ceaseless and irresistible. It always moved in the direction of the removal of the statutory and social disabilities of women. It established their individual liberty and freedom; they were in fact gradually passing from subjection to independence.

That Millicent managed to remain positive and optimistic and that she loved her work was a key to her success in the end.

Returning to the Lords to witness the short ceremony when the Bill was enacted, she described it as 'a gorgeous ceremony'. Her dream had come true and she needed to turn her attention to the clamour about how to celebrate it. The suffrage societies pressed for a large meeting, over which Millicent was asked to preside. It took place in London in March 1918 at the Queen's Hall, and the speakers included three politicians – one Labour and two Liberals – as well as Maude Royden, one of the pacifists who had disagreed with Millicent earlier and left the NUWSS executive. Millicent recognised the role of the war in achieving votes for women and underlined the need for consensus, saying:

We do not triumph over our opponents; it is much better than that. We did not threaten them; it is better than that. But the great searchlight of war showed things in their true light and they gave us our enfranchisement with open hands ... [which] will contribute to the true and permanent welfare of the country.

As well as rousing speeches, it had been agreed that great music should be played as the best way of celebrating. Millicent asked for Beethoven's 'Leonore Overture No. III', an ode to freedom and the power of love; she had wanted the last movement of Beethoven's 'Fifth Symphony' too, which in the end was not included. The London Symphony Orchestra played and Agnes's old friend Sir Hubert Parry conducted. For many years, William Blake's poem 'Jerusalem' had been used as their suffrage hymn but without any music. By then, Parry had agreed that he would set it to music; few realise that it was possibly played for the first time to a very large audience at the suffrage victory celebration in 1918.

Although Millicent was moved by the event and considered it a success, the war had still not ended and, assuming she walked home to Gower Street, she would have found the streets were dark, and if she went out the next morning past shops, she would have seen people queuing for food. She believed her duty was to continue working to defeat the Germans, so she became involved with the recruitment of women to the armed services, which was taking place on a large scale, advising on how best to organise it. When the war ended in November 1918, Millicent's relief was combined with her nationalistic pride and love of country. The Armistice fulfilled her hope that women would be able to reap the benefit of citizenship in a free world. Yet she was fully aware that further campaigning was needed to secure the vote for those women excluded in the

1918 Representation of the People Act. Young soldiers returning from the war could vote, but young women leaving the munitions factories had to wait until they were thirty. Four general elections took place before that was rectified, the first of which was in December 1918 following the dissolution of Parliament as soon as the war ended.

For the first time, Millicent herself could go into a polling booth and put her cross next to her favoured candidate on the voting slip. When being interviewed in 1912, she said she could not be a Conservative because she was not a protectionist, she could not be a Liberal because she was not a Unionist and she could not be Labour because she was not a socialist. Now she would have to make up her mind who to back. During the latter part of the war, she had become increasingly impressed by Lloyd George. She admired his qualities as a war leader, going as far as to say that 'the PM's vigour, courage, insight and driving power have saved the country'. She even told the *Daily Chronicle*, a pro-coalition newspaper, that if she had twenty votes, she could give them all to the government. While Lloyd George's leadership might have accounted for ten of the twenty, his decision to accept the recommendations of the Speaker's Conference on Franchise Reform would have accounted for the other ten! She was always going to contrast him favourably with Gladstone and Asquith, the other Liberal leaders who were on the wrong side about votes for women; even though Sir John Simon had been one of her strong supporters during the parliamentary battles, she refused to provide him with a letter of support in the 1918 election because he was not a coalition candidate but stood as an Asquithian Liberal.

Wanting to capitalise as much as he could on his popularity with suffragists for ensuring the passing of the Representation of the

People Act, Lloyd George invited Millicent to chair a women's election rally, where she praised him lavishly. How far this contributed to women's support for the coalition is unclear, although many women did vote for it. Nevertheless, as David Rubinstein records, in a manifesto written for female electors, Millicent asked them 'to support candidates of all parties who promised equality of employment, pay, morality, education and guardianship'. This list comprised many of the issues she believed had to be addressed in the post-war years. Unfortunately, there were very few female candidates in the election and only one of them was elected, which meant there was not even a small core of female MPs to start campaigns within Parliament in the pursuit of equality issues. However, Millicent was sanguine about this. It had, perhaps surprisingly, never been part of the NUWSS campaign to fight for women to be allowed to stand in general elections. What mattered was the vote. The 1918 Representation of the People Act gave it to 8.5 million women, around 40 per cent of an electorate of 21.4 million in 1918.

Without external pressure, Parliament did legislate to entitle women to sit as members in late 1918, but it did not go through until just three weeks before the dissolution and the start of the election campaign. In these circumstances, Millicent was surprised that there were as many as seventeen female candidates. They had far too little time to organise effectively in the constituencies where they stood. Moreover, they were nearly all selected for seats where they had no hope of winning. The one candidate who did win was Constance Markievicz, but paradoxically, as a Sinn Féin candidate in Dublin, she did not take her seat. Christabel Pankhurst, the only candidate who stood for the Women's Party, came closest of the other sixteen to winning. She lost by 775 votes. Four or five long-standing suffragists stood for various parties, one of whom was actually slightly older than Millicent. One of the strongest candidates was Mary Macarthur, the pioneering women's trade unionist, who stood for Labour and was backed by Millicent. In 1919, Nancy Astor, a Conservative, was the first woman to be elected and take her seat (in a by-election). The first real inroads on the parliamentary representation of women were not made until the 1929 election, when sixty more stood and fourteen were elected.

Millicent herself had many of the qualifications needed to be a successful Member of Parliament, but by the time the opportunity was open to her, she was seventy-one and would have seen herself, and probably been seen by others, as being too old to put herself forward. She never appears to have contemplated this at any point in the early years of her campaigning. Her object was always votes for women, not a career for herself as an MP. Partly, perhaps, because she did not have much sympathy for party politics. It had taken just over fifty years since the great hero of her early life, John Stuart Mill, had written on the subjection of women and tried unsuccessfully to persuade Parliament to enfranchise them. After so many years dedicated to this cause, Millicent might have questioned whether it had all been worth it. She never did. Even when victory for her cause came, she knew it was incomplete until every woman could vote on exactly the same basis as every man. Yet she had always been confident that once the principle of women voting had been established, this would follow, so she could now relax a little more.

11

HINTERLAND

In January 1919, Millicent decided to stand down from the presidency of the NUWSS and its Executive Council at its annual meeting in March. She was over seventy, had been in the role for many years and had guided the movement through the war to the parliamentary victory described in the previous chapter. She knew this victory was not complete and that some of her colleagues would put pressure on her to start to campaign for universal suffrage for women immediately, to which she was opposed. She thought some time should be allowed to elapse and for the new Act to bed down first. Further, her view was supported by many colleagues. She thought it was time someone younger took over to lead the debates on such issues. I find it easy to sympathise with her wish to move on from sitting through long and tiring meetings with the responsibility of ensuring they reached acceptable conclusions. She also did not want to take on any more speaking tours, which required a lot of time and energy. There were plenty of other ways to spend her time which she would enjoy more, as I will describe in this chapter.

Before she bowed out of the leadership of the NUWSS, she still had another task to fulfil. She took part with other female leaders from the Allied countries in a deputation to the Versailles Peace Conference. The deputation's aim was to lobby Presidents and Prime Ministers on the appointment of an international commission of women to enquire into the condition of women and children, and the need to take into account the views of women in establishing peace. The idea for this commission came from American and French suffragists, who believed that no time had been allocated to issues of concern to women at Versailles. The lobby did not focus on suffrage questions as they might be deemed to be a domestic matter for national governments to decide. Rather surprisingly, according to Millicent's memoirs, they gained access to the most important Allied leaders starting with Woodrow Wilson, the American President, who was encouraging and told them to talk to as many leaders as they could. Millicent was particularly taken by Georges Clemenceau, the Prime Minister of France; he apparently was known as the Tiger, but she appreciated his amusing repartee, saying, 'He did not growl, he purred.' Although Clemenceau said he was interested in the subject of women's suffrage, he was perturbed by 'the dangerous power of the clergy over the minds of women' in Catholic countries.

The meetings did not achieve much for Millicent. President Wilson politely wrote to her after their meeting saying he had found his colleagues sympathetic to the causes of women's suffrage when he took it up with them in part, but he was unable to get acceptance for a Commission of Women, noting the strong opposition of India and Japan. One positive gain was secured by Robert Cecil, a British delegate, who persuaded the Versailles Peace Conference to agree that women should be eligible as delegates or officers in all the positions in the League of Nations, which later became the United Nations, and that was written into the covenant. Millicent came home from Paris convinced of the value of the League of Nations and was pleased when asked to help with setting up a British League of Nations Union and even went on a speaking tour on its behalf in 1920.

Resigning from the leadership of the NUWSS was not a prelude to retirement. It would never have occurred to her to stop working altogether. She had worked hard all her life and to be unoccupied and without new challenges would have bored her. After her election as Vice-President of the League of Nations, she was the only woman of the eight British delegates to attend a League of Nations Union conference held in Brussels late in 1919, which was a somewhat frustrating experience. She was also involved in drafting a women's manifesto in support of the league, which emphasised the need for well-informed public opinion as a force for peace, claiming that 'if women share this duty with men, they will help to create a new force in the world, which will strengthen the foundations of peace'. Given subsequent history, this was over-optimistic. Her views on the League of Nations were shaped by her lifelong patriotism and belief that a healthy nationalism was a prerequisite of a healthy internationalism but that this must be based on 'the fact of nationalism, and not the spurious, academic internationalism which produces patriots of every country but their own and decries and belittles the love which ordinary healthy human beings bear to their own land'. This is surely a narrow-minded and unfair definition of internationalism and shows how unprogressive Millicent could be when she was on her patriotic high horse.

A quite different area in which Millicent became involved was the admission of women to the legal profession from which they were barred, a practice which had always offended her greatly. Her favourite brother Sam, who earlier had been the President of the Law Society, chaired a committee on ways to remove the bar. It met in the House of Commons and Millicent joined it as a member. When the Sex Disqualification (Removal) Bill came in during 1919, it was accepted that the Bill should make it possible for women to be eligible to be solicitors, barristers, jurors and magistrates. After it became an Act, Millicent sat as a magistrate on the Holborn Bench, not far from her Gower Street home. She was one of the first group of 200 women who were appointed in the summer of 1920 and soon after chaired a conference for female magistrates, where she said she had come to learn more about the role; there does not seem to have been a properly developed system for training magistrates at the time. She found the work interesting, including cases where parents were brought to court for failing to send their children to school. Using the extra time she had by then, Millicent followed up some of the former truants, helping them to secure jobs.

At the NUWSS council meeting in 1919, she made an emotional farewell speech designed to challenge the sense of anticlimax felt by many members after their victory. A little 'over the top' and, as so often, brimming with optimism, she said the successful struggle to get the vote was 'one of the most wonderful times in the whole history of the world' and suggested that the future held 'nothing dismal [but] ... a real certainty of a greater and better time to come'. At the same meeting, a decision was made to change the organisation's name to the National Union of Societies for Equal Citizenship (NUSEC). Millicent endorsed this decision as it would better describe the new goals of the union to promote equality for women across a wide range of areas, including equal employment opportunities. She realised how much still had to be done to make improvements to women's lives. She backed the NUSEC's list of items identified in 1919 for immediate action in their campaigns: equal pay for equal work; equal moral standards in laws dealing with solicitation, prostitution and divorce; widows' pensions; the return of female candidates to Parliament; equal rights of guardianship for women as parents; and the opening of the legal profession to women (this was attained later in 1919). Lastly, at the meeting, Eleanor Rathbone was elected to replace Millicent as president.

Millicent retained her membership after relinquishing the leadership and took part on a somewhat ad hoc basis in various events to promote these goals. She remained the public face of British feminism as well as continuing to be recognised internationally as an important figure. She opposed the threatened break-up of the IWSA at the end of the war. After all, the international movement needed to be supported as there were still many countries where women were not yet enfranchised. Eventually relinquishing her formal role, Millicent still stayed in touch. An indication of her international reputation was the award of a Belgian medal, citing in particular her support for Belgium during the war. At around the same time, the University of Birmingham awarded her an honorary degree recognising her 'honourable, sane and wholesome' leadership of the women's movement! Sometime later, in the New Year honours list of 1925, Millicent was awarded the Dame Grand Cross of the Order of the British Empire (GBE). There had for some time been speculation about her being honoured, to which Millicent's reply, when questioned, was that she knew nothing about it. She was awarded the GBE along with Ellen Terry, the actress. Louisa Aldrich-Blake, the pioneering surgeon, was awarded a Dame Commander of the Order of the British Empire. In replying to the vast number of letters of congratulation Millicent received, she said it was for her suffrage work and that many others therefore shared it. There were a number of events celebrating her award, including a garden party that the NUSEC held for her at the house in Kensington where she had first attracted the attention of Henry Fawcett sixty years earlier. Anti-establishment though he was, he would have been proud of her not just for the award but for the achievements which led to it.

Having fewer committee meetings to chair and fewer lecture tours to undertake gave Millicent more time for occupations she had loved above all as a young woman: reading and writing. She read extensively throughout her life and often quoted great writers in her speeches. Many of the photographs of her, which have survived, show her reading or, if not actually reading, with a book in her hands. She established the habit early. When she returned from school, she immersed herself in Shakespeare and in the great Victorian novelists. After she married, she read more widely, both to support her early writing on political economy and to provide Harry with the reading material he needed for his own academic and political work. Her early success with her economics textbook must have given her the confidence to embark on more writing projects. Between 1870 and 1895, she was the author or co-author of four books as well as a number of articles. Her early work was published by Macmillan, helped no doubt by Harry's friendship with Alexander MacMillan, who owned the publishing house. These books would have had a readership confined to those with an interest in political and economic questions and would not have led to her attracting widespread recognition as a writer. They did, however, help her to become known in some intellectual circles. In 1875, she had enough confidence to try something quite different. She wrote a novel.

To recover from her riding accident (see Chapter 4), Millicent had to cancel her engagements and recuperate at home. Enforced idleness did not suit someone whose normal life was full of activity, including an active social life in both London and Cambridge. Empty days were anathema; she had to work. Whether she had thought of writing a novel before being confronted with being confined briefly at home is unclear. The result was *Janet Doncaster*, the story of a young woman pushed by her mother into marriage to an alcoholic. She is soon driven into separating from him by his drunken behaviour but finds work as a translator and later falls deeply in love with another man. Her strict Victorian morals prevent them from living together and she insists they separate. The book ends with the death of her husband four years later, which frees her to marry the man she loves, and the reader is left to assume they live happily ever after.

Ray Strachey's verdict 'that the book as a whole was not written with the skill of a great novelist' is indisputable. Parts of it read like a tract against alcoholism. There is little action in the book to excite or interest the reader and most of the characters are not well developed. The exception is Janet herself. She is portrayed as a woman devoted to high principles and strong and decisive in pursuing them, as well as earning her living successfully. It is revealing about Millicent's perceptions of admirable women living in difficult circumstances. The book was not a complete failure; it was quite widely reviewed, attracting an especially favourable notice in *The Times*. Friends and family thought it a good story and no doubt recognised in its heroine many of Millicent's qualities of determination and certainty that she was right. Elizabeth even went as far as to say that it would make her sister rich and that 'we shall see you and Harry careering in the Park every day on steeds of your own buying and feeding'.

There was no such outcome and, moreover, Millicent thought that any success that it had was due to her name, her friends and the relatively high profile she had amongst the reading public. She decided to test this out by writing another novel secretly and had it published under another name. It was a flop, which confirmed her worst fears. From then on, she would read the novels of others, rather than write them herself. This story reveals that she had some insight into her own limitations, although it might have been easier to seek objective advice about whether she could succeed as a novelist, rather than to check whether she had the talent required by investing time and effort in writing a novel under a pseudonym.

She turned instead to biography (see Chapter 7) and the history of the struggle for women's suffrage, although she had no more books published until sometime after the death of her husband. Most of her biographical work was on women whom she admired for their contributions to social and political reform or for their success in challenging male supremacy. The very last book that she wrote, jointly with Ethel M. Turner, right at the end of her life at the age of eighty, was also a biography. Late in 1927, she published a biography of Josephine Butler to coincide with the 1928 centenary of Butler's birth. She had long been a great admirer of Butler, the social reformer and champion of women's rights, especially in public health and education; and the first sentence of the book stated that Josephine Butler 'was the most distinguished English woman of the nineteenth century'. It is impossible to know how much of it was the product of her co-author's work. However, it did not match the quality of Millicent's previous biography of Sir William Molesworth, and she admitted that she had found it difficult to write. She delivered her manuscript for typing to the Association for Moral and Social Hygiene, which kept alive Butler's work. The staff were astonished by Millicent's ability to climb fifty stairs up to their offices without any sign of being out of breath at the top and were charmed by her lack of grandeur, her ability to form easy, equal relationships and her talent as a witty raconteur. She had aged well.

The rest of her biographical work on women took the form of short essays, most of which were published as a series in a magazine and then collected together and published in book form. The first of these collections was published in 1889 and entitled *Some Eminent Women of Our Times: Short Biographical Sketches*. The twenty-three essays included great female literary figures such as Jane Austen and the Brontë sisters, as well as legendary reformers such as Florence Nightingale and Elizabeth Fry. In her preface, Millicent said, 'The sketches were intended chiefly for working women and young people; it was hoped it would be an encouragement to them to be reminded how much good work had been done in various ways by women.' Short and accessible, they would have engaged their readers and were not as overtly fixated on the theme that women could be great achievers as writers, scientists or reformers without losing their womanly concern for others or their femininity as her preface implies.

Her second collection, published sixteen years later and called *Five Famous French Women*, was a strange aberration. With the exception of Joan of Arc, these women were French royals or aristocrats, who were distinguished by their superiority in comparison with their weak and feeble spouses, in some cases taking over from them as rulers. Millicent quite often referred to her admiration of Joan of Arc for her independence, courage and nationalist spirit, but it is difficult to fathom why she thought it worth writing essays on medieval and Renaissance French women, which would have taken her time to research. The volume did not even have much value as a piece of suffragist propaganda.

Understandably, Millicent was determined to record the history of the fight for women's suffrage. The first book on this topic was published a little prematurely, perhaps, in 1912 and was entitled *Women's Suffrage: A Short History of a Great Movement*. Six years later, she recognised that it needed to be brought up to date and in 1920 she published *The Women's Victory and After*. This little book of 170 pages, illustrated by *Punch* cartoons and with an apt quotation from a wide variety of sources at the beginning of each chapter, represents Millicent's writing at its best. It is both rigorous and readable, and marked by her powerful optimism and hope for the future. Her quotation from John Bright, the great Victorian orator and campaigner for free trade and the abolition of the Corn Laws – 'If we can't win as fast as we could wish, we know that in the long run our opponents cannot win at all' – sums up the general tenor of Millicent's account.

In concluding her chapter on the last phase of the struggle, she referred to those who were dismayed by the fifty years it had taken to acquire votes for women in the following way:

The time we had taken to win household suffrage for women had been just two years less than the time men had taken to cover the same ground. For taking 1832 as their starting point with the Reform Bill of that year, it had occupied them fifty-two years before they won household suffrage for themselves, and they started with the advantage of about one million voters already in existence … [whereas] we had not one vote between us … [and a] tradition of unbroken subjection and subordination.

She ended the book by citing the seven Acts that had been passed which were of direct benefit to women, during the short period between women being granted the vote and the end of 1919, the date she completed the manuscript. She said this legislation had gone through Parliament without any trouble, which demonstrated the difference that votes for women had made.

Millicent's writing did not come to an end with the publication of this book. Soon after, she turned to a quite different topic for a book: travel writing. If asked to list her hobbies, she would certainly have included music, travel and walking, sometimes separately and sometimes combined. She had loved classical music ever since she lived with her family in Aldeburgh and became a regular concert-goer when she moved to London and Cambridge. She also greatly enjoyed opera and could walk from 2 Gower Street to the Opera House in Covent Garden in less than fifteen minutes, a route I often took when I lived there myself, and usually went there and back on foot. She became an ardent Wagner fan from making many trips to the festival in Bayreuth, usually accompanied by one of her sisters. Obsessive as Millicent was about working for the women's movement, she made clear that she would not sacrifice her love of travel to it and took annual holidays abroad or in Britain.

Trips to Europe were made with members of her family and friends from early adulthood, continuing throughout her life. In the early years, her sister Elizabeth was a frequent companion. Later, she was accompanied by nieces and nephews and Philippa too. Harry preferred to go fishing in Scotland or in the trout streams of Wiltshire than to visit the Alps, so during her marriage more often than not she went to Europe without him. Her visits to Switzerland and Austria involved strenuous climbing and walking in the mountains. On one of the rare occasions when Harry came too, he spent a whole day consumed with worry about Millicent climbing a huge mountain with one of their companions on the trip. She immensely enjoyed it but felt guilty on her return when she discovered how anxious Harry had been and regretted going. She also realised that endless talk about the beauty of the scenery on these trips excluded Harry from the conversation, a rare failure on her part to take into account his blindness.

In her memoirs, she says she particularly enjoyed her many holidays in Italy. Her first visit to Rome in 1874 was especially memorable. She claimed in her memoirs, 'The moment when one sees Rome for the first time is as memorable as the first sight of Jerusalem.' Her travels in Europe and later in life further east were remarkable for her determination to absorb the history and culture of the city or region she was visiting. She dedicated time to reading up about the architecture, paintings, sculpture and musical life of wherever she was going before she set off. She planned her sight-seeing carefully but advised others not to overdo it by cramming too much into one day. It was best to do it in the morning and, after a proper lunch, to rest in the afternoon, perhaps going out again in the evening before an early night. There was nothing impetuous nor much 'spur of the moment' activity about Millicent's travels, nor was lazing about or just sitting in the sun doing nothing much part of her repertoire. This is not to say that she was unadventurous. She took risks and enjoyed adventure, as I will illustrate later.

The intellectual curiosity she demonstrated on her travels extended to both politics and the daily life of people. When she went to Italy for the first time, she was impressed by the fact that 'the air was throbbing with political excitement and enthusiasm' in a relatively recently united Italy, the very old and rheumatic Garibaldi had just taken the oath in Parliament. A hero of her youth,

Millicent managed to visit him at his home, describing him afterwards as 'simple and majestic, without pose or any sort of affectation' and 'inherently noble'. She was certainly not bowled over by every grandee she met. In contrast to Garibaldi, after she went to an audience given by Pope Pius IX, she pronounced him to be no more than 'a kind, stout, commonplace old gentleman'. Her judgement fitted with her scepticism about the creeds and dogma of organised religion, although she did identify with the pursuit of goodness. It is hard to understand quite why she wanted to go to an audience with the Pope other than curiosity and her chance to see some of the paintings in the Vatican to which she refers in her memoirs. She may have been influenced by her sister Elizabeth, who was with her and wanted to get a rosary blessed by the Pope for her kind old cook, who was a Roman Catholic.

Millicent visited Italy many times, if not with Elizabeth then with friends or other relatives, such as her much-loved sister-in-law Maria Fawcett. Millicent said that if she knew she were about to die, one of her regrets would be that she would never see Italy again. She even became a writer of two chapters about different parts of Italy in the *Orient Line Guide* of 1885, in which she emphasised the debt of western civilisation to Italian history and how much better it was to see Italian art and architecture in the country itself rather than in galleries in a museum in South Kensington. Surely no one would disagree with that, although many people might not have the resources she had to travel there so often. Twelve years later, she went on a holiday to Egypt and Greece and again wrote about this trip for the *Orient Line Guide*. In spite of the preparation Millicent did beforehand in the British Museum and its library, whether she was sufficiently knowledgeable to have her travel advice published is questionable, although admittedly she spent some weeks in each place. In Egypt, unsurprisingly, she was dismayed by the position of women, including the lack of education for girls and arranged marriages.

Her last excursion into travel writing took place in the 1920s, when she wrote about her visits to Palestine. How these came about is interesting. On several occasions after the votes for women victory, collections were made to celebrate Millicent's leadership in securing them. The money collected was used to support medical or educational improvements, such as hospital beds or scholarships for girls, which were named after her. However, on one occasion, the fundraisers insisted that the money collected should be spent by Millicent on herself. She then asked if this gift of £500 (£18,700 in today's money) could be used to contribute to the costs of a visit to Palestine with Agnes alongside her. Her travelling scholarship, as she called it, was quite successful and they set off for the Middle East. They enjoyed it so much that they returned on three more occasions. These visits combined sightseeing with investigations into politics and the cultural and religious diversity of the region. They were impressed by a school where Jewish, Muslim and Christian children studied together and by the agricultural settlements they visited. On their second visit, they made a monumental journey to Jerusalem, going via Beirut across Lebanon to Baalbek, and from there to Tiberias and then Nablus. On these journeys, Millicent had no difficulty in gaining access to the British administrators in Palestine. She was an admirer of Sir Herbert Samuel, who was the High Commissioner there for five years, and she and Agnes were entertained at Government House.

They were also adventurous in the journeys they made around the region, staying in uncomfortable inns to visit out-of-the-way places. During one of their later visits to Palestine, when they were both in their early eighties, they hit terrible weather on their way to a Roman site not far from Amman. Pouring rain turned to snow overnight and they could not leave their cheap hotel, but Millicent reported that they were fortunate to have writing materials, needlework and a copy of the weekly edition of the *Manchester Guardian* with them! When they tried to return to Jerusalem the next day, their car got stuck in a snowdrift as it was getting dark and they had to wait for some time for it to be dug out before turning back to their primitive accommodation. Millicent made light of it, saying there was plenty of food, oil stoves to keep them warm and that they had come to no harm. This event took place after the publication of her book *Easter in Palestine* in 1926, an account of their two earlier visits. She did not embrace Zionism as a creed, but following the 1917 Balfour Declaration, she considered that a Jewish national home could be created without infringing the rights of the non-Jewish population. The condition of women, educational opportunities and attitudes towards democratic forms of government all led her to greater sympathy for the Jewish than the Arab population. Nevertheless, she believed that when Muslim, Christian and Jewish populations were brought together, they could work in harmony. Her optimism was justifiable, since this had been the case for hundreds of years in other parts of the Middle East, and she cannot be blamed for failing to predict what has happened more recently.

Her walking holidays in Europe continued long after the unsuccessful Swiss visit with Harry described earlier. They appealed to her passionate love of challenging exercise and she was often accompanied by the younger generation who were more likely to be able to keep up with her. Philippa came sometimes with her friends, as well as various nieces and nephews. Elizabeth sometimes came too, leaving her husband either at work or playing golf. On a visit to Austria, Elizabeth wrote home that when resting from strenuous climbing, she and Millicent did needlework and read aloud to each other. Amongst their reading matter at the time was Erasmus, the Renaissance scholar who was one of Millicent's intellectual heroes. There is no evidence of anything approaching frivolity in her reading. While self-improvement motivated her, it did not seem to make her an over-earnest companion, as she was often described as a splendid raconteur whose storytelling amused those who heard it.

There were plenty of walking holidays in Britain as well as abroad. Elizabeth and her husband, who was a Scot, had bought a cottage at Newtonmore in the Highlands, which Millicent visited from time to time. On one visit, her niece Louisa was there with her friend Evelyn Sharp, another militant suffragette, who wrote about the visit later:

> There was a strong family likeness in all the Garretts ... Miss Agnes Garrett used to accompany Mrs Fawcett everywhere and when they joined us at Newtonmore, the conversation became notably more racy, enlivened as it was with many excellent anecdotes gathered in their wanderings about the world. Nothing seemed to daunt these doughty women.

Evelyn described how they would tuck up their considerable skirts and 'don indescribable boots, before starting out to brave inclement weather and face really difficult rambles in the mountains above Speyside'. At the time, Elizabeth was in her mid-seventies and Agnes and Millicent in their mid-sixties.

Millicent also used to visit her youngest sister Josephine, known as Joey, who lived in Yorkshire, and walk there. On one of these visits, an anecdote describes her walking six miles from the station and back during the war in order to avoid taking any form of transport that was needed for the war effort. In the south of England, Millicent enjoyed walking in Hampshire and Wiltshire when she visited Harry's family. She was an early advocate of biodiversity (without, of course, using that term) and protecting forests and woodland. She strongly backed their preservation for public use against commercial interests and condemned the felling of 300 ancient yews by a government department as 'wanton acts of vandalism'.

She was a frequent visitor to Aldeburgh both before and after her parents died. With the arrival of the second generation, the size of Newson Garrett's family outgrew the capacity of Alde House and he allocated houses from his estate for the use of several of his children, including Millicent, which encouraged her to come back to stay. Eventually, Elizabeth, as the oldest surviving child, inherited Alde House and reconstructed its garden. Well before that happened, on Christmas Day, there might be forty or more family members to celebrate at the family home. According to Ray Strachey, Aunt Milly, as she was known in the family, was 'an important figure on these occasions'. Her advice was sought by her nephews and nieces and she was thoughtful in providing it. Unsurprisingly, they appeared to find her somewhat intimidating, as she did not hold back from expressing her disapproval when she thought it was merited, but she was genuinely interested in them, which they recognised and were especially pleased when she did approve. Outspoken as she was in her criticism, her praise was appreciated.

When she took time off from writing and campaigning, she

often left London to explore other places. When she was back in London working at 2 Gower Street, she also found time to pursue her serious cultural interests. Although classical music was the most important of them, she was also a regular theatregoer and visitor at exhibitions. She admired the Pre-Raphaelites and extolled the virtues of Holman Hunt. There is no record of her going to see the impressionists, but since most of them were French, they did not have the patriotic appeal of British painting. After seeing an exhibition of English paintings, which covered a fifty-year period, she was so moved that she said she could not help feeling 'we are a very great people'. Millicent's taste might well have been mocked by some later critics of British painting of the Victorian era.

She was a loyal friend and shared her interests with those to whom she was closest. More often than not, her friendships were built on her suffragist activities. She would have found it hard to build a lasting friendship with anyone who did not share those passionate views. This even applied to her family, so of her four brothers, the only one she was close to was Sam, who, unlike the others, was an ardent feminist; it helped too that he was easily the most intellectually able. Ray Strachey was a good example of a younger colleague who also became a close friend and continued to work for feminist causes in Millicent's old age and beyond. Strachey claimed:

It was not only her public virtues which made her popular. There was a steadiness in all her ways which made people admire and trust her, and an evident kindness which, in spite of all her reserve, drew them towards her. And then, too, there was a spice in her talk which was very refreshing. She had an immense store of good stories, which she told with evident enjoyment and used with an appropriateness which was in itself entertaining, and the mixture of the homely and the comic with the difficult and serious was always evident in her talk.

Even allowing for an element of hero-worship in Strachey's approach to Millicent, this description does chime well with other people's. In Brian Harrison's book *Prudent Revolutionaries*, he draws on an interview with Mary Stocks, a critic of Strachey's biography for being over-indulgent but who nevertheless suggested, in Harrison's words, that Millicent's 'general expression reflected her infectious enjoyment of life, her receptiveness to new ideas, her wide interests, and her many hopes for the future … This quietly spoken, equable, and good-humoured woman was welcome in many circles … Everyone relished her delicate sense of humour.' Millicent made a good companion whether walking in the hills somewhere or exploring a foreign city. She was also a generous giver of gifts to her friends and provided financial support to those who were needy. What she was never able to do was to reveal her own deep emotions and to seek support from friends about her inner conflicts or fears.

Not everyone liked her. She could be dogmatic and unforgiving and admitted as much herself. Once she had made up her mind about something, she was inclined to dismiss or ignore any counter-arguments rather than adjust her position. Lady Frances Balfour, the aristocratic suffragist who worked closely with her for many years, said that when she disagreed with Millicent, she never contradicted her. Presumably, Frances Balfour thought it was not worth the trouble. Edith Palliser, another sympathetic suffragist, wrote in a profile of Millicent that she 'was not demonstrative; her feelings do not lie near the surface; nevertheless the strong motive power is there, the fire, the force, the passionate belief in the justice and expediency of women's claims.' Frances Balfour summed her up, stating that 'she is the most extraordinary mixture of emotion, with a steel control'. These judgements seem closer to the truth than the view of some of the militants that Millicent was all brains with no heart. She had a heart, but her determination, her self-control and her intolerance of fools and knaves often meant it was hidden.

12

MARCHING ON TO THE
FINAL VICTORY

Millicent was active in supporting feminist causes throughout the last decade of her life. Although the pace of her work was much reduced, she did not retire. When at 2 Gower Street, she got up early and sat at her desk every morning, dealing with her extensive correspondence and her writing. Part of her self-discipline entailed answering letters by return. She usually wrote them by hand, which she thought was more polite than sending typewritten letters. She did not employ a great deal of secretarial assistance, although she could afford it; thrift was one of her attributes.

In early 1920, she became involved in establishing a new women's paper. The transition of the NUWSS into the NUSEC meant the demise of the former's newspaper, the *Common Cause*, which had focused on reporting on the fight for votes for women. The new paper was called the *Women's Leader* and aimed to cover a wide range of feminist issues. Millicent agreed to chair the board. Her long experience of article-writing for a range of publications made her an apt choice and she continued to chair it until 1925, as well as writing occasional articles for the paper. It did not succeed in its promotion of the retention of women's wartime contribution to the labour market. After the end of the war, opportunities for women to work declined rather than expanded. Neither the government nor the trade unions were prepared to challenge the post-war drift back to male dominance. In spite of the earlier triumph of the Sex Disqualification (Removal) Act in 1917, a committee set up by the government to examine employment conditions for the civil service reached depressingly reactionary conclusions: it opposed equal pay for women and even proposed reductions in the salaries of some job categories, nor was there any commitment to promote more women to senior positions. The committee had no female members. A little later, in the mid-1920s, Millicent addressed an international meeting of women in science and industry at the Wembley Exhibition Centre. She told her audience that, during the war, women had 'done such wonderful things that surprised everybody … Where has that all gone now?' She admitted that their lowly position in industry was 'one of the disappointments of my life'.

There were, however, some reforms in other areas which gave her great pleasure. One example was the passing of the Matrimonial Causes Act, which had a huge majority at its third reading in the House of Commons in 1923. The Act redressed unequal access to divorce for women. Millicent had bemoaned the terrible injustice of this inequality for many decades. She saw the Act's passing as an example of why the suffragists had fought so hard for women to be able to vote to ensure that their rights would be respected, and she said it was 'a wonderful piece of good fortune for me to have lived to see my dream come true'.

She was also pleased that more girls were completing secondary education and going to university, although they were still in a small minority on undergraduate courses. In the early 1920s, she returned to Cambridge to take up the cudgels on their behalf, so that their degrees would be properly recognised and they could become full members of the university. She wrote to as many eminent male graduates as possible whom she knew, to persuade them to make the effort to go to Cambridge to vote in favour of reform. The effort was to no avail. The vote was lost and women continued to be denied full membership of the university, provoking Millicent's fury. It was not until 1948 that women were awarded their degrees on the same basis as men and Girton and Newnham became colleges of the university along with the male colleges, though it was too late for Philippa Fawcett, who died in 1948.

Millicent's interest in international aspects of the pursuit of women's suffrage also continued. As she put it, 'British women were not really free themselves as women in other countries did not share that freedom.' In 1923, she took on a wider role as a member of the headquarters committee of the IWSA. There was still a long way to go to secure globally the freedom about which she spoke. Australasia, most of the Scandinavian countries and Canada preceded the United Kingdom in giving the vote to women, as did Russia following the revolution in 1917. The European countries of Austria, Germany, Poland and the Netherlands did so at the end of the First World War at more or less the same time as the United Kingdom. The United States and Sweden followed soon after in 1920 and 1921, respectively. It was not until around the end of the Second World War that women were given the vote in France, Italy, Belgium and Japan. India, today the world's largest democracy, gave women the vote in 1947 at independence. It took until 1971 for Swiss women to get the vote. Today, in theory, every country in the world allows women to vote. Millicent would celebrate this, but she would be greatly concerned about how difficult it is for many women to exercise this right in some countries, of which Afghanistan is the obvious but by no means the only example.

Another issue in which Millicent became embroiled in her late seventies was financial support from the state for families. As I reported in the previous chapter, her successor as President of the NUWSS, soon to become the NUSEC, was Eleanor Rathbone, a social scientist interested in social policy, whom Millicent warmly welcomed when she took over. Rathbone had strong convictions of her own and pursued them both inside and outside the NUSEC. Only too aware of the poverty faced by many families, particularly where there were large numbers of children, Rathbone promoted the idea of family endowment, which later became known as family allowances. Millicent's brand of laissez-faire liberalism, combined with her stern belief in parental responsibility, led to her strongly opposing welfare benefits of this kind. She castigated those who wanted the state to subsidise motherhood for associating themselves with 'a socialist nightmare'. Her line was consistent with one she had taken fifty years earlier when she had opposed free elementary education on the grounds that parents should contribute to the cost as a demonstration of parental responsibility (see Chapter 3). Once free universal elementary education was established, she dropped this fight. Indeed, by the 1920s, Millicent saw the distinction between the provision of services such as health and education, which she accepted should be provided without charge, and cash benefits to families, which she opposed.

The original committee Rathbone set up to provide state support for families had seven members, of whom four were drawn from the leadership of the NUWSS. By 1924, when Rathbone published her book entitled *The Disinherited Family* advocating family allowances, the NUSEC had debated the issue on a number of occasions. Many participants in this debate saw it as a new development in feminism – to support mothers. Millicent had made up her mind, was not persuaded and would not budge. At the 1925 NUSEC council, she received a standing ovation for her award of a GBE and her motion to pursue equal suffrage, which would include women under thirty. Yet the following day when she stood up to denounce a motion moved by Eleanor Rathbone to commit the NUSEC formally to family allowances, her opposition went nowhere. The motion to support the allowances was won by 111 to forty-two. The respect and affection in which Millicent was held as the suffragists' leader did not prevent her from being soundly defeated on this issue. Her position denoted inflexibility and a strange lack of empathy for the financial struggles of many families on low incomes.

Following her defeat, she resigned as a member of the NUSEC and from her role chairing the board of the *Women's Leader*. On this occasion, unlike the split over peace and war in 1915, there was no bitterness. Millicent had mellowed. Not only did she stay on friendly terms with Eleanor Rathbone; but she also contributed quite regularly to the pages of the *Women's Leader*. Moreover, she wanted to remain close to the NUSEC on the unfinished business of securing the vote for all women. She also continued her connection with the old London Society of the NUWSS, with which she had been associated for many decades. She succeeded her daughter as its president in 1923 under its new name of the Women's Service, which focused on promoting employment opportunities for women, as well as equal pay; and she encouraged her younger colleagues to pursue them vigorously.

Eminent people at the end of their lives are frequently invited to ceremonial occasions of one type or another. Millicent was no exception. Her presence was sought at celebrations of various kinds, many of which were close to her heart. The *Manchester Guardian* was the newspaper which gave the greatest support to her campaigns and she spoke at its centenary dinner. She took the chair at a mass meeting in Central Hall, Westminster, to celebrate women gaining the vote in the United States. Her sister Elizabeth had died some years earlier, having crowned all her medical achievements by becoming the first female mayor in England in her hometown of Aldeburgh. At a jubilee dinner of the London School of Medicine, Elizabeth had been praised for her great contribution to breaking down the barriers against women in the medical profession and securing training for them; Millicent was there and replied to the toast to 'women's' work.

In her spare time, as well as going to concerts and exhibitions, Millicent went to lectures and debates where she was happy to listen rather than to be a speaker. Her interests were broad, covering international relations, political economy, law and history, and she particularly enjoyed the proceedings of the Royal Statistical Society. Writing to a friend, she said she appreciated just being able at last 'to stand and stare'. She found it impossible to be idle, so it was a very active form of standing and staring and more like a programme of lifelong learning. Even as she approached old age, taxicabs and omnibuses were deemed an unnecessary luxury. She scurried off from 2 Gower Street most afternoons, weaving in and out of the traffic at the fast pace which marked her out all her life as a walker. On one occasion, Agnes came home to find Millicent sitting by the fire reading. Agnes interrupted her to tell her that she had just been knocked down by a taxicab. Noting that she was unhurt, Millicent replied that she hadn't intended to say anything, but she too had been knocked down by a taxicab the previous week!

Although growing older did not dim Millicent's zest for life and her curiosity, like others in her age group, she spent time writing the obituaries and going to the funerals of relatives and friends. In the mid-1920s, she mourned the deaths of her sister-in-law Maria Fawcett, to whom she was very attached; her sisters Alice and Josephine; and her brother Sam, whom she missed most of all. After struggling for several years with dementia, Elizabeth had died earlier in 1917 and Millicent's youngest brother George also predeceased her, leaving her and Agnes as the only survivors of the ten siblings, although they stayed in touch with nieces and nephews, in particular Louisa Garrett Anderson. It was with Louisa's backing that Millicent and Agnes ventured abroad again, going to Ceylon, which was further afield than ever before.

Why she went to Ceylon rather than to India, in which she retained a strong interest over many years, is not entirely clear, other than that they would be able to join Louisa, who was calling in there on the way back from Australia. Therefore, Louisa's two elderly aunts could meet her in Ceylon and they could all return to England together on the same boat. Millicent may have been attracted by the fact that there was a women's suffrage movement there, although given her seasickness, it was surprising that she was willing to embark on such a long journey by sea (being a terrible sailor myself, I could never have done it). However, she bravely rationalised when she wrote home that constant sunshine meant that it was 'nice to be warm without taking any violent steps to be so' and it provided an 'opportunity of seeing places one has never seen before'. Nevertheless, she was glad to arrive in Ceylon and to be met by a picturesque women's suffrage deputation. As well as her usual energetic sightseeing, including travelling to Kandy, Millicent spoke at a public meeting on votes for women and was confident that they would quickly win the fight. Her confidence was justified. Women gained the right to vote there in 1931, just two years later.

After the celebrations of the suffragists' victory in Britain and voting for the first time in 1918, Millicent was well aware of the need to finish the job so that all women were enfranchised, but she discouraged those who wanted to start campaigning immediately. She believed in the need to focus on maintaining the employment of women after the war ended, in a context of growing evidence that they were being pushed out, even more apparent in the economic depression of the early 1920s. She was concerned about trade union restrictions on what she called 'industrial freedom for women'. She claimed that there was no reason why 'because women were not allowed to build ships before the war it must be illegal for them to build aeroplanes today'. Such arguments were of no avail and while women were making some progress in the professions, in the wider economic world they were not, which was disheartening for feminists.

Lloyd George's coalition government collapsed in 1922 and the Conservatives won the ensuing election, which did not help the cause of equal suffrage. Claims were made by Conservative MPs that in 1918 the enfranchisement of women had been settled for at least a decade, and several Private Members' Bills on equal suffrage did not succeed during this period. At least in the next election in 1923, five new female MPs were elected, bringing the total number of women sitting in Parliament to eight; slow as it was, this was progress. There was yet another election in 1924 whose outcome was a minority Labour government, which improved the prospects of a Government Bill to give the vote to the younger women, who had been excluded earlier. Labour ministers such as Arthur Henderson and Philip Snowden had championed the cause for many years, which gave Millicent hope. The sudden collapse of the Labour government in the autumn of 1924 dashed these hopes and the Conservatives were back in power.

Alongside Eleanor Rathbone and other younger suffragists, Millicent started to campaign again, not mainly in mass rallies as had happened before any woman could vote but through letter-writing to newspapers and the lobbying of politicians. There were two exceptions: a NUSEC rally at Central Hall, Westminster, early in 1926 and a larger open-air demonstration in the summer of the following year, which Emmeline Pankhurst also attended. Millicent argued that the age of thirty was always arbitrary and it had been accepted by many at the time that it would not be a permanent restriction to women voting. Why, she asked, should young women be discriminated against? Some of her more conventional former colleagues, such as Lady Frances Balfour, disapproved of the changes in style of the new generation of young women, saying that their garish make-up made them look like courtesans. The New Woman attracted controversy by challenging traditional views of appropriate feminine behaviour. She was associated with a range of unconventional or 'fast' behaviours ranging from the adoption of daring fashion, smoking and bicycle-riding to sex outside marriage. Millicent disagreed with her colleagues, admiring their short hair and short skirts, which displayed their legs, 'I like their legs and I like their short petticoats. There is nothing wrong with their legs, they are perfectly beautiful. Such nice straight legs are a credit to us.' She picked out their pink stockings for particular praise. She also defended young women from the criticism that they were constant imbibers of cocktails, and when presented with a bottle of some kind of cocktail, she saved it for a Sunday evening. Agnes disliked it, but she said she had tasted worse things. More seriously, Millicent praised the modern girl for her independence, sincerity and frankness.

Her openness to the cultural change of the 1920s and her admiration of the new generation of young women, along with her determination that young people should be given the rights they deserved, were some of Millicent's attractive qualities and suggest that she was not as 'prim' as some people had assumed. The fact that she made no concessions to new fashions in her own dress is clear in a photograph of her and Agnes leading a procession of women in short skirts and cloche hats on their way to put flowers in front of John Stuart Mill's statue in 1927. She is wearing an ankle-length skirt, a fox fur and a flowery hat, looking truly Edwardian.

Millicent's endorsement of the 'flappers' contributed to her view that young women should be given a more powerful voice in public affairs. She genuinely liked young people and had often spent time in their company when she took the younger generation in her own family on holiday with her. Accepting that age and experience were valuable, she did not hesitate to criticise her own generation. She argued:

> The old are sometimes slow to learn, may even become sordid and callous. But we don't disenfranchise them. Let us give the young a chance ... and benefit from their youth as long as it lasts for helping to the right solution of the great problems that lie before us.

Although the Conservative government had been in power for over two years, there was nothing on electoral reform in the King's Speech early in 1927. Earlier undertakings had been given by ministers, including the Home Secretary, as Millicent, along with twenty-one other high-profile women, reminded the government in a letter to *The Times*. Following this letter, Millicent sent a telegram to every member of the Cabinet and then another letter to *The Times* demanding action. After a long debate in the Cabinet, Prime Minister Stanley Baldwin announced in Parliament that in the next session, a Bill could be introduced to give the vote to women on equal terms to men. It was the commitment Millicent wanted, although there was still nearly a year to wait before it would be enacted. Yet she was confident enough about the likely outcome to return to Palestine for the fourth time and it was in Jerusalem that she received a telegram with the news that the second reading of the Bill had a majority of 387 to ten. So delighted was she that she danced around the room with Agnes. She was slightly concerned about the number of abstentions but reasoned that 'the antis' abstained because they feared that voting against the Bill would antagonise many of their constituents.

On her return to London, she went to the Lords again, as she had in 1917, to witness the passage of the Bill there. This time there were no anti-suffragists sitting with her and the speakers were resigned to change even where they reflected disapproval. In summing up the debate, Lord Birkenhead, like Lord Curzon had done a decade earlier, opposed the Bill, but rather than abstaining, as Curzon had done, Birkenhead voted for it and advised others to do the same, if in a spirit of resignation. Millicent went back again to the Lords for the Royal Assent on 2 July 1928. As extraordinary as it now seems that victory took so long, Millicent reflected that she was fortunate to have been involved in sixty-one years of campaigning and that she was lucky 'in having seen the struggle from the beginning'.

There were many events celebrating the new Act where Millicent played a prominent part. She went to services of thanksgiving at St

Martin-in-the-Field and Westminster Cathedral; and apparently looking very young for her eighty-one years, she went to a lavish garden party given by Nancy Astor at Cliveden, her country house. True to the courteous approach Millicent had always adopted, she wrote to Stanley Baldwin to thank him for his government's role in putting the Bill through. In an article, she acknowledged the important part the suffragettes' militant campaign led by Emmeline Pankhurst had played.

It is worth dwelling briefly on what part Emmeline played in the final victory. As I described in Chapter 9, during the early years of the war, Emmeline strongly backed the participation of women in the war effort and spoke frequently to promote this. However, during the second half of the war, this work was interrupted by her departure for North America for six months in 1916 on a speaking tour to earn as much as she could to improve her own dire financial situation. This had been exacerbated by her rather ill-thought-out decision to adopt four so-called war babies from an orphanage; they were the illegitimate children of soldiers and young women who were unable to bring them up alone. Although Emmeline loved small children, her style of life and lack of resources were not commensurate with providing these children with a stable home and, some years later, they were readopted by others, with one already having become Christabel's daughter. In 1917, Emmeline went abroad again, this time for three and a half months to Russia. Her purpose was patriotic and she was backed by Lloyd George. Her intention was to try to persuade the Russian government under Alexander Kerensky to continue with the war against Germany. This interlude, although certainly interesting, achieved little or nothing.

On her return to Britain, Emmeline did briefly re-engage with women's suffrage, as revealed by her attendance at the large deputation to Lloyd George, described in Chapter 9. Yet unlike Millicent, Emmeline did not do very much to further the cause of equality for women during the decade between 1918 and 1928, in spite of embracing a similar feminist agenda. She briefly espoused a Woman's Party, which she helped to set up in 1917 and for which Christabel stood unsuccessfully in the 1918 general election. Essentially, the Women's Party was a relaunch of the WSPU, which had been women only in contrast to the NUWSS, where Millicent and her colleagues had always espoused the inclusion of men. Unsurprisingly, therefore, Millicent greatly disliked the concept of the Women's Party, but it petered out in any case within two years, soon after Emmeline left in autumn 1919 for North America, where she stayed for six years as an itinerant lecturer on feminist causes.

After Emmeline returned to Britain late in 1925, Nancy Astor offered to resign her seat for Emmeline to stand in her place as a Conservative. Emmeline declined, although indicated she might stand in a vacant seat. Her political position had shifted; she was especially perturbed by the industrial relations climate, with growing conflict between trade unions and employers, and was opposed to the General Strike, which started in early May 1926 but only lasted for a few days. Emmeline was impressed by the way Prime Minister Stanley Baldwin had handled the strike, which probably influenced her remarkable decision to stand for Parliament as a Conservative. In the words of her biographer, June Purvis, 'Emmeline had turned to the Conservative Party as the key political force that would uphold the British constitution and Empire, support democracy, advance the cause of women, and resist communism.' Her socialist daughter Sylvia was horrified; many others, including the press, were very surprised. Nevertheless, Emmeline's decision was consistent with the views she held. She could not stand as a Labour candidate because of its closeness to the trade unions, its pacifist and anti-empire leanings and its advocacy of state socialism.

Emmeline had certainly not abandoned her commitment to equality for women and claimed that if she became an MP, she would focus on a wide range of issues affecting women, such as better housing, new electricity schemes and better employment opportunities, as well as the quite different issue of strengthening the British Empire as already mentioned. She also took part in the big demonstration for an equal franchise led by Millicent and Eleanor Rathbone in 1927, as well as helping to persuade Baldwin of its importance. Indeed, she was asked to propose the vote of thanks to him at a Conservative event in the Albert Hall, where he confirmed that the government would implement it. However, she was never able to pursue in Parliament what she intended, because she died in 1928 before the election took place the following year. As it happens, the seat where she was selected to stand in east London was probably unwinnable even with the benefit of her striking personality. Sadly, she did not live to see the Royal Assent of the Act giving the vote to all women, which occurred just two weeks after her death at the age of almost seventy. Nevertheless, once the various stages in Parliament had had positive outcomes, Emmeline would have known that victory was close; it was a shame that she did not live to hear Millicent's acknowledgement of the enormous contribution she and the militant suffragettes had made.

Millicent herself was only to live another year after the Act came in, but she remained in good health up till three weeks before she died. Once the celebrations of the new Act were over, she went back to letter-writing and reading and was soon busy with two or three new projects. One of the letters of congratulation she received after the Act came into force was from newly enfranchised young women who belonged to a group formed to advance women's prospects. In a letter thanking them, Millicent warmly encouraged them and recognised how much they were doing for the advancement of women. She knew how to deliver praise and encouragement, highlighting her commitment to younger people, her abiding optimism and her hopes for the future:

> It is very splendid to see you taking up your responsibilities and carrying on our work into the new fields where it must now be pursued ... I look upon the formation of your Council and its achievements with the greatest pride, and I feel that the future of the movement will be safe and triumphant in your hands.

Millicent's various new projects included getting a statue of Queen Elizabeth I restored. Millicent was a great admirer of Queen Elizabeth, who she thought demonstrated what women could achieve if given the chance to exercise power. She helped to raise the money and unveiled the cleaned-up statue and was pleased with the press coverage. An activity of greater importance was the campaign she led to change the age at which marriage was allowed from thirteen to sixteen for both sexes. Although the existing legislation allowed marriage at far too early an age, it rarely happened. Nevertheless, it was an absurd anomaly in the laws of the land and needed changing. There was little or no resistance in the House of Commons. Millicent also spotted an opportunity for some international work when the suffrage-supporting Greek Prime Minister, whom she had met at the Versailles Peace Conference, was returned to power in a general election in Greece. Millicent worked at collecting a number of signatories to a letter reminding him of his obligation to secure votes for women in the country he led. Women did not get the vote in Greece until 1952, so it looks unlikely that her letter had any influence.

In Britain, the general election of 1929 returned thirteen female MPs and was won by the Labour Party. The numbers were still small, but at least they were increasing. Millicent was especially pleased that Margaret Bondfield became the first female Cabinet minister as Minister of Labour under the premiership of Ramsay MacDonald. Like Millicent, Margaret was one of many children, but unlike Millicent, Margaret grew up in poverty. She made her way through the trade union movement, was elected to the council of the Trades Union Congress and became the first woman to chair it. Millicent knew her because she was also a women's rights activist, although like many in the Labour movement, Margaret favoured adult suffrage for all. Millicent was delighted to write to her as the Right Honourable Margaret Bondfield, to which Margaret replied that it was her official title 'but I am the same as usual'. Millicent's final public appearance was to go to a lunch at the House of Commons to celebrate Margaret's appointment and the election of the thirteen female MPs.

Three days later, Millicent fell ill, dying three weeks later on 5 August 1929 at the age of eighty-two. She left £23,000 (over £1.2 million in today's money) in her will, a lot of money following prudent investment in various stocks and shares. Her estate was left to her daughter. Agnes, her loyal companion for so many years, received an annuity of £500 (£26,600 in today's money); she lived for another six years, until just before her ninetieth birthday, remaining at 2 Gower Street with her niece Philippa.

Millicent's many obituaries praised her for her sixty years of dedication to women's rights, although there were a few exceptions to the many positive accounts of her life. For example, the *Catholic*

Herald attacked her as 'excessively anti-Catholic' and 'one of the most bitter enemies of Irish freedom'. Her memorial service was held in Westminster Abbey. It was attended by fifty MPs, five Cabinet ministers and two former Prime Ministers, Lloyd George and Stanley Baldwin. Many of the congregation were her colleagues from the fight for women's suffrage. There were also representatives of over eighty national women's organisations, including many professional groups. It was an establishment occasion, and the writer Vera Brittain thought it 'official and impersonal', a verdict others disputed, although it may have lacked, in Brittain's words, the passion and emotion which characterised the memorial for Emmeline Pankhurst.

Before my final assessment of Millicent and her achievements, I want to conclude a comparison with Emmeline, which I began in Chapter 9, but at this point I will focus in particular on the last fifteen years of their lives after militancy had ended. As earlier, they had much in common as well as ways in which they were different. The decision they separately made at the start of the First World War to put their respective campaigns on hold is a further demonstration of what they had in common: in this case fervent patriotic support for the war. Emmeline and her daughter Christabel took a more extreme position than Millicent in denouncing young men for not joining up, presenting them with white feathers.

In the first year of the war, Millicent was preoccupied with the split in the NUWSS between the pacifists and the patriots. While there were also pacifists within the WSPU, including Emmeline's second daughter, the socialist Sylvia, Emmeline as an autocratic leader forcefully dismissed their arguments. In the WSPU newspaper, *The Suffragette* (which was later changed to the patriotic-sounding *Britannia*), Emmeline called for national unity with the slogan that it was 'a thousand times more the duty of the militant suffragette to fight the Kaiser for the sake of liberty than it was to fight anti-suffrage governments'. Not long after, she was amazed to be approached by her earlier enemy, Lloyd George, wearing his Minister of Munitions hat, to ask for her help in organising a procession of women to demonstrate their commitment to war work, especially in the munitions factories. Emmeline agreed to the request. Twenty thousand women marched from Westminster to Blackfriars, carrying banners proclaiming messages such as 'Shells made by a wife may save her husband's life', and were accompanied by a band playing patriotic music and hymns of the Allies. Thousands lined the streets and watched the public rapprochement of Emmeline and Lloyd George on a platform in the garden of the Ministry of Munitions.

The War Service Procession, as it became known, was proclaimed by the press as a great success, but I have found no evidence of Millicent's opinions about it. Although during this period Emmeline carried out speaking engagements round the country on the vital need for war work by women and campaigned on their behalf for equal pay, this march was to be the last great rally that she led in London. She became distracted by other issues: the need to support Serbia, which had been attacked by Austria; and a campaign to support illegitimate war babies, for which she failed to get either political or financial support and which led to her rash and ill-thought-out decision to adopt four of them herself.

During this year, it was Millicent rather than Emmeline who began to raise the issue of suffrage for women again. Dogged and consistent, as she nearly always was, Millicent wrote to Asquith on the need to consider reform, and it was she, not Emmeline, who sought to influence the all-party committee set up under the chairmanship of the Speaker of the Commons. However, Emmeline did attend the 1917 meeting with Lloyd George, although not leading the delegation, as mentioned earlier. For several months in 1917, Emmeline was distracted, this time by her long visit to Russia. Its main aim was to discover whether, after the fall of the Czar, the Russian regime could be persuaded not to pursue peace with Germany, which the Allies feared. Emmeline returned without securing such a commitment, and with a deep loathing of Bolshevism. What the visit did demonstrate was that continuing the war until Germany was defeated had become a much higher priority for her than fighting for votes for women.

Having both agreed that it was better to go for the government's more limited proposal than to risk going for total enfranchisement only to end up with nothing, it was Millicent, not Emmeline, who worked tirelessly to maximise the vote on the measure in the Commons, and thereby help its passage through the Lords. Did Parliament back it with such a large majority because of the fear of a return to militancy? It seems unlikely. After all, in the two years from 1911 to 1913 when militancy was at its height, Parliament was not cowed into introducing suffrage legislation. Rather, violence had led to public alienation, of which the politicians were well aware. As the war drew to a close, the contribution women had made was far more likely to have swung the vote. Above all, it undermined anti-suffrage arguments and their reactionary stereotypes of women as passive creatures made for domesticity rather than employment who were unsuited to holding political power. Both Millicent and Emmeline helped to dismiss such stereotypes by campaigning for women's war work.

They both also accepted that the 1918 Act was unfinished

business and that more campaigning was needed to secure the vote on an equal basis with men. However, both women reduced their campaigning roles after the 1918 election. Millicent was over seventy, as mentioned earlier, and handed over the leadership of the NUWSS under the new title of the NUSEC to Eleanor Rathbone. Emmeline left with her adopted daughters for nearly six years of public speaking on feminist causes in North America. Meanwhile, her daughter Christabel had found religion, becoming a fanatical Adventist preacher. Christabel abandoned her attempt to become an MP, eventually going with her adopted daughter to live in the United States too, where she devoted her life to religious proselytising. As described earlier, Emmeline supported the Conservative Prime Minister Stanley Baldwin. It was an extraordinary journey from the radical socialist she had been in her early adult life. And it was Baldwin who, in 1930, unveiled Emmeline's statue in Victoria Embankment Gardens next to the Parliamentary Estate, although it had been paid for by subscriptions from her supporters.

Both Millicent Garrett Fawcett and Emmeline Pankhurst deserve our praise and admiration for the campaigns they mounted over many years to obtain acceptance that women have the right to vote on equal terms with men. Yet over nearly a century since that victory in gaining universal suffrage for men and women, it is the suffragettes who have consistently caught the imagination of the public through their dramatic, though short-lived, campaign, rather than the suffragists, who campaigned for so much longer and so much more constructively.

Brian Harrison's compelling comparison of them, written as an introductory chapter in his book about interwar feminism, elaborates on the public perception. He claimed that 'for the Pankhursts, politics and theatre were never distinct; they knew how to capture the headlines, although without always distinguishing between politics and notoriety'. He claimed that Emmeline's magnetism had little to do with 'the content of her speeches, which were not powerfully reasoned and usually involved no more than appealing to familiar experience and common humanity. Her impact stemmed from the combination of personality, appearance and expression ... and she knew how to vary emotion and pitch.' Inspiring speeches have great value, but they are not enough to force reform. Millicent knew how to work the system, whereas, in Harrison's words, 'Pankhurst was too eager for the fray, too prone to the dramatic gesture, to grasp the realities of the parliamentary situation'. It was, he went on to say, 'absurd for Pankhurst to argue that the British public, let alone its government, would enfranchise women simply to rid itself of a militant nuisance; the suffragettes' strident tone towards politicians reflects weakness and inexperience'.

Emmeline was memorable because she was a charismatic and inspiring speechmaker as well as being autocratic and impulsive. In contrast, Millicent disdained drama and sensationalism; instead, she was dogged and self-disciplined, rational and thoughtful, a persistent lobbyist and an effective rational writer and pamphleteer. Admittedly, these qualities did not appeal to the public imagination or make her as memorable in many respects as Emmeline. She herself recognised Emmeline's contribution and, at the time of her death, described her as 'very able' although 'impossible to work with'. Both women demonstrated qualities of leadership, resilience and determination and should have their place in history, and neither of them should ever be written out of it.

As we approach the centenary of universal votes for all women in 2028, I would like far more people to recognise Millicent's unique contribution and for her greatness to be appreciated. It was not just, as Harrison said, that she 'contributed so much more than Pankhurst to winning the vote'. She also fought for women to have their rights to far wider educational opportunities, to entry into the professions, to better employment conditions and fair pay, to equal rights in divorce, to freedom from sexual exploitation and to the recognition of their right to live fulfilled lives beyond the domestic sphere. She was also a generous donor towards the causes in which she believed.

Millicent was a reliable colleague, if at times dogmatic in her views and tediously uncompromising in her patriotism. Her desire for self-improvement, her self-discipline and her powerful work ethic might have made her a bore. She found it hard to reveal her inner feelings and express her own emotions, which may also have made her a less interesting companion than she might have been. Yet underneath the steely exterior, she was passionate and truly cared about the issues that mattered to her. She was interesting rather than boring. Beyond her work, her wide interests, which she was determined to find time to pursue, were shared with her close friends and family. She was happily married and deeply felt the loss of the husband she loved. She cared for her clever but colourless daughter and loved many members of her large family. They, in turn, loved and admired her. In her long years of widowhood, she built a fulfilling life for herself, not just through work but through travel, walking, music, opera and exhibitions, as well as wide reading and her own writing. Many years ago, on the radio programme *Any Questions?*, I was asked who I would choose to be with on a desert island. Were I to be asked again, I would answer Millicent Garrett Fawcett. We would have so much in common and so much to talk about.

EPILOGUE

I have never admired statues either as a form of art or a form of remembrance. In a painted portrait, it is so much easier to convey the essence of a person by the use of colour or the deployment of light and shade. Brush strokes bring facial expressions to life through a twinkling eye or a touch of a smile. There is a sense of movement as the sitter leans forward, sometimes engaging with their environment, whether by reading a book or by looking through a window. In contrast, images in stone seem heavy and static, even dreary in their greyness and lack of colour. Their weight and their size make them hard to move and therefore difficult to lend to other places, instead staying for ever where they were initially installed.

For these reasons, it would never have occurred to me to campaign for a statue of someone, not even of Millicent Garrett Fawcett or any other woman to make up for the huge disparity in the number of statues of women compared with men. Some other people feel differently, and I respect their view that statues, which are erected in someone's honour, signify the admiration and respect in which they are held, even if often of limited artistic merit. The place where a statue stands is clearly of great importance because it symbolises what the subject's life meant. Moreover, some locations are in themselves prestigious. Parliament Square is a good example. Looking out at Big Ben and the House of Commons, it is a public place in which to recognise the value of parliamentary democracy. In the second decade of the twenty-first century, it contained eleven statues of historical political figures, all of men and British, with the exception of Abraham Lincoln (1920), Jan Smuts (1956), Nelson Mandela (2007) and Mahatma Gandhi (2015).

In 2016, a campaign was launched to rectify the absence of a single woman amongst them and to claim a place there for a statue of Millicent, who some thought had been neglected compared with Emmeline Pankhurst, whose statue still stood close by, just to the south of the Palace of Westminster, a few yards from where it was originally unveiled. The main controversy about the proposal derived from Emmeline's protagonists, who wanted her rather than Millicent in Parliament Square.

Activist and author Caroline Criado Perez had already campaigned for women to be portrayed on banknotes following the Bank of England's decision to put Winston Churchill on £5 notes as a replacement for Elizabeth Fry, the campaigner for improved prison conditions. In 2017, Criado Perez won this battle, and the Bank of England agreed to portray Jane Austen on £10 notes. When Criado Perez discovered that there were no statues of women in Parliament Square, she did some research, which revealed that only 2.7 per cent of statues in the United Kingdom were of women, excluding female members of the royal family. Indeed, according to English Heritage, there are more statues of animals in London than of women. The Mayor of London, Sadiq Khan, was then sent a letter signed by forty-two eminent women requesting his agreement to a statue of a suffragette in Parliament Square to mark the

2018 centenary of the Act giving votes to women. This was followed by a petition to Parliament signed by 74,000 people requesting a statue of a woman in Parliament Square. Supported by the Fawcett Society, which had been set up many years earlier to promote equal rights for women, Criado Perez suggested that Millicent should be its subject, stating that it was shocking that she did not have a statue of her own already.

Meanwhile, a rival campaign had already been started in 2014 for Emmeline Pankhurst to be represented in Parliament Square, initially by moving her existing statue there. In the end, after considerable debate, there was growing momentum for a statue of a new woman in the square and agreement was reached that it should be Millicent. This was backed by Westminster Council and the Mayor of London, and eventually by the then Prime Minister, Theresa May, who after the announcement in 2017 said, 'The example Millicent Fawcett set during the struggle for equality continues to inspire the battle against the burning injustices of today. It is right and proper that she is honoured in Parliament Square alongside former leaders who changed our country.' Her endorsement was deserved, but it did not prevent a few fringe misogynists from complaining about a woman being honoured in this way, nor some feminists who still wanted a suffragette and not a suffragist represented in Parliament Square.

The well-known artist and former Turner Prize winner Gillian Wearing was selected to design the statue, following a competition confined to women, to which some male sculptors briefly objected. Wearing's design was notably inclusive because she added to the sculpture's plinth the names of fifty-nine people (four of them were men) who had campaigned for votes for women. Many leading suffragettes, obviously including the Pankhursts, were listed, along with many of Millicent's suffragist colleagues. It was an inspired decision to celebrate the campaign for women's suffrage in this way. Wearing was advised on who to include by Professor Julie Gottlieb, a historian of the women's suffrage movement. Creating a list of this kind is no easy task, but they succeeded in devising a wide-ranging and diverse group of feminist activists in the fight for women's votes, some of whom continued to advocate for improvements in the status of women after the vote had been granted. They represented different geographical regions, social classes and approaches to campaigning. Maybe some experts would have omitted a name or two or added a few others. However, I have seen no controversy about the list. It was a brilliant device for greatly increasing the number of women celebrated in Parliament Square as well as underlining the fact that the struggle involved the participation of many people, since one person cannot achieve political and cultural change alone. Millicent understood this well, and although forceful and sometimes domineering, she was not vain. Once asked whether women ever told her that she had changed their lives, her quick reply was 'No, never,' as if the question was rather sentimental and silly.

Wearing also created an unusual image with Millicent holding a banner with the words 'Courage calls to courage everywhere'. This was a quotation from a 1920 speech in which Millicent describes the action of Emily Wilding Davison, the suffragette who was killed when she threw herself in front of the King's horse at the 1913 Derby.

When the statue was unveiled in April 2018, it was acclaimed as an artistically worthy addition to Parliament Square. It portrays Millicent at the age of fifty in 1897, when she became President of the NUWSS. She stands erect in one of the full-length coat dresses that she so often wore. Historic England warmly welcomed the statue and its 'historical and artistic contribution to this important commemorative landscape'. It also pointed out that Parliament Square is a public space where 'those recognised need to be perceived to have the historical status to be relevant peers of the other statues in this setting. Few, if any, have claimed that Mandela, Gandhi and Fawcett do not meet this test.' The BBC's arts editor, Will Gompertz, thought that Wearing's execution of her brief was 'exceptional', giving it a five-star rating and comparing it very favourably with most of the other statues in the square, which were made to look ridiculous or pompous in comparison with it. I have been persuaded that my scepticism about statues is not always justified.

The unveiling was carefully choreographed, with an all-female cast undertaking it. They included two girls from local secondary schools; an indirect descendant of Millicent; London's deputy mayor for culture and creative industries, Justine Simons; and Caroline Criado Perez, the woman who campaigned for it in the first place. Speeches were made by Prime Minister Theresa May; the Mayor of London, Sadiq Khan; and the Communities Secretary, Sajid Javid. Theresa May said:

> I would not be here today as Prime Minister, no female MPs would have taken their seats in Parliament, none of us would have the rights and protections we now enjoy, were it not for Dame Millicent Garrett Fawcett. The struggle to achieve votes for women was long and arduous and Dame Millicent was there from the beginning. For decade after decade, in the face of often fierce opposition, she travelled the country and the world, campaigning not just for the vote but on a whole range of issues … For generations to come, this statue will serve not just as a

reminder of Dame Millicent's extraordinary life and legacy, but as inspiration to all of us who wish to follow in her footsteps.

Both Javid and Khan also pointed to inspiring us all to further action. Javid said the statue 'will remind us all of how we must keep up the fight against inequality and injustice in everything we do', and Khan said, 'I hope this statue sparks further change across society – driving forward gender equality and inspiring women and girls across the capital and the UK.'

Were Millicent alive today, she would undoubtedly endorse the need to keep fighting for a fairer and juster world for women. Her legacy is the large agenda she identified to improve the lives of women, and her own part in demonstrating that committed and determined activism can lead to progress. She would have marvelled at much of the progress that had taken place. What a pleasure it would be to take her today into the gallery of the House of Commons and watch her delight in seeing more than half the Labour benches occupied by women as well as their strong representation on the front bench. Yet she might remark that the Conservative Party were well behind Labour and needed to catch up, although she would have been surprised but pleased to discover that there have been three female Conservative Prime Ministers. How enjoyable it would be to take her to Cambridge, for her to discover that there are almost as many female as male undergraduates and that women hold many professorial chairs and head numerous colleges. Yet if she dug a little deeper, she would be disappointed that women are less well represented in senior academic roles, and she would have views about what needs to be done.

Another part of Millicent's agenda was to open the professions to women. She would be pleased that more women than men now become doctors, lawyers and accountants, but she would be sorry that there are still so few female engineers and that women are still underrepresented in senior positions in large enterprises in the private sector. She would also want better promotion prospects for women, so that equal pay becomes a reality and not just an ideal. She would strongly endorse the expectation and indeed the acceptance that most married women with children will have jobs.

One of her disappointments would be that the sexual harassment of women continues. She would be horrified by female trafficking, the modern version of the white slave trade of her own time, and she would denounce all forms of sexual violence against women as abhorrent. She would, however, note that women could divorce abusive men more easily than in her own day, and she would approve of efforts to enforce divorced men's maintenance payments for their children. She would understand the needs of single mothers and ask that they should receive more support, especially with childcare.

To conclude, nearly a hundred years after votes were won for women on an equal basis with men, Millicent could justifiably say that she was right to be optimistic and to believe in the possibility of progress. Yet her thank-you letter to the young women who wrote to her after the Act passed (see Chapter 12) is still relevant today and deserves quoting in full:

It is very splendid to see you taking up your responsibilities and carrying on our work into the new fields where it must now be pursued ... I look upon the formation of your Council and its achievements with the greatest pride, and I feel that the future of the movement will be safe and triumphant in your hands. I believe, of course, that it will change and develop; you will probably find new methods and new needs, and your ways will be the ways of full citizens instead of the way of beggars and outcasts as ours for so long had to be. But I feel confident that you will find, as we did, that the cause of real freedom of women is a great one, worth one's best service, and that you will never lose sight of it even amidst your new opportunities.

It is not the only good cause in the world, nor the only one you will care for. But it does lie with you to care for it; and for all its changes it is the same that we older women cared for. And it does lie close to our hands, as women, and it must not be forgotten until it is wholly achieved. You know from your own experience that equal pay and equal economic opportunity are still withheld from us.

I shall expect to see you individually and collectively putting your shoulders to that wheel and pushing the car of progress along in your generation as we tried to do in ours; and I know you find that, in this struggle, there is enjoyment, pleasure and real interest as long as you believe in your cause and in your associates. And I am firmly convinced that justice and freedom for women are things worth securing, not only for their own sakes, but for civilisation itself.

The speakers at the unveiling of Millicent's statue were right to call for the continuation of the fight. There is plenty of unfinished business still to be done.

SELECTED BIBLIOGRAPHY

Crawford, Elizabeth, *Enterprising Women: The Garretts and Their Circle*, London: Francis Boutle, 2002.

Crawford, Elizabeth, *The Women's Suffrage Movement in Britain and Ireland*, London: Routledge, 2006.

Evans, Richard J., *The Feminists: Women's Emancipation Movements in Europe, America and Australasia, 1840–1920*, London: Croom Helm, 1977.

Fisher, Lucy, *Emily Wilding Davison: The Martyr Suffragette*, London: Biteback Publishing, 2018.

Garrett Anderson, Louisa, *Elizabeth Garrett Anderson, 1836–1917*, London: Faber & Faber, 1939.

Garrett Fawcett, Millicent, *Easter in Palestine, 1921–1922*, London: Fisher Unwin, 1926.

Garrett Fawcett, Millicent, *Five Famous French Women*, London: Cassell and Co. Ltd, 1905.

Garrett Fawcett, Millicent, *Janet Doncaster*, London: Smith, Elder & Co., 1875.

Garrett Fawcett, Millicent, *Josephine Butler: Her Work and Principles and Their Meaning for the Twentieth Century* (with Ethel M.

Turner), London: Association for Moral and Social Hygiene, 1927.

Garrett Fawcett, Millicent, *Life of Her Majesty Queen Victoria*, London: W. H. Allen & Co., 1895.

Garrett Fawcett, Millicent, *Life of the Right Hon. Sir William Molesworth*, London: Macmillan, 1901.

Garrett Fawcett, Millicent, *Political Economy for Beginners*, London: Macmillan, 1870.

Garrett Fawcett, Millicent, *Some Eminent Women of Our Times: Short Biographical Sketches*, London: Macmillan, 1889.

Garrett Fawcett, Millicent, *Tales in Political Economy*, London: Macmillan, 1874.

Garrett Fawcett, Millicent, *What I Remember*, London: T. Fisher Unwin, 1924.

Garrett Fawcett, Millicent, *Women's Suffrage: A Short History of a Great Movement*, London: T. C. & E. C. Jack, 1921.

Garrett Fawcett, Millicent, *The Women's Victory and After: Personal Reminiscences, 1911–1918*, London: Sidgwick & Jackson, 1920.

Glynn, Jenifer, *The Pioneering Garretts: Breaking the Barriers for Women*, London: Hambledon Continuum, 2008.

Harrison, Brian, *Prudent Revolutionaries: Portraits of British Feminists Between the Wars*, Oxford: Oxford University Press, 1987.

Manton, Jo, *Elizabeth Garrett Anderson*, London: Methuen & Co., 1965.

Moore, Wendy, *No Man's Land: The Trailblazing Women Who Ran Britain's Most Extraordinary Military Hospital During World War I*, London: Basic Books, 2020.

Oakley, Ann, 'Millicent Garrett Fawcett: Duty and Determination (1847–1929)' in Dale Spender (ed.), *Feminist Theorists: Three*

Centuries of Women's Intellectual Traditions, London: Women's Press, 1983.

Purvis, June, *Emmeline Pankhurst: A Biography*, London: Routledge, 2002.

Purvis, June and June Hannam (eds), *The British Women's Suffrage Campaign: National and International Perspectives*, London: Routledge, 2020.

Rubinstein, David, *A Different World for Women: The Life of Millicent Garrett Fawcett*, New York: Harvester Wheatsheaf, 1991.

Stephen, Leslie, *Life of Henry Fawcett*, London: Smith, Elder & Co., 1886.

Strachey, Ray, *Millicent Garrett Fawcett*, London: John Murray, 1931.

Taylor, Graeme, *The Remarkable Rhoda Garrett*, Woodstock: Graeme Taylor in conjunction with Writersworld, 2017.

Terras, Melissa and Elizabeth Crawford (eds), *Millicent Garrett Fawcett: Selected Writings*, London: UCL Press, 2022.

ACKNOWLEDGEMENTS

I am immensely grateful to those who encouraged me to write this book, and then provided me with advice and suggestions. The two people to whom I am especially indebted are my agent Clare Alexander and my assistant Linda Maynard. Thank you, Clare, for believing in the project and for your wisdom and clarity in all the advice you gave me. As I am so old-fashioned that I write by hand, Linda had to cope with typing up an untidy and sometimes barely legible manuscript. She also suggested improvements and undertook additional research. I would have been lost without her help.

My old friends Grant McIntyre and Helen Fraser, both former publishers, were enthusiastic about my proposal to write a book about Millicent Garrett Fawcett and gave me invaluable advice about getting an agent and who to approach. They continued to encourage me as writing the book progressed. My close friends Richard Layard and Tom Schuller boosted my confidence from the start. They also read the book as I drafted it, chapter by chapter, providing many helpful comments. I greatly appreciate how much time they spent on it and how positive they were. Another old friend, Nick Tucker, drawing on his expertise as a critic, gave me helpful advice about how to approach writing a biography of this sort, as did my friend, the feminist author Ann Oakley, whose own work is full of relevant insights from which I have drawn.

I am also grateful to Harriet Harman, the most passionately feminist of my friends, for reassuring me that the story of the suffragists' leader was one well worth telling. I turned to Professor Joanna Bourke for a professional historian's view about the project. She was adamant that the story of the suffragists had been relatively neglected compared with the 'glamorised' suffragettes, even though the suffragists' constitutionalist approach, as they called it, had done more to obtain the vote for women. She was therefore insistent that a new book about Millicent was needed.

This book is written without the help of diaries, which Millicent did not keep, nor with large collections of personal letters, which she certainly wrote but most of which have not survived. There have only been two published full-length biographies. The first was written by Ray Strachey, who became a close colleague and friend in Millicent's later life. Her book was published two years after Millicent's death in 1931. It was a full account of Millicent's life and, although too uncritical, it nevertheless provided me with invaluable information about how Millicent operated and what she thought. The second was written by David Rubinstein, an academic historian of late nineteenth- and early twentieth-century feminism. His rigorous research and his careful noting of all his wide-reaching sources – including parliamentary records, journals, newspapers, the minutes of the meetings of suffrage organisations and speeches by politicians and campaigners – have been hugely helpful for me. The fact that he did all this work saved me from having to spend many weeks tracking down all the information, which instead was readily available in his book for me to interpret in ways I wished.

Millicent was encouraged to write an autobiography, but she resisted, saying it would be too much about 'I' and that this did not appeal to her. Eventually, she caved in after the partial enfranchisement of women in 1918 and wrote a book with the title *What I Remember*, which was published in 1920. The title is an apt description of the book. She seems to have sat down and penned an anecdotal account of her life rather than trying to set out an intellectually coherent history of what shaped it and what challenged her most. Nor does she reveal deep emotions. She shied away from writing in depth about those to whom she was closest: her husband, her sister Agnes or her daughter Philippa. Although it is a frustrating source for a biographer, it does demonstrate her sense of humour, determination and political astuteness.

The last source I want to acknowledge is the work of Elizabeth Crawford. She is undoubtedly the most knowledgeable living researcher and historian of the work of Millicent Garrett Fawcett and of her wider circle. As well as publishing a collection of many of Millicent's articles and speeches, Elizabeth has published a meticulously researched and beautifully illustrated book entitled *Enterprising Women: The Garretts and Their Circle*. For readers who want to delve in much more detail into the extensive networks of which Millicent was a part, it is the place to go. I am also grateful to Elizabeth for the invaluable advice she gave me when I decided to write the book, as I am to Polly Russell at the British Library, who was delightfully enthusiastic about Millicent and even named her daughter after her.

The librarians at the House of Lords patiently dealt with all my requests, borrowed books from elsewhere for me and were indulgent in allowing me frequent renewals. I greatly appreciated their help.

I am also grateful to the Fawcett Society, the charity which commemorates Millicent's work by campaigning for a more just future for women and girls everywhere.

Finally, I want to thank Olivia Beattie and Ella Boardman at Biteback, for their enthusiastic backing of the book. And in Ella's case, for the generosity of her comments on the draft chapters and her hard work later in rigorously copy-editing the book.

I dedicate this book to female voters who exercise their democratic right as citizens to choose who will represent them, a right denied them for so long.

INDEX